Mountain to Mountain

Mountain to Mountain

A JOURNEY OF ADVENTURE AND ACTIVISM FOR THE WOMEN OF AFGHANISTAN

Shannon Galpin

ST. MARTIN'S PRESS

NEW YORK

Author's note: The names of the women in Afghan prisons have been changed.

MOUNTAIN TO MOUNTAIN. Copyright 2014 by Shannon Galpin. All rights reserved. Printed in the United States of America. For information, address St. Martin's Press, 175 Fifth Avenue, New York, N.Y. 10010.

www.stmartins.com

Map by Jeff Ward

Library of Congress Cataloging-in-Publication Data

Galpin, Shannon.
    Mountain to mountain : a journey of adventure and activism for the women of Afghanistan / Shannon Galpin.
        pages cm
    ISBN 978-1-250-04664-2 (hardcover)
    ISBN 978-1-4668-4705-7 (e-book)
    1. Galpin, Shannon.   2. Women—Services for—Afghanistan.
3. Women—Afghanistan—Social conditions.   4. Women—Violence against—Afghanistan.   5. Women's rights—Afghanistan.
6. Cycling—Afghanistan.   7. Women social reformers—United
States.   8. Women political activists—United States.   I. Title.
    HV1448.A3G35 2014
    362.83092—dc23

                                                            2014016897

St. Martin's Press books may be purchased for educational, business, or promotional use. For information on bulk purchases, please contact Macmillan Corporate and Premium Sales Department at 1-800-221-7945, extension 5442, or write specialmarkets@macmillan.com.

First Edition: September 2014

10 9 8 7 6 5 4 3 2 1

FOR DEVON,

you are my reason for everything.

Contents

viii   Contents

No matter how high the mountain, there is always a road.

—AFGHAN PROVERB

Mountain to Mountain

(1)

Single-Speeds in a War Zone

Afghanistan 2009

This *is a bad idea.*

Breathe. Just breathe. Steady.

Just let go of the brakes and ride through. You got this. You know how to ride a bike.

Damn, these rocks are sliding! Worst trail ever. Don't crash. Please, please, please. Not here.

The mountainside was more rock strewn than it had appeared. These barren slopes were not like those I was used to biking in Colorado. Devoid of trees, the slopes looked like someone had dynamited the mountain and left the rubble where it had fallen. My bike was rolling down what had started out as a narrow goat path farther up the mountain. Almost immediately the path disappeared, and there was no clear way up or down, just rocks in all directions.

The ground slid, and small stones sprayed underneath my tires. I tensed.

Whose idea was this?

Yours, my brain replied.

There's no path!

Yeah, well, there could be land mines if you ride off the path.

My heart pounded. I focused downhill. Picking a line through the rubble, I steadied my nerves and took a deep breath. I gripped my handlebars and tried to keep my bike upright. The school and the open courtyard sat at the base of the mountain, a small white oasis in the sea of brown. I shifted my weight over the back tire. I let go of the brakes and let the speed take me through. Shades of brown rushed by in a blur as I picked up speed. I bent my elbows deeper to allow my arms to absorb the bouncing. My teeth chattered with the vibrations. My tires slid more than they rolled, searching for solid ground.

You're almost down. Relax. Breathe. Just ride. You know how to do this. Breathe! Dust stung my eyes. My hair was sweaty and plastered to my head under my checkered head scarf. My heart pounded even harder—whether from fear, exertion, or the layers of clothing I wore that felt like a sauna, I wasn't entirely sure.

Suddenly the tires stopped sliding and I was on level, solid ground. The mountain had spat me out alive. As if a mute button was released, sound flooded my ears: cheering. Six hundred boys were cheering. I looked up for the first time since I'd started my descent and smiled in relief through the cloud of dust. Six hundred Afghan boys smiled back. And one threw a rock. Six hundred to one? I'll take those odds.

Travis was smiling at me from behind the sea of faces. "Nice job, mate. They loved it. They can't believe you didn't crash. It would have been more entertaining if you had, though."

I wanted to punch him, but in Afghanistan women don't punch

men, playfully or not. But, in Afghanistan, women also don't ride bikes.

In a remote village, in the heart of the Panjshir mountains, six hundred boys, their teachers, and a few random villagers who wandered over, had just watched a woman ride a mountain bike behind their schoolyard. This was the first time any of them had seen a girl ride a bike. What they maybe didn't realize was that they had just witnessed the first time *any* woman had mountain biked in Afghanistan.

I didn't go to Afghanistan planning to ride a mountain bike. Does anyone travel to a war zone and say to themselves, "I wish I had remembered to pack my mountain bike, helmet, and lycra! This would be an awesome place to ride." No, they probably don't.

But on my fourth trip in 2009, I decided to bring my tangerine Niner 29er single-speed and challenge the gender barrier that prevents women from riding bikes. Afghanistan is one of the few countries in the world that doesn't allow its women or girls to ride. But I'm not Afghan. Standing tall at five foot nine, with long blond hair, I am clearly not a local. While many back home assume being so obviously a foreigner is an inherent risk, it has become my biggest asset. A foreign woman here is a hybrid gender. An honorary man. A status that often allows me a unique insight into a complicated region.

Afghan men recognize me as a woman, but as a foreign woman. I am often treated as a man would be. I sit with the men, eat with the men, dip snuff with the men. I have fished with them. They have let me ride buzkashi horses. All while their women are often shut away in the family home, not to be seen or heard. I'm in a fascinating position, being able to speak freely with the men who make the decisions, while having full access to the women because, despite my honorary male status, I *am* a woman. It allows me a unique insight into both sides of the gender equation, which often have extremely divergent perspectives.

I have discussed this with other foreign women I know who live and work in Afghanistan and Pakistan—journalists, photographers, writers, and aid workers—and they all have the same experience. They are most often met with curiosity and a willingness to talk as equals. Unfortunately, too often they are also faced with overly flirtatious Afghan men. More than once I have been groped in close quarters by a man who thought he could get away with it because I'm American. The assumption that American women are promiscuous is an unfortunate and deep-seated stereotype that has preceded me in many countries throughout the Middle East and Central Asia. It has led to more than one unwanted advancement, and the occasional marriage proposal. Thanks to globalization, the only consistent exposure many cultures have to American women is through movies, television, and music videos. Do we realize that our gender is judged on the standards of rap videos, Miley Cyrus, and the Kardashians?

Shaima, a friend I met on my first visit, illustrated the gender issue succinctly. Shaima was an American from Boulder, Colorado, and was half Afghan and half Costa Rican. She was in the country for several months to work with an Afghan nonprofit. Because she looked Afghan, she often encountered men who wouldn't speak to her. She would be at a meeting discussing next steps with the program they were working on, a program she was in charge of, and Afghan men often wouldn't shake her hand or speak to her directly. They would speak to her male colleagues as if she were invisible.

Over time I began to embrace the access that my honorary male status allowed. I was frustrated by the double standard, but I soon recognized the opportunity to challenge the gender barriers as a foreign woman in ways that might not have been tolerated if I were an Afghan woman. My theory was that beyond illustrating what a woman was capable of to Afghans, I would also be able to experience Afghanistan in a way few others had before me. By sharing my experiences and stories back home, perhaps I could challenge perceptions in both countries.

So it was on October 3, 2009, that I first put the rubber side down on a dry riverbed in the Panjshir Valley. It was part of the small but strategic Panjshir province, its mountains so steep that they'd kept the Taliban out—one of the few areas able to do so.

Travis, Hamid, Shah Mohammad, and I were driving through the province on the main road that followed the Panjshir River. Our driver, Shah Mohammad, was a sweet man I'd met on my first visit. Short and stout, he had a solemn face framed by a neatly trimmed beard and an ever-present embroidered white taqiyah prayer cap. We had seen some goat trails and a truck path on the other side of the river, so we were keeping our eyes peeled for a bridge large enough for our car. When we spotted one that seemed safe enough, Shah Mohammad drove through a small village and over the water. He opened the hatchback of the white Toyota Corolla so we could unload our gear.

Travis Beard and I had also met on my first visit a year prior. He'd become a trusted friend and an advisor to my fledgling non-profit organization, Mountain2Mountain. Focused on women's rights projects, it was what had brought me to Afghanistan in the first place. Travis was an Australian photojournalist, rock musician, motorcycle tourer, and aspiring filmmaker, and he was on hand to document the trip. I trusted his opinions and advice, if not necessarily sharing his comfort level of assumed risk. As he spent a lot of time traveling through Afghanistan on a motorcycle, he supported my desire to ride and had encouraged me in previous discussions. Trav came across as a brash and cynical war journo, but he nonetheless cared deeply about Afghanistan. He's done more for mentoring young Afghan photographers, artists, and musicians than anyone else I knew. Unlike most aid organizations and embassies, he's done it without the stamp of approval or the desire for credit, and often out of his own pocket.

Also along with us was Hamid, Travis's Afghan "brother." Hamid was working for me on this trip as my translator. He looked like a young Lenny Kravitz, circa "Fly Away," with a short curly fro and killer good looks. He would break hearts wide open if he lived somewhere where dating was acceptable. Not only was he always up for adventures, but his family was also Panjshiri. It was important to have someone with us who was local and considered part of the province's social fabric.

On this visit to Afghanistan, I was staying with Travis and Hamid, along with their other housemates, Nabil and Parweez, in their large private house in Kabul's central Taimani district. Living with a group of young Afghan men for several weeks was proving to be interesting. When I arrived with my bike, Hamid and Parweez were curious about my plan to ride it, and they watched the assembly as I took it out of the Thule bike box in pieces. We discussed the components, the tools, and what did what. Both of them rode motorcycles, but neither rode bicycles, and they thought I was a little crazy to want to ride a mountain bike instead of something with a motor. We talked in broad strokes about my plan, potential obstacles, and what to wear on a bike to keep from offending people in a country where women don't ride. The beauty of staying with them was that their house, like most in Kabul, had a walled courtyard, and I could take off my head scarf and dress as Western as I liked. And so, wearing my halter dress and jeans, I pulled on my cleats and took the bike outside into the courtyard, to see if my reassembly was adequate or if I'd forgotten something important.

Their courtyard was small and contained a car, three motor-bikes, and one frisky stray cat they'd adopted named Mojo. So it was a bit like a small BMX course for three-year-olds. My handling skills are poor at best and I'm not great with tight corners and switchbacks, so this was actually a challenging environment. I soon realized I needed more air in my front shock and my rear tire, and my seat was too low, but the brakes worked, and I thought I'd done a damn fine job at the first-time assembly. This coming from a girl who rarely washes the mud off her bike and whose only maintenance is occasionally remembering to oil her chain. Very occasionally.

More important, in the courtyard I discovered that I could, in fact, ride in jeans and a skirt. Not ideal in the heat, but feasibly ride-able and socially respectable. I had a few Patagonia halter dresses that I liked to wear over pants and under a tunic around town, and the combination proved comfortable for riding—a big start toward figuring out cycling attire that wouldn't offend in rural villages on or off the bike. So I continued playing around, coming up with a little clockwise courtyard circuit, round the garden, through the carport, under the clothesline, over the grass, up the concrete porch, and down the other side over the loose pile of bricks. I got more confident on the loop and picked up speed.

The trouble came as I reversed direction. Not paying attention, I rode toward the carport between the pillars that supported the clothesline I'd been ducking under. From this angle, I could get more speed but also had to go up the curb rather than down. I rode toward it, focused on the curb and lifting my bike up it, forgetting about the clothesline. It cut me across my right eye and the bridge of my nose, whipping my head back. I swore loudly as I instinctively took my feet off the pedals to keep my balance and put them on the ground, on either side of my bike. I doubled over and tentatively felt above my eye.

It was official. In my desire to be the first woman to mountain bike in Afghanistan, I had injured myself on day one, in a private courtyard, with a clothesline.

My eye hurt, but one of the housemates, Nabil, was on the porch watching, so as I got off my bike to go inside, I felt obliged to chat with him. My eye was starting to throb, so I excused myself, and Najib said, "Oh, yeah, your eye is bleeding quite a bit. You should go clean that."

Uh, thanks?

How about telling me that ten minutes ago when I was trying to pretend that I'm okay and could have a coherent conversation with you?

So I went upstairs to take a look and sure enough—I had gashed the bridge of my nose and my eyelid and they were already swelling. Nice. Really smooth, Shannon. My penchant for clumsiness was front and center in Afghanistan.

I decided that I'd had enough humiliation for one day, so I went back downstairs to put my bike away in the front room.

Three days later, I was unpacking it from the hatchback of Shah Mohammad's Corolla, beside a dry riverbed in the Panjshir Valley. Behind my sunglasses, my eye was still sore.

While I put the wheels on the bike, Travis went up the road and perched on a small hill to shoot some video from above. Hamid hung back with me while I attached the wheels. Shah Mohammad watched quietly, obviously curious as to what I was going to do next.

I considered my bike helmet. Wear it over my head scarf? No head scarf? What if I had to take my helmet off? Did I even need my helmet? How do I do this with the least amount of offensiveness and the least amount of awkwardness? I was already wearing many layers: long pants under my long dress under a long-sleeved tunic. The helmet seemed to fit over the head scarf, which I pulled down and wrapped around my neck and tied behind it—checking the length of drape so it wouldn't kill me Isadora Duncan–style by getting caught in the back wheel and breaking my neck.

I did a quick once-over . . . all seemed to be in order. Glasses. Bike gloves. Two wheels. By this point a healthy crowd of men had gathered around, mostly workmen from the construction trucks we'd passed. Since we were off the main road, I'd assumed we would be mostly alone. Nope. Word spreads like wildfire when something unusual is going on. Great, no pressure.

A stormy gray sky was developing, but the clouds hadn't yet covered the sun. I looked around. The rugged mountains rose up on all sides, and ahead of me a dry riverbed offered a rocky path that I could navigate. When I got the signal from Travis that he was ready, I took a deep breath and started pedaling. And, voilà! I was riding my bike. In Afghanistan. On my thirty-fifth birthday. A huge, goofy grin pasted itself to my face.

The path was strewn with boulders and was bumpy as hell. Since construction trucks came through here regularly, we knew this area was clear of land mines. I played around, hopping my bike over rocks, just enjoying the experience, and riding around to see what the terrain was like, how it felt to ride it, and what sort of reaction I created among the men who saw me. I had to go through runoffs that crisscrossed the ground as I picked my way through the riverbed. Each crossing sprayed water as I splashed through like a kid, trying not to slide on the slippery rocks just under the surface. It felt almost like riding back home, where I hit puddles and water at every chance, much to the horror of friends who try to keep their bikes clean.

Many of the men who were working in the area shouted "*Salaam*" when they saw me, but most simply watched curiously. I was riding back and forth along one section that was smooth and fun to play on when I noticed a mother and young girl sitting quietly, almost hidden, under a tree watching me. I immediately thought of my daughter, Devon, four years old and half the world away. I wished she could be here with me. As I rode past them I waved shyly, and they both smiled and waved back. I smiled and put my hand to my heart, the way Afghans do when they are saying "*Salaam*" to show respect, and they did the same.

My heart happy and my pants muddy, I arrived back at the car boiling hot under the layers of clothing. I couldn't stop grinning. I took off my helmet and grabbed a bottle of water. Hamid and I talked to a few of the local men who had gathered around. They asked where I was from and what I was doing there. I asked about their work and families. One young man shyly asked if he could ride my bike. I smiled and offered it to him, nodding. "Bale"—*Yes*. He smiled back more confidently as he took my bike. He pedaled around in wide circles while the men laughed and joked with one another.

The clouds rolled in, blotting out the sun, so we said our good-byes, and I quickly took off the wheels to put the bike back in the car. We were heading to the village of Dashty Rewat and didn't want to arrive in the dark. We still had a few hours of driving ahead of us, much of it on dodgy dirt roads. Until now we'd been on paved or relatively smooth dirt roads just inside the entrance to the valley, and we'd made good time.

Unfortunately, when we hit the dirt roads, it became apparent that Shah Mohammad should not be driving outside Kabul. He couldn't see the numerous crudely constructed concrete speed bumps made to slow down traffic through the villages that dot the main road. His ancient Corolla was not meant to take on these things at high speed, yet he seemingly couldn't see them until it was too late. The lack of shocks in the car rattled our bodies each time the car made contact with the speed bumps. The problem came to a head as we were driving around the hill of Massoud's tomb. It sat in the middle of the valley overlooking the river. As we rounded a bend, Shah Mohammad overcooked the turn and suddenly the car was careening straight toward the cliff.

Travis had been sleeping in the seat next to me, holding his camera in his lap, when I screamed.

Luckily for us, a few months prior, as part of the ongoing construction work being done on the road, and on Massoud's tomb above us, rock barriers had been built along the cliff. I hadn't noticed them the last time I visited. Even more luckily, the barriers were solidly built. We busted off a chunk when the Corolla made impact, but the car didn't follow the rocks tumbling down the cliff side. Shah Mohammad quickly tried to reverse the Corolla so he could keep driving. We all shouted for him to stop so we could check the car, the barrier, and collect ourselves.

I looked over at Travis, he looked at me, and we both leaned forward to look into the front seat to check on Hamid. He appeared stunned. None of us had been wearing seat belts. I wasn't even sure there were any functioning in the car. We'd come inches from death, and I realized that in a so-called near-death experience your life doesn't flash before your eyes. You just think, "Oh, shit!" and everything else is blank.

Without saying a word, we all got out to look at the car and the barrier.

"What the hell, dude?" said Hamid in a low voice to Travis.

His years as an English translator for American troops and hanging around expats like Travis had honed his slang and timing, and I often forgot that Dari was his first language. The fender and wheel panel were smashed in, but there was far less damage than I'd expected. Judging from the rectangular barriers on either side, I guessed that the one we'd hit had lost half of its concrete. We looked at one another again, and then we all started laughing, the adrenaline leaving our bodies. Hamid and Travis peered over the edge. "*Daaaamn*," said Hamid.

"Uh, guys? You gotta look at this." They turned around. I pointed at the car.

Shah Mohammad had gotten a crowbar out and, as if to prove that Corollas were as resilient as the Afghans themselves, he hooked the curved end of the crowbar under the fender and pulled it back into place. He did the same with the wheel panel. Good as new! Sort of. Hamid shook his head in disbelief.

We piled back into the car and continued onward as if nothing out of the ordinary had happened. We got about an hour or so farther down the road, which had quickly become bumpy, rock strewn, gutted out, and four-by-four worthy. It was around this time that Shah Mohammad started complaining. He wasn't happy he had to drive so far, on such bad roads. Hamid, who sat beside him and was the only one of us fluent in Dari, one of Afghanistan's two national languages, took the brunt of it. About fifteen minutes from Dashty Rewat, we encountered a massive rock pile that we had to navigate across. Shah Mohammad told Hamid he wouldn't go any farther. The discussion became a bit of a kerfuffle, and I said I wouldn't pay the full day's rate if he turned around. I told Hamid to explain that we had hired him for the day to go to Panjshir. If he had a problem with the distance or the roads, he should have said so and we could have hired another driver. He continued to complain but he also continued to drive. I didn't blame him really. We were all getting cranky, hungry, and tired. The road was battering our bodies as well as our moods. But Travis continued to sleep, his camera cradled in his lap like a small cat.

Travis and Hamid had spent time in Dashty Rewat on their first attempt to summit the Anjuman Pass, which borders the back end of the Panjshir Valley. They traveled there by motorcycle with their good friend and fellow adventurer Jeremy Kelly. They'd randomly stopped here at dusk to ask if any of the villagers knew where they could spend the night. Idi Mohammad, one of the villagers, had immediately offered his home. In the time-honored tradition of Muslim hospitality, all three had received a warm meal and a place to sleep. It turned out that Idi Mohammad was the principal of the boys' school and Travis told him about me and the work I was looking to do with my organization, Mountain2Mountain. Travis, Hamid, and Jeremy were unsuccessful on their first attempt to summit the Anjuman Pass, and were stopped by the local police in Parion and forced to spend a night in their custody. They returned a few weeks later with a letter of introduction from the Panjshir governor to complete the ride, and again stayed with Idi Mohammad's family. Knowing I would be interested in meeting Idi and discussing education in a rural community, Travis had promised to introduce me to him the next time I was in Afghanistan.

Dashty Rewat looked much the same as any of the other villages we'd been driving through—crumbling mud walls and shipping containers that housed various shops along the dirt road. It had the general look of a village recently used for bombing practice. The only distinguishing feature was its remoteness and a new structure being built. Two men were on the roof of a two-story white building. One turned out to be Idi Mohammad, in a light-brown pakol hat, the type favored by the Northern Alliance mujahideen leader and Panjshiri hero, Ahmad Shah Massoud.

Panjshir is known as the Valley of the Five Lions, and Massoud was often referred to as the Lion of Panjshir. He was a powerful figure not just in Panjshir but throughout Afghanistan, a rare Che Guevara type, with iconic photographs on buildings, roadside banners, and even in the windows of cars. He was not just beloved by his own Panjshiris, but potentially had the ability to unite Afghanistan. He rose to fame as a mujahideen leader fighting the Soviet-backed central government. After the Soviets withdrew, the Afghan government collapsed. Civil war erupted and Kabul became the battleground for mujahideen factions fighting for control of the city and the country. Eventually, the Taliban took Kabul, and Panjshir became a key staging ground in the fight against the Taliban under Massoud's leadership of the Northern Alliance. The high mountains surrounding the narrow province create a natural defense, and Panjshir was not taken by the Taliban. Massoud was assassinated on September 9, 2001, by posing as a news crew under the orders of Osama bin Laden. When the United States was attacked two days later on 9/11, many analysts made the connection to the major terrorist attack Massoud had warned against several months earlier in a speech to the European Parliament. The United States soon found itself in Afghanistan, hunting Bin Laden, and fighting the Taliban on the side of Massoud's Northern Alliance. Revered in life, he is still revered in death. The tomb under construction on the hillside overlooking the valley is a symbol of the people's love, as are the men that still serve him and his cause. There is a pride and independence in Panjshir that comes from their love of their commander and his love of Panjshir, which is still plainly visible in every village.

Idi's face lit up when he saw Travis and Hamid stepping out of the car, and he shouted down at us, "*Salaam! Salaam!*" He quickly climbed down from the roof, beaming broadly, while we walked around back, gathering a crowd of children and men. Travis shouted up, "*Salaam,*" in his Aussie drawl, waving up at the men. "*Salaam,*

salaam," he said to the children, smiling and high-fiving some of them as we walked through the crowd.

After Travis, Hamid, Idi, and the second man, Idi's brother Fardin, embraced and shook hands, I was introduced and found myself, once again, mesmerized by the handsome features of Panjshiri men. Photos of Massoud highlight his charisma, and my Panjshiri friends are all striking. Idi Mohammad was no different. Idi was genuinely happy to see the guys and asked how their motorbike trip went. He'd been worried about them. There was no cell phone service, so he had no way of knowing if they'd encountered problems, if they'd been successful, or even if they'd gotten back alive.

The men were disappointed that Jeremy was not with us. Travis explained to me that they'd loved his red hair and beard. Hamid explained to Idi in Dari that Jeremy was working in Kabul, but that he was healthy and sent his best to everyone.

Idi asked us to come inside and join his family for dinner and to spend the night, since the sun was already behind the mountains. Hamid explained to him that we'd wanted to drive out to Dashty Rewat so that they could introduce me, but that we had to go back tonight, especially now as our driver was being such a pain in the ass. Idi Mohammad looked concerned and unhappy that we couldn't stay. He offered a second time in case we were simply being polite in declining, but we explained that our driver was the main issue and that we would come back next week and plan to stay longer. Idi agreed and we sat down to talk on a stone wall overlooking the road and the mountains as the entire village watched, or at least the men and the children. Not one woman was to be seen.

Idi explained to me that he was a teacher, and like many Afghans during the civil war, he'd spent years as a refugee with his family across the border in Pakistan. In Pakistan, he received an education, and when he returned to his village, he started up a school for the local boys with a few other teachers. It expanded as more and more families sent their boys, and they now had a school that provided education through high school. He was the principal and while they had a school and teachers, they lacked supplies. This was something I could potentially help with. We discussed the immediate need for paper and pens. Ironically, the simple lack of supplies is the unfortunate reason many children do not attend school in countries like Afghanistan. Families are often too poor to afford the twenty cents for a notebook. The school housed six hundred students on average. Amazingly, their other need was computers. I was surprised and asked why. Idi Mohammad explained that it could connect them to the rest of the world and allow their remote village to provide a better education. They already had a teacher trained in computer science, so it was simply a matter of machines. Many of their boys hoped to get into Kabul University, and basic computer skills could help.

When I asked about the girls' education, he replied that there was no school in the village or nearby.

"Would the village be open to the idea of a girls' school?" I asked.

"Yes, we would allow our girls to go to school. It is a very necessary thing for all children. Boys and girls."

"Is there land that could be used, or a building that could be improved? Are there any female teachers in the area?"

"Yes, we can discuss that more. There is a piece of land that used to be a girls' school before the Russians. There are no female teachers. But if it was just through year five, we could use male teachers."

"Could we discuss this more when I return?"

"I would be most honored to discuss it further, and I will help in any way I can."

During the last few minutes of the talk, we heard banging. Behind us, in the street, Shah Mohammad was striking the front fender with the crowbar. Was this passive aggressive behavior to get us moving along, or did he really think it would further improve the dents?

I shook my head in disbelief, but I reluctantly stood. I shook Idi's hand and the hands of many others in the crowd. "*Tashakur, Idi. Khoda al fez.*" Thank you. Good-bye. We all said good-bye, and I promised to come back the next week with school supplies as a start, and we'd stay for a few days.

Back in the car I was positively giddy. I was fully aware that this meeting wouldn't have been possible without the previous visits and cups of tea drunk by Travis and Hamid—opening the door for me to step in with solid connections already in place.

"Thank you, thank you, Trav. I am so grateful. You have made this the best birthday ever." He smiled amusedly and muttered in his dry Aussie drawl, "Yeah, yeah," and promptly fell asleep again.

I leaned back and sighed with contentment as we began the long drive home, dusk already setting in as Shah Mohammad bitched to an uninterested Hamid, who continued playing his role as seeing-eye dog in the front seat, pointing out speed bumps and upcoming curves. Strangely enough, Shah Mohammad was now wearing a pair of glasses. *Perhaps they could have been of use a few hours ago when we nearly died?* I thought to myself.

Five days later we drove back to Dashty Rewat in a rented four-by-four. We left Shah Mohammad in Kabul. Hamid was at the wheel. The back was filled with a thousand dollars' worth of school supplies and my bike, which I hoped to ride some more. We had a five-song playlist of American hip-hop in the tape deck and another tape with five Bollywood songs. "In Da Club" by 50 Cent bumped loudly on repeat halfway through the trip while Hamid sang along gangsta-like in his new black sunglasses we'd bought at Bagram's black market that morning. Travis was in front of us on his Honda dirt bike.

Once we got inside the Panjshir gates and completed the security check-in with the guards, we stopped at several places we'd spotted on the last visit where I'd wanted to bike but hadn't had time. Four or five times along the route, I unpacked the bike with Hamid's help. None of the paths connected, so I couldn't ride far, but I explored different areas and had discussions with new groups of men. On each ride, I gained more confidence and was soon enjoying the interactions with the men that gathered. Hamid answered questions while I rode and when I returned, he made introductions and the discussions continued. I was met with curiosity about who I was and why I was there. I answered and asked my own questions: Did their kids go to school? Girls and boys? Could girls play sports? Would they allow their girls to ride bikes? If not, why not? Impromptu discussions by the side of the road naturally unfolded and progressed down different rabbit holes. Each time, I had to tear myself away and decline offers of tea or dinner at their homes.

Several hours later, as we pulled into Dashty Rewat, night was falling. Idi Mohammad's brother, Fardin, welcomed us back. Thirty seconds after our arrival, flashlights came out of the courtyard and we were led back into the home. We'd let Idi Mohammad know when we were coming, but he was in Kabul for a few days to buy supplies for the guesthouse he was building. His brothers made us feel more than welcome. We were led into a large rectangular room, with traditional dark-red toshaks lining the floor and three sea-foam green walls. While seated on the toshaks and pillows, we were fed, watered, and introduced to a few neighbors who came to check out the foreign visitors. One in particular was a real comic. Older, missing a few teeth, he wore a traditional pakol hat and a pale-green shalwar kameez that matched the walls. He had the look of a real outdoorsman, Afghan-style. He brought an old boom box—circa 1970s. It was encased inside a burgundy velvet "purse" brocaded with mirrors.

"So Afghan," Travis said with a lazy smile, shaking his head in wonder at the scene that was unfolding. Laughing at the unexpected entertainment, I glanced over at him. Chuckling, Travis winked at me and stood up. He put the velvet-encased boom box on his shoulder to demonstrate how they were carried in the hood. As the entire room clapped and sang, Hamid perked up from his toshak, where he had been quietly watching. Travis handed the boom box back, grinning, and sat down to the appreciative laughter of the entire room. Our visitor was a natural comic. He left the room, and when he came back in, he strutted through the doorway with the boom box on one shoulder and his hat cocked over an eye—another Afghan gangsta. He sat with a big smile, and I took his photo, laughing so hard my iPhone shook. The entire room had erupted in laughter.

The family lived together in this compound, three brothers, four wives, two grandmothers, and approximately fourteen children, although I never got an accurate count. The women stayed in a separate part of the home. The young boys served dinner, so the women were still not seen. After dinner I was invited to go back and have tea and talk with them, but was told no camera, and no translator, since Hamid was a man. One of Idi's boys came along and offered to translate. His English was very basic and my Dari was even worse—but it was sufficient for niceties and general questions. The four wives were beautiful and the two grandmothers had heavily lined faces, full of character and with smiling eyes that made me feel welcome. Children ran around and were allowed free rein through the compound. They were curious, having never met a foreign woman before, and they gestured for me to sit on the floor. The oldest girl, maybe thirteen, brought me green tea and placed a dish of dried berries and walnuts in front of me. They sat, surrounding me on all sides—four wives, two grandmothers, and about a dozen children.

Only three men lived here so I assumed one had two wives, but didn't feel it was appropriate to ask so soon after meeting them. With the confusion my young translator had with family words—brother, cousin, mother, sister all interchanged randomly—I figured that I wouldn't understand the answer even if I asked. I didn't know if this was a case of two wives for one brother, or if perhaps one was a sister whose husband had died. Instead, I asked less complicated questions, mostly about the family. I complimented the children and learned how to sit quietly, smile, and drink tea with twenty silent faces watching me. I offered to answer their questions as well, but they didn't have many, were too shy, or didn't understand what I'd said. Sometimes I want to share that I, too, have a daughter, but then there's the husband question. Where is my husband? Why do you only have one daughter? Are you barren? I have learned to avoid this question simply by saying that he lives in the United States and takes care of my daughter while I'm in Afghanistan. This is essentially true, and the subject is dropped, but with the people I am building relationships with, it sometimes feels like a falsehood not to explain that I'm divorced and to allow them to think what they will. Divorce is rarely an option here, and women who are divorced are typically looked upon dishonorably. Family is everything in Afghanistan. Men may take many wives, but rarely will they request a divorce. It is rarer still for a woman to be granted one should she choose to request it. When a Muslim man decides he wants a divorce, he can just say the words, "I divorce you," and it is official under Islamic law. The courts are starting to hear women's divorce cases, but it is still rare. Yet, as with many other things, like riding a bike and motorcycle, or sitting with the men, I am a foreign woman and divorce isn't so shocking. But without the ability to communicate well, I didn't want to risk delving into this subject.

Despite my desire to sit and talk with the women all night—as I would in the United States—I'm much more comfortable with the men. I said good night to the ladies after an hour or so, and asked if I could come back in the morning to take photos. They told me that photos of the children and grandmothers would be okay, but the older girls and the wives were off limits. I wondered if it was an issue of simply not liking their photo taken, or if it was forbidden by the men. But the gorgeous wife of Idi Mohammad mimed getting slapped if I took her photo. It was forbidden. This still surprises me when I meet the wives of men I think of as more progressive, or at least less conservative. Idi Mohammad was a principal and teacher; he valued education, including girls' education. He treated me as an equal and yet had these deep-seated cultural restrictions firmly in place with his own women—always hidden away. That's not to say they weren't treated well by Afghan standards, or were even un-happy. That I couldn't answer. But they were not free. They did not have the same rights as men. Their lives were controlled by men, and often even by the sons they'd raised. And that was not freedom, nor could I believe that anyone could be truly happy without it.

Amid hugs, handshakes, and smiles, I again promised to come back in the morning to take photos. I walked through the inner courtyard to the men's side. I ducked under the low doorway and found Travis and Hamid laughing. One of the neighbors, the tooth-less one with the Afghan boom box, had expressed interest in purchasing me as a second wife. Prices had been discussed, half-jokingly. No harm or unease apparently, just a laugh on the boys' part. Apparently, they talked him up to $120,000. They were quite pleased with the amount and figured they could retire on the beach somewhere cheap. I played along halfheartedly, joking about selling women wasn't as rib splitting to me as it was to them. I told Hamid that I'm worth at least half a million. *Good luck raising that kind of cash in the rural mountains of Afghanistan,* I thought. Still, we were sitting in the heart of the emerald mining region, so who knew what was possible?

As we got ready for bed, I realized I had no idea where the bathroom was. Bathroom facilities are always an interesting experience in the developing world and seem to be a source of much discussion and comparison by travelers. In Afghanistan, they cover the entire spectrum: from the luxury of a flush toilet in foreign guesthouses and cafés, to porcelain squat toilets on the floor in restaurants and government buildings, to a concrete floor with a hole cut in it Porta-Potty style, to the horror of a facility that involves any of the above three, reeking of urine and with nothing but a watering can to clean up with. No toilet paper, coupled with no running water or soap.

Here, the outhouse was like many in rural areas, a small raised mud structure with a hole in the floor through which everything simply dropped on the ground below. I had a group of children following me everywhere to make sure I was okay, and that I had everything I needed. When I asked, *"Tashnab kujas?"* they offered me a small shared roll of pink toilet paper and even gave me their slip-on sandals so that I didn't have to put on my cumbersome motorcycle boots. It is a little unnerving to be the center of attention and the recipient of so much curiosity in the best of times, but to be the center of attention for a trip to the bathroom is more than a little awkward. We walked to the outhouse as a procession, and I smiled and thanked them as I went up the step and inside. Eight or so children waited for me. I closed the warped wooden door and blocked it with the rock placed there for that purpose. I hoped I wouldn't have performance anxiety as I could hear the kids chattering excitedly while they waited for me. When I emerged, eight smiles greeted me, and I couldn't help but smile back. I let them lead me to a pump where I washed my hands, and then they escorted me back to the main room.

Hamid, Travis, and I were invited to sleep there on the toshaks. Big heavy blankets were brought out from the corner where they'd been stacked neatly, and the men literally tucked us all in—even Travis and Hamid. It was possibly the strangest bedtime ritual ever, but quite sweet. I felt like a little kid and wondered if I'd get read a bedtime story. We slept in our clothes. I'd been mountain biking in mine all day and would be wearing them for two more—day and night. The men made sure we had a flashlight and everything else we needed and bade us good night. A couple of the older boys slept with us on the other side of the room, either out of curiosity or for security.

Travis and I woke up at a predawn six o'clock to do some biking in the village. I wanted to ride without attracting so much attention. I should have known better. Even at this early hour, we were the talk of the town. All the village men came out to watch and chat, and many invited me to breakfast. Throughout it all there was a lot of curiosity and no animosity. An old man in a traditional brown blanket worn as a shawl and a matching pakol hat stopped me in the street to talk. He mimed pedaling, and I understood that he wanted to know how I clipped my feet in, so I showed him the cleats on the bottom of my cycling shoes and how they clipped into the pedals on the bike. Several young men took turns riding my bike around the village street. One man who I stopped to chat with—and by "chat" I mean mime and speak with in my limited Dari since Hamid was still sleeping—apparently worked in the emerald mines in the mountains behind the boys' school. He mimed necklaces and bracelets and invited me to breakfast. Maybe I'd found Afghan husband number two? I explained that I had plans to visit the school and thanked him. A few minutes later, I was stopped by an older man with a striking long white beard, a kind wrinkled face, and twinkling eyes. He was strolling through the early morning in his traditional green striped Afghan coat, the ones with the long, skinny arms that aren't used but instead hang down the back; the coat itself is draped from the shoulders like a cloak. He asked if I was cold, and we commented on the weather and the beautiful mountains in the sunrise. He had the sort of face that spoke of stories to be shared, and I cursed Hamid in his bed for preventing me from a deeper conversation. Then I cursed myself for my dependence on a translator. I vowed to make learning Dari a priority. Whether from lack of focus and time, or simple laziness, I have struggled with foreign languages, despite having lived overseas for a decade prior to Afghanistan.

Many people peeked out of windows and came down from the fields to watch the crazy woman on the bike. Amazingly—just like on yesterday's ride—no one was hostile, offended, or annoyed. There were just smiles, laughter, joking, simple curiosity, and the desire to chat. "What is your name? Why are you here? Why are you riding a bike?" In exchange I got to share about myself—my love of bikes, my work with Mountain2Mountain, my desire to see Afghanistan and learn about its people. Men nodded and smiled, and invited me to have tea with their families. I asked questions about girls playing sports, if that was acceptable, and if so, which sports? Soccer and basketball were the most common answers, both sports that could be done in privacy, at school or behind courtyard walls.

I rode through rocky, dried-up fields, empty after the early fall harvest. I had to navigate piles of dirt as solid as concrete and practiced bunny hops, working hard to avoid crashing. I had a first aid kit, but I'd have preferred not to break it out. My future husband was there, this time strutting through town to show off his hunting rifle and prove his prowess as a skillful provider. He'd told us last night that he was a proficient deer hunter. Apparently, there were several hundred deer in the area, but he was in need of binoculars to spot their grazing areas. I smiled weakly, took a few photos, and when he saw I had the camera out, he again hammed it up, tilting his hat like a French beret and strutting, the rifle jauntily held over his shoulder. He then stopped and offered to take us fishing after we visited the boys' school. I knew that both Travis and Hamid would be keen to go after the school visit, and I was curious to check out the local fishing techniques. I had seen Afghans throw sticks of dynamite into the river to get fish. Another friend had watched RPGs launched into the river to catch dinner. Hoping for something less dangerous and more sustainable, I agreed that we'd come along. Fishing would be another experience that continued to link my life and work in mountain communities here to the mountain community where I lived in Breckenridge, Colorado.

I discovered a much better way to bike with the men's kaffiyeh scarves, which was what I began to wear on the motorcycle to look like a man. These were black-and-white patterned scarves often worn around the neck or wrapped around the head like a turban. I wrapped it around my head and my face, leaving only my eyes peeking out when I was traveling by motorycle. It helped keep the dust out of my nose and mouth, and disguised my gender. It was perfect for the bike, but instead of wearing it like a full-face turban, I wore it like a hadji from the nineties, or the politically incorrectly named "cancer patient" style, and then I simply added another scarf around my neck. If I could get away with it, I'd wear them all the time. They're much more my style than the women's head scarves, still respectful but edgy and much more functional. My walk is even different when I wear men's scarves. Women's scarves blow off in the wind, and I have to constantly hold them, so I tend to look down more to keep them in place and as a result I don't make eye contact with others. I wear the men's, and I'm actually more covered up—my blond hair all tucked away, the scarf so tight it doesn't slip like the women's, and my neck covered completely. Yet I walk like me, big strides, head up, athletic, with a more confident, almost defiant, demeanor. I stand out because women don't wear men's scarves, but I stand out anyway in the women's scarves that show much more blond hair and constantly fall back off my head. So it's a crapshoot. The men's scarves wouldn't work in the south or in more conservative areas, or for formal meetings, but for around Kabul and Panjshir they're perfect. Hell, with my reputation for forgetting to wash my hair in Colorado, they'd be perfect back home!

We went back to the house after an hour or so of biking and making friends. Immediately, Travis crawled back into bed, laying down on the toshak next to Hamid, who hadn't yet stirred. I needed the bathroom and a wash after two days of wearing the same clothes while biking in the Afghan dust. The bathroom processional followed me to the outhouse and again I listened to them giggle and chatter on the other side of the door. I walked back to the main room, and my young translator from the night before asked if I would like to wash up. He pointed to the door across from the room where we were sleeping. Inside was a small concrete cubicle the size of a Western shower but without a drain. A broken mirror was propped against a tiny window that let in a few rays of early morning light. I nodded gratefully with a "*Bale, lotfon.*" Yes, please.

He brought me a jug of blissfully warm water that the wives had warmed up. He placed it on the floor, and I closed the door with a "*tashakur.*" I washed my face and my feet but couldn't bear to take off all my clothes in the cold air just to put them back on again dirty. I would get a full shower soon enough. The warm water and the cold air on my face refreshed me, and I felt ready for the full day ahead.

We'd passed by the boys' school during the bike ride through town and discovered that we would have to cross a narrow bridge to get there. This made delivery of the school supplies more complex. After a quick breakfast of naan, fresh cream, and cherry jam with the men of the house, we drove the four-by-four along the road to the path that led down the hill to the bridge. As we unpacked the supplies and stacked them on the ground, various men gathered around to watch and help us unload. When the four-by-four was empty, the villagers stopped the young boys walking by on their way to school and had them help carry boxes. The young boys each took a small box, and the teachers and older boys took the heavier loads. We walked as a long procession down the steep path to the bridge.

The boys led the way across, and we walked up concrete stairs into an enclosed dirt courtyard at the foot of a mountain. I hung back as the boys went inside and took their seats in the classrooms, the courtyard briefly quiet. It was such a small gesture, giving school supplies. But if it meant these boys, who might have the chance and opportunity to go on to university, felt that others were valuing their education, then perhaps they would feel more valued in return and understand that an American woman cared whether or not they went to school. Or maybe they just thought, "Hey, you crazy infidel, thanks for nothing!" Hopefully, it was the former.

I knew some people might wonder why I would help a boys' school when my focus was on girls' and women's rights. This was a simple first step, a drop in the bucket, that could help the children at the school where Idi Mohammad and his brother worked. When I made this first step and then opened up a discussion of their views on girls' education and potential sites for future schools, they understood that my intention was sincere. I wanted to help the children of this area get an education. Educating boys often leads to more understanding of the value of education and can open the doors to educating girls. I continued to discuss land potentially available for a girls' school. Building a school was perhaps not necessary if we could find available rooms in the village. The real issue is that there simply aren't enough female teachers in Afghanistan. Doing a little bit to support the boys and visiting the school would give me more leverage to say, "The boys already have a school, teachers, and education through high school, but the girls have nothing right now." Both Idi Mohammad and his brother had girls—none of whom were in school. I wanted to ask them bluntly, "If you believe in education so much, then why aren't you working to get your girls in school? Why aren't you teaching them at home? Why are they worth less than your sons?" But I didn't. Instead I looked for a back door into that discussion.

Distributing the supplies was bizarre. I wanted to get photos and film a little so that I could show the images to donors back in the United States. But trying to get the teachers and administration to "do it for the camera" was hilarious. I hated having to do these things for the camera. It felt false, and I was sure they were wondering, "Why are we pretending to unpack the boxes here when we want to do it over there?" Though I'd like to do the work without fanfare and let the work speak for itself, I needed to document it to build support for Mountain2Mountain back home so that I could fund future projects. The video camera is a powerful tool to share stories and engage supporters.

Distributing the supplies in a second-grade room, I encountered a stern teacher in camo fatigues. He didn't smile or shake my hand when we greeted each other, and I wasn't sure what he thought of me or the situation. We were led to a fourth-grade class. As I began to distribute supplies with a couple of the teachers, the room quickly became chaotic, with notebooks, pens, and pencils being passed in all directions, one gruff teacher shouting at the boys. They looked dumbfounded, as if they were wondering what was going on. No one had made an introduction or an announcement to explain what we were doing there.

Down the hall, we visited a twelfth-year class with their English teacher. He was very interested in getting computers for the school. He'd studied in Pakistan and recently returned to Dashty Rewat. He stood at the front with me, and we talked to the boys. When I asked how many wanted to go on to university, all of them raised their hands. Most wanted to study to be doctors and engineers, but there was a journalist as well. I asked how many thought they would need to use computers to reach their career goals. All of them raised their hands, but when I asked how many had used a computer before, only one raised his hand.

After visiting several classrooms, I sat down to interview the head of the teachers, but the conversation was stilted, and I struggled to get answers from him. The English teacher was also there and replied to a few more questions. Sitting next to him was the Islamic teacher, who said nothing. He didn't smile and was impossible to read. Oh, the questions I had for him . . . but most of them were inappropriate for a first meeting and too deep for an informal discussion. I couldn't think of any questions for him that weren't controversial. During these trips to Afghanistan, I was often stepping into the shoes of a journalist. I was excited by the opportunity to have conversations with remote villagers, government officials, school teachers, members of Parliament, and prisoners, but I'm not a trained journalist. I'd prefer to have meandering conversations inspired by my curiosity about their lives, families, communities, and thoughts.

Outside, the students gathered in the courtyard to sing for us while the teacher in camo fatigues tried to bully them into some form of order. After they finished, I let a few of the older boys take turns riding my bike. They rode it around the courtyard, narrowly missing the younger boys, scattering them like bowling pins.

We said our good-byes and walked back across the bridge to the four-by-four. Idi Mohammad's youngest child was in the backseat. He'd been there since we started to unload more than an hour ago. He was sitting quietly, looking as if he'd been left there as a gift or a bodyguard. As we unloaded the boy and loaded up my bike, men gathered around to discuss the day's events thus far, and as if on cue, my future husband turned up to take us fishing.

Travis, Hamid, and I walked with our personal fishing guide through town, and went down a small path that led behind his house. We stopped in the patch of yard behind his house and watched him don green waders and matching rubber boots. He grabbed his weighted net and nodded at us with a mischievious smile. We followed him to the river just below his house. He had a large Afghan dog with pale blond fur and black markings on its face, and it followed us to the water's edge. I reached down to scratch his head. Our guide waded to the middle of the river and expertly threw his net. On the second throw, he aimed into the current and pulled the net back with a fish. He smiled triumphantly at us. He threw the fish onto the beach where a young man, maybe his son, picked it up and speared it on a stick. He caught six fish in about half an hour, and I was presented with them all strung up on the bendy stick, some of them still thrashing. I was unsure whether by accepting I would be accepting more than just the fish, but as no money had exchanged hands and I didn't see Travis and Hamid high-fiving or discussing vacation plans, I assumed that I was still a free and single woman.

We walked back to our house, and when the men saw the fish, they took them to the wives, who cleaned them and packed them in plastic for our journey to Kabul. I would have been happy to leave them there as a gift, but alas, they were returning with us in the four-by-four.

We stayed for lunch—not that we had a choice. It was already planned so we gratefully sat down and stretched out on toshaks. While we waited, we chatted aimlessly, and the men pulled out tins of naswar and shaped small balls that they then slipped into their mouths. Naswar is essentially snuff. The ball of powdered tobacco sits against your gums for a while and then gets spit out. Travis said it was like a really intense cigarette, and the men offered some to me. After checking that it was straight tobacco, not mixed with hashish or opium, I accepted.

Fardin handed me the tin, and Hamid used the lid to section out a small amount that he put into my hand. The technique is to use the forefinger and thumb of the other hand to squeeze the powder into a tiny ball and place it into the crease of the bottom lip. Hamid laughed as I tried, unsuccessfully, to make a ball like Fardin's. He poured a little more into my hand, and this time I squeezed it properly. I pulled my lip down and placed it where they showed me, and sat back. The men smiled and nodded, and Travis and Hamid were laughing. A slight burning began at my gumline then spread; my entire bottom jaw became somewhat numb. Travis told me about being given a large portion of naswar by a villager last year. It was so strong he had to run to the toilet and vomit—this coming from a man who smoked cigarettes and marijuana regularly. I laughed, then realized my head was spinning. I felt very mellow and a little sleepy. Hamid joked that we'd get home faster this way since I'd be sleeping in the car and we wouldn't have to stop to bike or take photos. I would have laughed out loud if my head wasn't so woozy.

After about five minutes, I discarded the little wad into the spittoon as directed and spat a few times. The naswar tasted awful, and I didn't want to swallow any.

I sat back. I was starting to break out in a cold sweat. I decided I should go to the outhouse. I stood up—a little wobbly—and immediately realized I needed to move quickly. I thrust my feet into my motorcycle boots and hurried to open the front door. Two big rocks were blocking it, and the children were all signaling that I should duck under the other door that led to the inner courtyard of the women's area to get to the outhouse. One handed me the pink roll of toilet paper, and they all followed. I felt the bile rising and was desperate to figure out which direction was the correct one, never having been this way in the daylight. I burped, the taste of bile in my mouth, but I controlled myself. I saw the outhouse and raced inside, barely having time to put the stone in place before I hurled into the hole.

Vomiting is unpleasant enough into a clean toilet. Vomiting into a hole with a mound of feces so high that my face was mere inches away took things to another level. I spat a few times, then slowly stood up. I steadied myself with a hand on the wall and looked out the open hole at the chickens wandering around the dirt courtyard. One of the little girls was chasing them with high-pitched squeals. I wished my head would stop swimming. I breathed deeply but immediately regretted it as the stench alone was enough to bring on another round of vomiting. I slid the rock out of the way with my foot and stepped down into the courtyard. The women and the children were all waiting to see how I was. They waved me over to the water pump so I could rinse my hands. I smiled weakly in gratitude, then splashed my face.

"*Tashakur, tashakur,*" I said, thanking them. Two of the wives came over to the water pump and started talking quickly. They were either miming eating, washing my face, or vomiting. I tried to keep up, but my head was still fuzzy, and I didn't have my little translator with me to fill in the gaps. I mumbled, "*Naswar?*" and they mimed the mouth action again. I took it to mean vomiting. I nodded, and they giggled, and I nodded some more, said *tashakur* one more time, and turned to leave.

As I walked slowly back, I wished I could just find a quiet corner and sit down for a few minutes alone. The emotions and experiences were swirling around. The constant yin-yanging of fear and exhilaration was playing havoc with my emotions. The constant questioning and the feeling of being a specimen under a microscope, being examined and judged, was more overwhelming than I had anticipated. I just wanted a little space to get grounded and absorb everything that was happening. I was experiencing Afghanistan in a way few get a chance to, and it was opening up so much. I wanted to do so much, but the learning curve was still wickedly steep—much like the mountains I tried to conquer on my bike.

As I explored rural Afghanistan, the bike was proving to be a valuable tool. I'd wanted to engage here in unique ways. I wanted to share the beauty of the land and its people back home. But more than that, the bike had become an icebreaker among the Afghans I met in ways I could never have imagined. The idea that I could ride a bike—something that symbolizes personal freedom and mobility—in a place known for war and oppression was amazing. It was even more amazing that I could challenge this particular gender barrier as a foreign woman. I was struggling to reconcile that joy with the knowledge that the women here were still confined to the back part of the home and couldn't leave without wearing a burqa.

I took a deep breath to steady myself and reminded myself that each step brought me a little closer to understanding what I wanted to do here.

I entered the room where the men were all still seated, feeling sheepish, and sat back down.

Just in time for lunch.

2

Genesis

Colorado 2006-2009

A week later I was back home, cuddling on the couch with my daughter, Devon, while we watched *Ratatouille*, a movie about a rat who dreams of being a chef in Paris. Of the children's movies we had, it was one of my favorites. I was struggling to keep my eyes open. Jet lag made it hard to stay awake past 6:00 P.M., so we were curled up on the couch under a blanket, and I dozed with my arms around her, her hair smelling sweetly of her sweat from a day of playing outside. I was exhausted but happy. Devon didn't mind I had fallen asleep. When it was over, she turned her face up and kissed my cheek, and I squeezed her. I was so tired.

"Okay, chica. Let's get you to bed. And me. Go brush your teeth, okay?"

"Okay, mommy," she replied, kissed me again on the nose, and crab-walked down the hall. I listened for the sound of running water to signal she was actually brushing her teeth. Feeling like a zombie,

I sat up and stared numbly into space as I waited for her return. A few minutes later she came back and crawled onto my lap.

"Come on, Mommy!"

"Okay, I'm up. I'm up." I laughed. She slid down and grabbed my hand pretending to help me stand up. Then she reached up and I held out my arms in prep for her to jump up. I carried her to bed, luckily only a few feet away from the living room.

"You're heavy!" I groaned, half serious.

She giggled.

"What did you eat while I was away?" I joked, and she giggled more.

"Cheese!"

"Shocker. No wonder you're heavy. You must have eaten fifty pounds of cheese. I think you got taller, too. Did Daddy stretch you out each night?"

"Yup!"

I hugged her close as I staggered into her room, and then I laid her down heavily on her bed with a bounce, and she dove under her turquoise fleece blanket.

I sat on the edge of her bed, and her head popped back up from underneath her blanket. She sat up for a big hug, and as I squeezed her, I said, "I love you, chica."

"I love you more," she replied, squeezing me hard and pulling me on top of her.

"Nope, not possible. I'm bigger. Therefore, I have more room to love you with." I squeezed her hard and then sat up and smiled tiredly, loving our nightly tuck-in banter.

"I love *you* more because I'm smaller." I laughed. You can't argue logic with a five-year-old.

"*You* are awesome. Good night, sweetie. Sleep tight." I stood up to leave and kissed her on the forehead. "See you in the morning. Okay?"

"Okay. Good night, Mommy."

"Sweet dreams, princess," I said as I shut the door.

I walked to my room two doors down the hallway and crawled, fully clothed, into bed and pulled the down duvet over me, closing my eyes with a sigh as exhaustion overwhelmed me. I took the contact lenses out of my eyes and flicked them to the floor. Ten seconds later, I was out cold.

The two ends of the spectrum in my world are extreme. Mountain biking and activism in Afghanistan and being a single mother in Breckenridge, Colorado. I didn't set out to build a life around extremes or seemingly divergent paths, but when you allow life to unfold, it has a flow that invites you in. Soon you find yourself living day by day in ways that from the outside seem insane but to you feel as normal as a nine-to-five and a white picket fence do to other people.

I didn't always want to work in Afghanistan, though. Originally, I wanted to be a modern dancer. So determined was I to pursue this path that I didn't even bother taking the SAT or ACT. I'd filled out applications to colleges with strong dance programs, but I didn't send them in. I knew that wasn't for me. I saw my life, and it didn't involve me living in a college dorm. I couldn't explain why, but I knew that going to college wasn't my first step. During my senior year in high school, I auditioned for a placement as an apprentice at Zenon Dance Company in Minneapolis. I got a spot and applied for a job at the Gap in the downtown. Three months later, I was living in a studio apartment in a brownstone just off Nicollet Avenue, while everyone else I knew was starting their freshman orientations.

I had no idea that fourteen years later I would have given up dancing, lived in Europe for ten years, worked as an outdoor guide, become a sports trainer, had a daughter, married and divorced, raced mountain bikes, started my own nonprofit, and begun to work and travel throughout Afghanistan. Years filled with mistakes, triumphs, fuck-ups, and victories, heartache, heartbreak, love, and laughs, and joy. Life reveals itself in fascinating ways when you let it do its thing.

It was Thanksgiving week in 2006, and I was visiting my parents in Bismarck, North Dakota, with my soon-to-be ex-husband, Pete, and nearly two-year-old Devon. Sitting in the living room of my childhood, I announced to family and childhood friends that I was starting a nonprofit organization, and I was naming it Mountain2Mountain. Its first baby step was to raise money for the Central Asia Institute, a nonprofit organization founded by Greg Mortenson that focused on education for girls as a way to facilitate peace in Afghanistan and Pakistan. I had read his book *Three Cups of Tea*. Intrigued by the cover—a photograph of three young girls in head scarves reading books—I'd bought the hardcover on a whim from my local bookstore and finished it in a few days. Soon after that I read John Wood's *Leaving Microsoft to Change the World*, and Rory Stewart's *The Places in Between*. I was inspired by the willingness of these men to experience countries many choose to avoid and to focus their lives on helping them. But more than that, I was struck by the perspective of men working for women's rights, and until I read *The Blue Sweater* by Jacqueline Novogratz, I was struck by the lack of female voices.

This was before Nicholas Kristof's *Half the Sky*, before organizations such as Girl Up, UN Women, and the Girl Effect. The idea that investing in the education of women and girls was not only the right thing morally and a human rights issue, but that it could also lead to greater overall community viability and stability, was not yet so widespread. Investing in women and girls as the key to economic growth and peace was not being looked at seriously by the mainstream public or media.

Something sparked, and almost overnight I was discussing the idea of raising money to help an organization whose work inspired me. It could be my first step while I figured out how far I wanted to travel down the rabbit hole I was looking into. Could I rally my own mountain community to care about building a school for girls in rural Pakistan? Could one mountain community come together to support another half the world away? This wasn't Nepal where many Coloradans travel to climb and explore. This was a country known for terrorism, not tourism.

Yet, rally the community did, and quickly. During a seven-month period, we put on two events, an author event with Greg Mortenson attended by more than six hundred people, and a trail running race I dubbed Race for the Mountains. I had no event planning experience but did have the ability to envision and put together an event. Thanks to the logistical skills of my friend, Tara Kusumoto, and the support of the Breckenridge community, we raised over $105,000 for Central Asia Institute to build two schools for girls in Pakistan. I was overjoyed, encouraged, and motivated.

I immediately leaped into another partnership with an organization that worked in Nepal and India, hoping to replicate what had been accomplished in the first attempt. But those seven months I'd spent fund-raising for CAI—coupled with continuing to run my own business, a Pilates and wellness center, raising a toddler, and moving out of my home as I started the process of divorcing Pete—had left me severely burnt out. My efforts and my energy stalled, and we raised $20,000 for the organization—nothing to sneeze at, but their expectations were that we could at least match the effort I'd made for Central Asia Institute, and they were disappointed and frustrated. They were not willing to recognize that Mortenson's then rocketing star power, book sales, and compelling story were a huge factor in the success of the initial fund-raising initiative.

My energy and creativity in the tank, I found refuge on a mountain bike. For years, I'd been a runner. I'd started running in Germany around the same time I began working as a sports trainer and outdoor guide, and soon I started racing to see what I was capable of. I'd gotten the idea that I wanted to run a half marathon, and thanks to the network of forest trails in the Odenwald, only a few minutes of jogging from my apartment in central Darmstadt, I quickly built up mileage and speed. My first half marathon was in Trier, a beautiful German town with cobblestone streets and stunning architecture. My second half of the race was faster than my first, and I finished close to my goal of 1:30, with 1:33. I was energized and euphoric, hooked on running, if not racing. I did half marathons, 10k, and local 5k races—mostly to push myself further and as a way to see nearby towns and villages differently. But it was my evening runs, surrounded by the forest's beauty, that fueled my spirit and gave me a sense of peace. Running stuck with me when I moved to the mountains of Colorado, and I took to the trails as a way to lose myself in the mountains and in myself. I learned to embrace the pain that came with the uphills and the altitude.

Running was put temporarily on hold when I showed up for my first pregnancy doctor's appointment on crutches. I'd twisted my ankle running with Pete on the trail behind our house earlier that morning. My doctor asked me to stop trail running but said that I could continue on the road if I wore a heart rate monitor.

"Have you used a heart rate monitor before?"

"Yes," I replied. "I'm a sports trainer, but I've never used one on myself."

"Okay, well, you'll need to wear one for any physical activity. Running, hiking, etc. I'd prefer you don't bike, but that's entirely your call. Essentially, I'd like you to work out with sports that don't elevate your potential to fall and hurt yourself or the baby."

"Okay, got it."

He looked at me, holding my gaze. "I'm serious about the heart rate monitor. The higher your heart rate, the higher your internal core temperature rises. Let me put it simply: you don't want to cook your baby."

"No microwaving my baby. Got it." This put a whole other spin on "bun in the oven."

I tried to road run for the first month or so, but it was just too hard to keep my heart rate down to the acceptable non-baby-cooking level. So I starting hiking every day with our dog Bergen, a German shepherd–chow mix we had gotten two years earlier from the pound.

After I had Devon, I quickly regained strength and speed thanks to the resistance training that jog strollers, bike trailers, and nordic sleds provide. I raced on dirt trails in the summer and on snowshoes in the winter. I did well. I podiumed often and won occasionally. Running made me feel strong, and I loved the challenge of going longer, farther, faster, as well as the seemingly endless options for trails in Breckenridge. But I didn't realize that running was also a means of escape. Lately, it was an escape from marriage. Never an early morning riser, I found myself getting up early to run, which eliminated the chance of morning intimacy. Looking back, I realize that it allowed me to escape all sorts of things: monotony, weakness, fear, and my past.

Then I was challenged to ride a single-speed bike. Brent approached me after a late-season snowshoe race in Frisco. We'd both finished at the head of the pack, and he asked if I wanted to ride bikes sometime. I was in the chaos of the Mountain2Mountain fund-raisers, and I was leaving Pete, but we stayed in touch. After my two fund-raising events were done for Central Asia Institute, I took him up on the offer to ride. I needed a challenge and a distraction from the chaos in my life, and I wanted to try something new.

So in June 2007, I drove up to Boulder, and Brent loaded two DEAN custom titanium single-speeds and we headed to Hall Ranch in Lyons. A little apprehensively, I mounted the 29er frame and clipped in. I had grown up riding bikes around the neighborhood, and in Europe I rode a bike for commuting and for weekend rides along the forest trails in Germany and France. But mountain biking, particularly mountain biking in Colorado, is something altogether different. The trail was narrow and winding, carved into a hill scattered with clusters of boulders and stones called rock gardens. Here was a new kind of riding that was a world away from the wide, dirt-packed forest trails I'd ridden with friends throughout Germany and France. It was more akin to riding through a trail of sharp objects determined to draw my blood. The only bike I owned was a heavy Cannondale, with grip shifts, that cost me $350 new in Garmisch, Germany. It was perfectly suited for forest trails and rides to beer gardens, but not for steep inclines and rock gardens that begged for a lighter, more agile ride, and an altitude that begged for bigger lungs.

It took me at least thirty minutes to get up the front side of Hall Ranch through its infamous rock garden of boulders and puzzle-like rock formation "problems" that riders better than I tried to "solve" in an attempt to get through without dismounting. My right shoe didn't release smoothly from the clipless pedals and more than once I found myself fighting and failing to unclip fast enough to put my foot down, leading to many bruises, some blood, and a few cactus needles embedded in various parts of my body. Not to mention having to dismount every few yards to hike, lift, or crawl over massive boulders or around tight switchbacks. I finally got to the top, exhausted but smiling at the challenge. Brent was sitting on a park bench, helmet off. He'd obviously been there awhile. I rode over, red-faced and panting. My helmet was slightly askew as I hadn't tightened it enough. I took it off and fully expected steam to release from my head. I drank water, assessed the congealed blood on my knees and shin, pulled out a cactus needle, and wondered aloud if I had much more of this ahead. I felt more than a little embarrassed, but I wasn't defeated; I was determined for more. This was definitely not like the forest roads in Germany.

"You did remember that this is the first time I've ridden a single-speed when you picked this trail, right?" I asked in between gulps of water.

"Yes. But my car has been at the mechanic's for the past couple of weeks, and I've been itching to ride out here. Since you had a car that could carry the bikes, I figured I'd seize the opportunity."

"And, you didn't think this would be a little over my head?" I was slightly incredulous at his reasoning. It was akin to taking your non-skier friend (whose car you needed to get to the slopes) to the top of a double–black diamond run, and telling him to just point his skis downward.

"You seemed tough enough to handle it."

"Yeah, whatever. Fine. Are you ready to roll yet?" I joked.

Brent glanced at me. "You sure you want to continue?"

Indignant, I replied, "Are you kidding me? Yeah, I'm sure. I didn't come here for a thirty-minute ride. Hike. Whatever. "

"Okay then, tough girl. Well, that was the tough part. This section is smoother, and you can probably stay on your bike."

"That's a novel idea, a bike ride where I actually ride my bike," I replied, and punched him in the arm.

"Just follow me, smart-ass. You should be good at this section. You're built like a hill climber, and you've got the lungs from running."

I took a deep breath. "Okay, let's do it." I put my helmet back on, and Brent looked over at me.

"What are you, twelve? This thing is huge on you!" He tightened it up the best he could.

"Yeah, yeah, yeah." I brushed him off. "Let's go."

Ten minutes later, I was still on his wheel, keeping up with his pace, and starting to climb. He was right: *this* I was good at. I sat until I couldn't push the pedals smoothly, and then I stood, and it wasn't that different from running. The simplicity of a single-speed appealed to my running nature. I could concentrate on pushing my body hard to climb the hills, and when small rock piles emerged, I didn't have to think about what gear to use. I just rode my bike. I was in love.

We stopped briefly for me to catch my breath at a little bench, at the start of a short loop that would take us to the top of the hill. The climb was harder, and it was now hot as hell, but if I pushed myself, I could keep Brent in my sight. We started to head back down to the car. Brent had a surprise for me.

"Let's go down the backside. You'll like it more than trying to get down the rock garden."

"There's a backside?"

"Yeah, it's pretty fun. Rolling switchbacks."

"You mean we could have come up a different way?"

"Yeah, but my grandmother rides the rock garden. In her wheelchair. So I figured you could, too."

"Fuck off." I shook my head, trying not to laugh.

He was right again. It was tough to negotiate the switchback turns as my bike-handling skills were less than stellar, but the roller-coaster swoops and turns were smooth, rideable, and fun as hell. When we hit the pavement to ride back to the car through the town of Lyons, I was chattering away nonstop about building up my own bike, the wind rushing in my ears.

Two weeks later, I found myself purchasing a tangerine Niner 29er single-speed frame at the Golden Bike Shop. Brent had written out a list of parts I needed to build it up. Instead of purchasing a fully assembled bike with stock parts, I would assemble it myself, which would allow me to get better-quality parts that suited the style of riding I was doing—things such as a seat post, lighter wheels, stronger brakes, a front suspension fork, and handlebars were self-explanatory. But the list was also full of things less obvious: bottom bracket, stem, spacers, and seat clamp. I didn't even consider gears; the simplicity and the challenge of the single-speed fit me like a glove. I couldn't imagine riding anything else. Little did I realize what an important role the bike would play in my life and how it was a metaphor for everything that was changing.

I spent that summer riding trails in Boulder and Breckenridge, building my stamina and my confidence. Beyond the physical challenge, I loved the mental reprieve. Unlike running, where my mind could wander, mountain biking required my full concentration. The mental attention each ride demanded allowed my brain to rest. I felt sparks of creativity punch through my burnout. The strength and confidence I felt building in my body allowed me to continue down the path I'd started on. But my path often felt so empty that I often wondered if I'd ever see anyone else on it.

In my typical "all or nothing" approach to life, two months after my first ride, I entered my very first mountain bike race at Winter Park, the Tipperary Creek race. Thirty-three miles of cross-country racing over single-track and steep fire roads. Lining up at the start, I was petrified. What had I gotten into? I had a better-fitting helmet now, and mountain biking baggies over my chamois, and a camelback. I looked like a mountain biker. Actually, I looked like a single-speeder. Instead of matching lycra jersey and shorts, covered in sponsors, like most racers were wearing, I wore skull-and-crossbone black knee-high socks and a bright purple top. Even the male single-speeders look different than the other racers. Instead of a race jersey, some had mechanic's shirts on. Brent was wearing pink, striped knee-highs and a Tinkerbell T-shirt, insisting that pink was the new black. I was petrified with all the riders in lycra surrounding me. I didn't want to be "that girl," the one that held up better, faster riders, or be stuck behind a slow train of granny gears. I didn't want to crash. I didn't want to make a fool of myself.

I looked around the lineup. Single-speed women lined up with the semi-pro and expert women. I looked down at their bikes to see how many were single-speeders. I saw one, then another, the knee-highs giving many of them away. Two minutes later it became obvious: the long hill climb separated the geared semi-pro and expert women and our small clump of single-speeders. The other girls took the time to say hi as we climbed, since they knew one another from previous races. Once we hit the trail, two of us separated from the rest, and we found ourselves in a friendly game of cat and mouse. She was a fast and competent downhiller, but I was a stronger climber. Riders passed me, and I passed riders, to a constant theme of "Hey single-speed, go get 'em," "Hey Niner, nice work." The welcome camaraderie on the trail kept a smile on my dirt-covered face and made me feel part of the community of riders. By the time we were on one of the last fire road climbs, I was nearing my redline—there was nothing left in the tank. I got off my bike and hiked, alongside many others who were also defeated by the long procession of steep climbs. I found I could hike it up pretty fast and catch my breath. At the moment I was in front. What if I could just stay in front for the upcoming descent?

Coming across the finish line, I was elated, and my front wheel was rattling. . . . Apparently, my skewer was coming loose. I may have come in first, but I was chided by Brent to remember to check rattles so that I didn't end up a bloody heap on the side of the trail when my front wheel flew off.

I kept pushing my own boundaries and conquering my fear on the trail into the fall, with my first trip to Moab, Utah. The trip was an example of the strength and determination I had to "not be a girl" and be tough as nails. I drove out with a group of guys, all strong riders who invited me to join for a one-day ride of the White Rim, a hundred-plus-mile trail inside the Canyonlands National Park. The trip started with a stopover in Fruita to ride Mary's Loop/Horsethief, a trail that has become my go-to ride to and from Moab every spring and fall—a trail that makes me smile from the moment I start climbing the rock at the trailhead to the dirt road traverse back to the car at the end. It's a trail that has taken more than its fair share of blood, my first flat tire, and hamburgered my entire forearm on a descent. A few hours later I found myself on my first "double" as we added in a second ride of the day—a seemingly endless sufferfest in Moab on the Golden Spike jeep trail, with deep sand and endless climbing on a wide slab of slickrock that led to the top of the cliffs high above town. Day two, we rode Amasa Back, another trail that is now a go-to ride that I've never skipped on a Moab trip. Instead of an afternoon ride, we rested our legs while packing and shopping for supplies. Day three was the one-day unsupported ride of White Rim: more than a hundred miles of slickrock, single-track, and dirt climbs with no potable water. Looking up the description for the trail before I left, I found this online: most riders spend three or four days to ride this trail, spending the night at campgrounds. (Two days = Monster. One day = Lunatic.)

Great, I thought, *that's fitting.*

In the end, it was the most-challenging three days of desert riding I could have imagined, in an otherworldy terrain unlike anything I'd ever seen—striated rock formations that looked like the movie set for a science fiction movie. Throughout the four epic rides, I emerged relatively blood-free despite descending rock gardens and drops I had no business attempting, but being the only girl in a group of guys, I wasn't going to let inexperience dictate my choices. Thanks to the strength and skills I'd built during a summer of intense single-speed riding, I was always near the front of the group. I was hooked. The bike was my new love and possibly my sanity.

The following spring I was still feeling the full effects of a mental and physical burnout from my fund-raising efforts for the second nonprofit I'd been supporting, the one that worked in Nepal. Against my better judgment, I'd agreed to do a fund-raiser for it only weeks after wrapping up the two fund-raisers that I'd spent six months creating for Central Asia Institute. I was running on adrenaline and passion, with no foundation underneath me to support my energy, and no amount of biking was going to offset the emotional drain. My work may have stalled there, and I would have gone back to full-time sports training and Pilates had it not been for a fortunate cup of coffee in Breckenridge that I had with one of CAI's staff members, Christiane Leitinger, a few months earlier. Christiane had driven to Breckenridge to meet and discuss the author event I was creating as a fund-raiser. She was the director for the Pennies for Peace program that engaged students and schools in a service learning program that benefitted CAI's programming in Pakistan and Afghanistan. She was also the only staff member who wasn't in Bozeman. She lived nearby in Evergreen, Colorado, and wanted to discuss the event and how to maximize the community's involvement so that it would be a success.

My friend Tara and I met her at Cool River Café in Breckenridge. Christiane arrived in a cobalt blue Patagonia puffy jacket that matched her large blue eyes. Her long brown hair was pulled back in a ponytail, and she had a graceful look illuminated by the lack of makeup, her bone structure much like that of a ballerina. She pulled out her laptop and began to discuss what we were planning and how she and CAI could help. Throughout the next seven months, she checked in periodically, and she was at the event itself to handle the two book signings we'd planned for Mortenson as well as his schedule, which was starting to become chaotic.

Months later, we met for coffee as friends, and when Mortenson was speaking at Colorado University's Mackey Auditorium, Christiane invited Tara and me to come. Short on volunteers for an event in Evergreen, she asked if I could help out. Her thin frame seemed even thinner than before, and after a late-night event, she was supposed to drive to Telluride with her two girls the next day to speak at two schools. I asked if there was anything I could do to help her.

She looked at me, her blue eyes tired, and said, "Any chance you could drive me to Telluride in the morning? I am not sure I should be driving."

I paused, looked at her, and found myself wanting to help her and take something off her plate.

"I have to pick up Devon, but if your girls and Devon can get along in the backseat for five hours, I think we could make that happen." I was half kidding, half serious. I had very few female friends, none with children, and never arranged play dates.

Christiane's eyes lit up. "Really? Do you think you could?" Her husband, Charley, came over ten minutes later and gave me a huge hug—the type of hug that I learned to love and appreciate in the years that followed, the kind that makes you feel like you are family. "Thank you for helping out Christiane. You have no idea how worried I was about her making the drive."

I smiled, slightly embarrassed. "It's the least I can do, she seems so tired, and I have the weekend free. I'd love to help."

We made plans. I drove back to Breckenridge, and the next morning I picked up Devon from Pete at my old house. I met Christiane and her two girls, Isabel and Eva Sophia, in Frisco to combine cars. For five-plus hours, we talked like old friends while the girls read to one another and played games in the backseat. We spent two nights in Telluride and turned around. It was during the drive home that the lightbulb flickered.

I'd been telling Christiane about my frustration with the organization I was fund-raising for. I'd created a photography exhibition that I'd named *Views of the Himalaya*. The exhibit was a collaboration of world-renowned photographers famous for their work and insight into this region of the world from varying perspectives. Among them, Nevada Wier, Beth Wald, Jimmy Chin, and even the trust that managed the late Galen Rowell's photography contributed images to create an exhibition that could serve to inspire and educate viewers. I'd reached out to the photographers involved to ask for a contribution of images, and local photographer Kate Lapides had offered to advise with the printing and framing—something I knew next to nothing about.

I was beyond thrilled with how the exhibition had developed, and I loved using photography to tell the story of the region we were fund-raising for. Beyond the exhibition itself, I'd created a book online to complement the exhibit with its photos and an artist statement from everyone involved. Yet the founder of the organization I was working to support was more focused on the dollars used to support effective programs, not the vision of storytelling. Understandably, this is the norm; the end goal is money in most organizations, as more money equals more projects and growth. I felt frustrated at every conversation and just wanted to get through the events we'd committed to and move on. My heart wasn't in it.

All of a sudden, Christiane spoke up. "There's a silver lining here, don't you think?"

I looked at her incredulously. "Oh, yeah?" I smiled. "Do tell."

"Well, you know what you don't want to do now. You realize what you don't want to be. That's almost as important as realizing what you *do* want to do because it's more specific."

"Yeah, I don't want to be *that* guy. I don't want to be focused on the 'sale.' I want to be focused on the stories, the connection, the change of perspectives. I think I'm more passionate about the shift of perspectives that can create a bigger ripple than I am about a traditional sticks-and-bricks approach."

"No, you're right. And you know that you want to be creative in how you engage people."

"Yeah, it's weird. It's like I want to connect the people here to the people I want to work with over there in a visceral way. I want them to be inspired to get involved. I don't want to just raise money. I'm sure a fancy event with thousand-dollar-plate dinners would be more effective at that, but I'd blow my brains out. That sounds boring and staid. If I am choosing to do this, I'm going to do it my way. Otherwise, why bother?"

I was getting riled up. "Why can't I work in ways that inspire change, that inspire communities, and do good work? I mean, there are a gazillion organizations much larger than me that can focus on the big stuff. Why can't I focus on ways that engage people and communities—that challenge stereotypes and perception? Engaging people and inspiring individuals could create a bigger ripple effect than just writing a check."

"Exactly," Christiane said with a big smile. "*That's* exactly it. You see the power in storytelling as a way to connect people to a cause. So do *that*. Do what matters to you. If you are going to put your drop in the bucket, make it yours."

I watched the white lines go past as we continued to drive back to Breckenridge. The rabbit hole was opening up wider, and I saw myself diving in headfirst.

Back home, I mulled over all that we'd talked about: starting my own nonprofit, rallying the masses to care, working for girls and women in conflict zones *as* a woman, sharing their stories in unique ways, connecting communities and cultures.

Throughout the months and years that followed, Christiane became my soul sister, the big sister I never had. An advisor, a confidante, and family. The single best thing that came out of my initial decision to raise money for Central Asia Institute was the friendship that was forged with her and her family. Her friendship would allow me to tap into a sisterhood of amazing women and open up my deeply buried vulnerability to my own sister and daughter. This would change my life profoundly, in a myriad of subtle ways.

And I rode my bike. A lot.

3

Inshallah

I looked over at Tony sitting beside me and then back out the window again. The airplane was losing elevation and the gridwork of mud walls below revealed themselves through the haze of thin clouds. The expanse of jagged peaks we'd been passing over retreated, and one snakelike road led across the mud-colored grid toward square patches of green. The first color I'd seen since we left Dubai. It was not until we were practically skimming the rooftops of single-story houses that colors emerged below in turquoise blue, red, green, and yellow, and began to take shape as fences, gates, shops, and cars.

I tugged at my scarlet head scarf, feeling as though the silk covering my hair was less a sign of modesty and more like the A the heroine was forced to wear in *The Scarlet Letter*. Rather than helping me blend in, it felt like a harlot's cry for attention. I craned my neck to look at the other two foreign women on the plane. One wore black, the other white. Damn. I pulled the front of the scarf farther down my forehead, as if I could crawl inside.

The photographer and friend, Tony Di Zinno, was with me for my first trip. This was 2008, one year before I would become the first woman to mountain bike in Afghanistan. He'd joined me to document the journey and bring back images that could help rally support for our yet-to-be-determined projects. Tony was a sensitive soul with an eye for seeing things and the ability to capture them through his lens. We'd been friends for a few years, and the ease with which he traveled the world, his excitement and pride in what I was setting out to do, and his desire to see Afghanistan firsthand, made it a no-brainer to bring him along. In addition to being my documenter, Tony would be my shadow and companion for this foray. The fact that he was a large, bearlike man of Irish-Italian descent didn't hurt. After a couple of weeks without shaving, he blended in so well that most Afghans assumed he was Turkish. I had my own personal Mafioso strongman watching my back, albeit a nonviolent, Buddhism-practicing one.

The plane touched down, and as soon as the brakes kicked in, seat belts were being unclipped. Turbaned men were standing and opening overhead bins, the plane still speeding down the runway. Chatter erupted around us as cell phones were pulled out of pockets and bags. By the time the plane came to a stop, the aisle was blocked with men and bags. I wouldn't have been surprised if a goat or two jumped out of the overhead bins.

We'd arrived from Dubai, and the juxtaposition of wealth and poverty had never felt so extreme to me as it did between the two terminals. Arriving on Emirates into the fabulously ostentatious Terminal 3 was like entering the Las Vegas of the Arab world, minus the tassels. We collected our luggage and spent an hour trying to find out where our connecting flight was departing. We got at least three different suggestions from airport information staff. No one seemed to have heard of our connecting airline, Kam Air. We left the glitz and glamour of Terminal 3, and when the sliding glass doors opened to let us outside, the heat and humidity slammed into us. We took the shuttle to Terminal 1—the international terminal on the other side. It was 8:00 P.M. and well over ninety-five degrees.

After wandering around Terminal 1, I asked at the information desk out of where Kam Air was flying. I was then finally directed to the third and final terminal—Terminal 2—which was surprisingly a substantial cab drive away. Why isn't it just called a separate airport with a different name? Why doesn't anyone know how to give us directions? This is insane. Calling it Terminal 2 implies it lies somewhere between Terminal 1 and 3. With a sigh, I changed some money into Dirhams, and we climbed into a cab for a twenty-minute drive through Dubai at night to the terminal that time forgot.

A more dreary and empty airport terminal I'd never seen. Far from the hustle and bustle of Dubai's other terminals, this one seemed like a different country: one barren corridor, a bathroom, an information counter, and no food or drink to speak of, as the lone newsstand was closed at this hour. We settled in for the ten-hour layover. As far as I could tell, I was the only female, and Tony and I were among three Westerners crowded around an ancient television mounted on the wall that by some miracle was broadcasting the U.S. election results as they came in on BBC World. The entire world was watching, it seemed, to see if Barack Obama would become the next president of the United States. As the election results trickled in, the departure gates opened and we were allowed to go through security and check-in. I looked up at the departure list on the screens above us and laughed. It was the departure list to hell: Baghdad, Kabul, Kandahar, Kuwait, Fallujah. As we joined the crowd queuing to board, mostly Afghans, mostly men, I felt my excitement building.

We emerged from the airport in Kabul with our bags in hand and no idea of where to go next. We followed the crowd that was walking across a deserted parking lot toward a gate. I kept my head down so the head scarf wouldn't slide back, my hands constantly checking it. We went through the narrow doorway and saw in the crowd a small man with thick glasses holding a sign with my name on it. Najibullah—my fixer, translator, and guide for this visit. "Good morning, Shannon. You are most welcome to Kabul. Your new president is Barack Obama," he informed me with a smile. I sighed with relief, knowing that from here on out, I was in his hands.

Our guesthouse was in a remote area of town, run by the NGO Afghans 4 Tomorrow. It was accessible only after going through a double barricaded checkpoint on either end of the street. The guards recognized Najibullah and waved us on. Our driver, Shah Mohammad, the same one who would nearly drive myself, Travis, and Hamid off a cliff a year later, slowly maneuvered the white Corolla through. Inside, we were greeted by the severe face of the housekeeper, a man dressed all in black. The stone floors echoed as we made our way through to our rooms and were told that there was only one other guest. We dropped our bags, then followed Najibullah outside.

Najibullah walked us to the breakfast room, a separate structure at the back of the courtyard. We sat down to discuss our plans and goals for the weeks ahead over a pot of green tea.

Shah Mohammad, Najibullah told us, was an ex-military commander. Ironically, he'd been in the transportation department, but it took the help of Najibullah's guidance and directions to steer between buses and around donkey carts and pedestrians in the complete and utter chaos of the Kabul streets. It was a free-for-all in every direction, people crossing between cars and buses that came at each as if in a high-speed game of chicken. Drivers didn't yield to anyone: human, donkey, bicycle, tank, or bus. Yet the littlest car would confidently pull in front of oncoming vehicles, the wrong way, calmly beep his horn, and somehow melt into the multiple lanes of traffic.

What I hadn't expected when I arrived was the city's deteriorated infrastructure—one hundred times worse than what I'd seen living in Beirut. Buildings were gutted and crumbling, without rooms, windows, or complete walls, often with people and businesses still occupying them in some fashion. There was only one paved road we'd been on thus far, the newly fixed one from the airport; the rest required off-road driving skills. This was six years after the Taliban had been pushed out. If this was the capital city, where most of the money was concentrated and most of the reconstruction was focused, what did the rest of the country look like?

Everything in Afghanistan is done on the streets. Need to change money? There's a guy at a roundabout that changes my $200 dollars into the local currency, Afghanis, or Afs—not to be confused with Afghans as a people. Afghani—money; Afghans—people. The rate was fifty-one to one which reminded me of working in currencies like Lebanese pounds that required more head space when I switched back and forth. You can use U.S. dollars or Afs to pay for things, and you may get either back in return, or a combination of the two, depending on the establishment. Currencies are like the New York Times crossword puzzle—a frustrating but effective brain exercise to stave off Alzheimer's.

Need to buy a phone card for the cell phone? There's a guy on the side of the road at a busy intersection with whichever phone card you need: Rohsan, Etisalat, or MTN. The markets are street-side. Carts with apples, bananas, nuts, fresh-squeezed lemonade, balloons and children's toys, scarves, construction materials, and pretty much anything else you could need are set up each morning inches from the traffic.

It was quickly apparent that Najibullah was well connected and that any meeting I requested was possible, from school tours to visits with members of Parliament. I made a mental note to send photographer Beth Wald a thank-you. Beth had worked with Najibullah several times and generously shared Najibullah's information with me when I met with her for coffee to discuss my upcoming plans for Afghanistan. Najibullah also offered great advice and direction, but he did lean to the conservative side with security, to the point that I got a little claustrophobic at times.

We quickly settled into a routine. Each morning I returned to consciousness with the local Imam's call to prayer through the loudspeakers of the neighborhood mosque. His warbling voice was a cultural alarm clock that put a smile on my face despite the predawn hour. I grabbed my contacts and pulled a blanket off the bed to wrap around me in the drafty, cold room. I turned on my computer and sat in the dark, checking e-mails and writing thoughts and observations from the previous day.

After a chilly shower to remove the previous days' Kabul dust, I greeted TLC and grabbed breakfast in an outbuilding across the courtyard. I'd dubbed our guesthouses's resident puppy TLC, "Tastes Like Chicken." He was sweet and needed TLC, but I held a suspicion that our cold-hearted housekeeper was tolerating him only to fatten him up for a cold winter night's feast.

Breakfast was a crapshoot. The first day it included naan bread, spreadable cheese, jams, peanut butter, and, if we asked, runny eggs.

Day by day, it became scarcer and more unusual. The naan was always there, but the cheese varied and then disappeared, and once jars of jam or peanut butter were finished, they weren't replaced. The only constant was the giant thermos of green tea. The cook and the guesthouse manager didn't communicate well, it seemed, so if things ran out, everyone waited for someone else to replace them. Pretty soon we were down to naan and the occasional runny eggs.

TLC typically followed us back to the guesthouse where we shut down computers and grabbed our stuff in time for Najibullah to ring the bell. Greetings were passed back and forth in Dari, each day getting a little smoother. We loaded bags and camera gear into the back of Shah Mohammad's car and then it was time for round two of endless Dari greetings. Shah Mohammad liked to mix it up, which kept us on our toes for the rapid-fire greetings and replies that were issued in quick succession. *Salaam Alekum, Hubisti, Chitoristi, Jonnyjuras, Tashakur.* He grinned when he threw in a new phrase or simply changed up the order to see our furrowed brows as we concentrated to keep up and respond appropriately.

The days varied in purpose and activity, but not in the nonstop pace. From the moment we hit the road, eyes and ears were trained on the scenes that unfolded before us. Najibullah pointed out landmarks and let us know the current Afghan news on the radio. Many mornings we were discussing the latest attack in the southern provinces, a kidnapping at the school around the corner from our guesthouse, or a recent foiled bombing attempt. I hardly missed my morning coffee, but the adrenaline shot Najibullah delivered was more effective than any espresso shot.

One morning we heard that a group of girls were attacked walking to school in Kandahar. Eleven girls and four teachers were splashed with acid by three men on motorcycles. Months before the attack, there had been posters placed around local mosques stating,

"Don't Let Your Daughters Go to School." My thoughts immediately went to Devon. What would I do if my daughter risked an acid attack just for walking to school?

Full mornings, adrenaline, and the randomness of our breakfast worked up an appetite, and that meant kebabs, fresh yogurt, Kabuli rice with lamb and shredded carrots and grapes, and a meat dumpling called mantu. Sometimes we were seated cross-legged around the meal in traditional Afghan style, and sometimes at a table. The meal was always delicious. Shah Mohammad would join us and smile broadly as Najibullah schooled us with impromptu Dari lessons, connecting thoughts and phrases from the morning's work.

I wrote the phrases and words in my notebook phonetically so I could try to commit them to memory. Languages had never been my strength. I lived in Germany for six years, and I wasn't even close to being fluent in German. I took three years of French in high school, and spent years visiting various areas of France, and several months living in Paris and Beirut, and my French remained abysmal at best. I found myself wishing I could upload languages directly to my brain via a Matrix-like database.

Tony and I came up quickly with a shorthand for photos and descriptions. It started with the blue burqas worn by many women in Kabul. We called them bluebirds—as if they were free to fly about if we thought of them that way, making the burqa a thing of beauty. We came to refer to the Afghan police as the parrots, since they were green and squawked loudly. The white burqas were doves, symbols of peace as they swirled around the dust-covered city. The badass private security, spilling out of jeeps dressed all in black, with their mirrored sunglasses and extensive firepower, were the blackbirds. Ever present, flitting about the city looking for spare crumbs were the sparrows, the street children that swarmed around asking for money, offering to shine your shoes, sell you a map, or waving their smoky cans of "good luck." Street children often wander between cars in slow traffic waving cans of burning incense meant to ward off evil in exchange for a few Afs.

The sparrows hung out by the doors of several kebab houses we frequented for lunch, and afterward we handed them leftovers that Najibullah had wrapped up. He unfailingly had several small bills of ten or twenty Afs—a few cents worth—that he would hand out. Occasionally, we bought their gum or pencils. Najibullah took us to several schools, including one specifically for street children. He was always generous and patient with those that gathered around us.

In the afternoon, the pace ramped up until dark, when Najibullah tried to have us home for security reasons. We took a different route each night and entered the first of two security gates guarding both ends of our street. After a few days, I realized that Najibullah still had a long drive home to his family and that his days were at least two hours longer than ours with his commute both ways. Yet he always arrived bright-eyed and ready to work.

We dropped our bags and headed straight to the outbuilding again for dinner. The saving grace was the fresh naan bread, as the main course varied in its sparseness and sliminess. Praise Allah for the incredible lunches at kebab shops and teahouses that fueled us and kept us going!

After dinner, the work continued. Tony retreated to his room to download and back up the day's captured images, and I went upstairs to organize interview notes, write blogs, and interpret new layers of cultural understanding. The first few nights I attempted to light a fire in the little metal stove in the middle of the room, the only source of heat, but the fuel briquettes smoldered more than burned. I gave up and put on a few extra layers of clothes instead. The room grew colder and colder as I worked, with the solar generators giving their warning bell around ten o'clock. There were two beds in my room, and after I shivered and froze on the first night with no heat, I stripped the extra bed to pile on more warmth to mine. I had a few hours to work off my computer's battery and turn on my headlamp for a last-call bathroom run. Then sometime around midnight, when the room was dark and cold, I crawled under the layers of covers, already dreaming before my head hit the pillow.

I wasn't looking at buying real estate, but despite the chaos, stress, and security threats, I was exactly where I wanted to be.

One of the first meetings, and the only one I'd specifically planned ahead of time, was with AINA Photo Agency. For decades, the people of Afghanistan had endured war and chaos. In 1996, the Taliban gained complete control and placed the Afghan people under Sharia law. Citizens were forbidden to participate in a free press, and it was considered a crime to take or even possess photographs. Truth and communication were suppressed. After the Taliban were pushed out of power in 2002, AINA, Afghanistan's Independent Media and Culture Center, was established by Reza Deghati. This foundation was born out of the desire to develop photojournalism from within Afghanistan and to find outlets to allow the truth to be seen. The offices shared space with *Kabul Weekly*, a trilingual newspaper run by Faheem Dashty who also served as the president of AINA Photo.

AINA was a key part of my decision to go to Kabul. Through filmmaking, photography, radio, journalism, and design, AINA trained, produced, and empowered individuals and communities to speak out and make sustainable changes in civil society. This was Afghanistan's first and only Afghan-owned and -run photography agency. Now, a group of talented men and women photojournalists were developing AINA's talent pool to further the country's ability to tell its own stories.

I hoped to support the work of AINA Photo and reach out to local Afghan photographers so that I could include their work alongside that of Western photographers in a cultural exhibition I wanted to create. *Streets of Afghanistan* would showcase the country from a variety of perspectives.

We met Faheem Dashty in his office to discuss the project and learn more about AINA, freedom of the press and artistic expression, and in the process get a history lesson dating back to the time of Massoud. He told me of death threats, some subtle, others more blatant due to the unbiased content of *Kabul Weekly*. He worked hard to maintain his job as editor in chief and not be swayed by politicians, leaders, and warlords. His office wall was taken up by an imposing life-size portrait of Massoud, the leader of the Northern Alliance, who fought the Taliban and inspired a nation. The Lion of Panjshir served as a moral compass for Dashty, who referred to him as "Chief." If not for journalists and editors such as Dashty in countries like Afghanistan, corrupt and violent groups and individuals would run rampant without fear.

Around the world, the work of journalists and photographers serves to tell stories that would otherwise remain hidden—whether atrocities normally swept under the rug or individual bravery and kindness that can inspire others. Yet telling such stories often puts the storytellers at great risk. Corrupt governments, bribed policy makers, and others don't want their story told. And Afghanistan has no shortage of corruption, violence, and atrocities. But it also has its share of brave souls, storytellers, and artists.

Beyond storytelling and the ability to educate and inspire, media can be a powerful weapon against tyranny and violence. Photography takes that one step further. It reaches us on a visceral level. It can combat the apathy and tell stories in ways words often cannot. The idea of the *Streets of Afghanistan* exhibition was to use photography to galvanize individuals and communities to believe that change is possible in Afghanistan. It aimed to build support for projects that could help the next generation of storytellers.

Faheem pointed to the portrait of Massoud behind him. He explained that he'd served as his press secretary. Three days before 9/11, Massoud had been assassinated by Tunisians posing as a television crew. The bomb was in the camera. Faheem was nearly killed as well, and he was still haunted by his decision to grant access to the false media team that killed a great leader. He continued to work as an editor for *Kabul Weekly*, despite the threats, so that the truth could emerge, so that corruption could be fought, and so that Afghans could hope for a better future.

We were soon joined by the majority of the AINA photographers, mostly men, but two women attended the meeting. We had been speaking in English with Faheem, but now we reverted to Dari, and I asked Najibullah to explain to the room what we were doing and what I hoped to accomplish.

Fifteen minutes into the meeting, the door opened and in strode Travis, who I'd only communicated with by e-mail. He was assisting and mentoring at AINA, and was my first line of communication in setting up the meeting to discuss the exhibition. He was dressed in a black North Face puffy coat, black pants, and a black-and-white checkered keffiyeh scarf. I didn't know what I'd expected but not someone that looked as if he'd just climbed off a motorcycle.

He listened while we discussed the project and suggested that the photographers each pull their top ten images for me to look at the following week. I could then get a better sense of their work since the agency database was slow at best and nearly impossible to use. I could negotiate image use fees with AINA after I decided how many I wanted. Travis would also put me in touch with Farzana Wahidy, a female photographer that was originally with AINA Photo but was now represented by Agence Française, a French photo agency.

After the meeting, Faheem invited us to have lunch with him and his family in the Panjshir Valley, to see more than Kabul and meet his father. I agreed enthusiastically, though at that time I had no idea how prominent a role the Panjshir province would come to play in my life.

Afghanistan is visually heartbreaking in both its beauty and its devastation. The Afghans have endured hardship with incredible resiliency, and it's easy to fall into the trap of looking through rose-colored glasses at the ancient aspects of the country, from the herders along the busy streets of Kabul, their goats intermingling with the cars, to the elaborate turbans and timeless faces lined with history. Often, it feels as if you've stepped back in time to the days of the silk roads and camel caravans. But the security restrictions soon temper that. Suicide bombs, kidnappings, and acid attacks occurred during our visit—a harsh reminder that this is a war zone and a warning to stay alert. The tendency to romanticize the dust, the call to prayer, and the mountains is quelled when you meet women living as modern-day slaves, kids forced to beg in the street, and men hobbling along, one of their legs having been blown off. The violence and oppression is as overpowering as the beauty.

Tony captured the image that perfectly illustrates the beauty in the heartbreak. We were driving to Panjshir province to meet General Dashty, Faheem's father, at their home in the Panjshir Valley for lunch. As we were leaving Kabul, we saw a woman in a burqa with her baby begging in the middle of the street. The woman was directly in the line of fire from traffic in both directions, but she sat there unflinching as traffic whizzed by, peaceful in the eye of the storm. Dust swirled, and Tony grabbed his camera at my request to shoot through the windshield, catching this bluebird in the road.

That image is the one that has stuck with me throughout numerous visits to Afghanistan. The haunting quality of the woman and child is offset by the blurred line of Shah Mohammad's hand on the steering wheel giving a real sense of impending conflict. It's an image that I used years later as a cornerstone of the photography exhibition *Streets of Afghanistan*. There was heartbreak and beauty combined in one beautiful frame.

Then I pushed my luck and asked Tony to get a shot of the road behind us as we passed. Bearing in mind that Najibullah had warned him not to shoot photos from the car—at least not when there were police around—Tony had been uber stealthy. My big-mouthed request meant that he lifted his camera just in time to get us waved down by the police. I shrunk in the backseat and apologized to Najibullah. Luckily, they let us off with a warning and didn't confiscate anything. Tony laughed at me and my big mouth and shook his head ruefully. "You are supposed to be keeping a look out, not getting us in trouble."

I shrugged my shoulders sheepishly. "Sorry!"

The rest of the drive passed without incident, and as we drove north out of Kabul, we went under a checkpoint with a large sign that arched across the road. It had been put there by the Ministry of Health, and Najibullah explained that it referred to family planning and said that space between children was good for both the mother and child. "In other words, don't try to knock up your wife a couple of days after she gives birth," I joked to Tony. I may have a dark sense of humor, one that has gotten darker after years of working in Afghanistan, almost to a point of inappropriateness, but we were talking about a country with one of the highest rates of maternal and infant mortality. I had to crack jokes to keep from wallowing in the insanity around me. Commonsense practices surrounding family planning weren't common sense. Over the years that followed, I often met young women with six and seven children. The mothers were missing teeth and malnourished, their bodies exhausted from the constant demands of feeding newborns while pregnant and living in rural communities already lacking food and resources.

As we continued north, the Shomali Plain spread out in front of us, a brief landscape of wide open views. We arrived at the gateway to the mountains several hours later. We saw land mine clearing on the left and stopped to buy some grapes from one of about twenty or so men selling them. They stood in a line at the side of the road, with small gnarled grape vines spreading out behind them into fields I hoped were free of land mines. A couple of hours later, the mountains closed in as the valley narrowed and followed the river, and we came to the entrance to the Panjshir Valley.

Najibullah asked Shah Mohammad to slow down. On the right-hand side of the road was a small shack, about the size of a police checkpoint. An old man with red hair was standing there. Najibullah rolled down his window and exchanged greetings with him, then handed him some Afs. The old man looked inside the car, then put his hand on his heart and nodded when he saw Tony and me. I did the same in return with a smile.

"Who is he?" I asked Najibullah as we drove off.

"He is one of Massoud's men. He still stands guard every day at that little hut as a first watch before the gates of Panjshir. Everyone who comes to Panjshir gives him a few Afs. He's almost seventy years old now."

The gates of Panjshir are not just a metaphor for the narrow valley opening where the Panjshir River runs through the mountain ranges that surround this narrow province just a mile or so past the old man's checkpoint. The proverbial gates have a literal gate, an official police checkpoint that the Panjshiri still maintain to see who is coming in and leaving. This checkpoint was manned by a serious-looking bunch of uniformed men. They peered through the driver's window and asked a few questions. I put my right hand on my heart, nodded, and said, "Salaam." One of them responded in kind and smiled, allowing Tony to take his photo. He told us he'd been a commander under Massoud and now worked this checkpoint to continue his loyal service to Panjshir. The guards invited us to join them for tea, but Najibullah explained that we didn't have time as we were expected for lunch farther down the road. I was a bit disappointed. How often was one invited for a roadside cup of tea by ex-mujahideen fighters?

The dirt road, interspersed with short sections of pavement, followed the river through the valley while the mountains looked down on us from both sides. We periodically munched on the slightly wrinkled, anemic-looking grapes in the pink plastic bag. Suddenly, we arrived at a village that screamed, "You're not in Kansas anymore." The road narrowed and market stalls pressed in tightly on either side. A cow was getting cut up on the street in front of the butcher shop. *Can't ask for fresher than that,* I thought as my stomach growled at the thought of lunch. The Corolla wove through the crowds of animals and people, and all I could think was what I would give to get out of the damn car. I was aching to stretch my legs and get closer to this experience. Stands selling liter bottles of Coca-Cola, fresh yogurt in clear plastic bags, butchered animals, fruit, and clothing had their wares hanging by strings and ropes tied to the low roofs of the metal shacks.

Slowly the neutral, dusty landscape we'd been driving through since Kabul developed some splashes of color as trees with golden yellow leaves appeared in great clusters along the sides of the mountain across the river. We'd caught the last few days of autumn in Panjshir. The foliage was a welcome sight after the muted shades of brown we'd become accustomed to.

We arrived at Faheem Dashty's family home by way of a narrow alley off the road. On both sides were steep rock walls, and I couldn't see any other houses nearby, but I could hear the river raging. Faheem welcomed us at the gate and directed us to the garden, where a table and chairs were set on the lawn. The house had mountains on both sides and a flowering garden overlooking the river. It was hard to believe that this was the stronghold of Massoud's resistance against the Taliban. It was too peaceful—an oasis, really.

Faheem's father, introduced to us as simply the General, came out. Compared to the slightness of Faheem, his father was large, with a kind, grandfatherly face. He greeted us and warmly shook my hand between both of his, welcoming us to his home.

We sat in the garden, my eyes drinking in the color. A servant brought freshly pressed apple juice from their own trees in the orchard out back. Thick and pulpy, the juice was the first I'd had in days and it tasted as though I'd just bitten into a sweet yellow apple. A refreshing break from the constant stream of watery green tea.

Faheem and the General shared many stories of the family home, the Panjshir Valley, life during the Soviet occupation, and their relationship with Massoud. Faheem still referred to Massoud as the Chief and smiled mischievously, recounting a story about getting caught smoking after the Chief had forbidden it.

The General told us how Massoud asked him to blow up the road near the valley entrance when the Taliban were trying to enter. The road collapsed into the river, boulders and rubble making it impassable for vehicles. The Taliban that survived were either captured or killed, or they fled back to Kabul. Ironically, the General's government job was road building for the Ministry of Transportation.

After a couple of hours sharing stories, the General guided us to a small outbuilding on the other side of the garden for lunch. We entered a tiny foyer with a red afghan rug just large enough for us to slip out of our shoes, and we walked into a small rectangular room with cobalt blue pillows lining the four walls. We sat cross-legged on the floor, and a tablecloth was spread in the middle of the empty space. Food and water were brought in from the kitchen, and Faheem passed along plates, then platters of food. I sat next to the General, and he gestured that I should serve myself first.

I adore Afghan food. It is a great joy to be invited to a private home for a home-cooked meal, no matter where you are in the world. My favorite meals in Paris, Beirut, and Germany were served in the intimacy and familiarity of a private home. Here it was all the more special as so few foreigners experienced the hospitality in such an intimate way. On the floor in front of us was an array of dishes that the General's wife had cooked. Rice mixed with raisins and carrots covered tender hunks of lamb. Another platter was stacked with fresh-baked naan bread. A bowl was filled with quorma, a slightly spicy Afghan stew of lamb chunks and potatoes. A tiny condiment bowl contained spicy green peppers crushed with garlic, and yet another bowl contained tomatoes, onions, and fresh basil. Lastly, there was yogurt, freshly made that day. Everything from meat to vegetable to naan bread had been produced on the family land.

I was in heaven as the General gestured for us to "eat more, eat more!" Tony joked with Faheem that his mother's cooking would be famous tomorrow as I would surely write about it. I suggested that perhaps I should simply return for some cooking lessons.

After a post-lunch walk around the garden with the family dog, a gorgeous German shepherd, we said good-bye to the General who insisted firmly, but with a wide smile, that I must return to see him. Faheem offered to drive us to visit Massoud's grave to pay respects, so we walked through the inner courtyard and piled into the General's Toyota four-by-four. We stopped first at Massoud's family home. The driveway was blocked by a thin chain that a child removed when we pulled up, and we drove up the steep dirt driveway. Faheem showed us around the house of the most famous Afghan in recent times.

The grave was not much farther, and as we got closer, we could see construction in progress on a large marble structure around Massoud's grave. This was the same hillside where I would almost meet my demise when Shah Mohammad crashed his Corolla a year later. It overlooked the Panjshir Valley in all directions, a unique vantage point and one that was chosen to allow the Lion of Panjshir to continue to look over his flock. People had been coming here since 2001 to pay respects or to picnic.

Faheem stopped to say hello to a group of workers, and I pressed my right hand to my heart and said "Salaam" quietly to each of them. We followed Faheem toward a covered casket under the roof of the uncompleted tomb. I hung back in respect as he bowed his head for several minutes while Najibullah and Shah Mohammad prayed silently across from him. The mood was somber as we walked slowly to the car.

Two days later in Kabul, the somber mood was replaced with nervous excitement. Najibullah set up two "interviews" for Tony and me with two prominent female leaders and activists. The first was with the former minister of Women's Affairs, Dr. Massouda Jalal. She ran for president against Hamid Karzai in the first post-Taliban elections in 2002. As we drove to the meeting at Dr. Jalal's home,

I looked over at Tony and said quietly, almost whispering, "What the hell am I doing? This is the equivalent of sitting down for a meeting with a cabinet member and senator back in the United States. I'm seriously out of my element here."

"You are going to be great. Just let her do the talking. You want answers. Here's someone who may have them. Just breathe and be yourself."

"Lame," I joked, smiling over at him while rolling my eyes.

"Nope, not lame. You want to know what's really going on here? You want to show others what Afghan women are capable of? This is exactly the sort of woman you've been looking for."

I nodded and looked down over the hastily scribbled questions in my notebook.

I needn't have worried. Dr. Massouda Jalal was not a wallflower. Dubbed the Mother of Afghanistan, she set an example for women looking to challenge their position in Afghan society and promote the role of women in government. After exchanging pleasantries in her living room over tea, we started in. Her answer to my first question about her work as minister of Women's Affairs took over fifteen minutes. The second, about her run for president against Karzai, another twenty. This part was fascinating. Though she didn't have the international support or financial backing that Karzai had, she came in a relatively close second. She talked a lot about the role that women could have in politics. "Women are peacemakers. Men are the fighters. Men hold grudges and work on ethnic boundaries that go back generations. Women don't have the same grievances and generational resentments. We can negotiate and build alliances better than men." Her English was fluent, so Najibullah excused himself to pray in the corner. Five or six questions later, I had said very little but had gotten a solid overview of her life and government work. I asked a few follow-up questions about her newly established organization, the Jalal Foundation, and its work with women's issues, and then we were finished.

Relief poured out of me as Tony and I ate kebabs afterward. I steeled myself for an interview with a female member of Parliament, Dr. Roshanak Wardak.

Dr. Wardak was not an easy interview. Here was a woman who had stared down the Taliban. Even now, in Parliament, she worked alongside warlords who preferred not to see women in politics. I got a heady dose of how intense her gaze can be, perhaps made more so by the Parliamentary room we were meeting in. Red leather chairs surrounded four long, polished dark-wood tables arranged to form a large square. The Afghan flag stood solemnly in the corner. Where Dr. Jalal was motherly and animated, Dr. Wardak was tough and blunt. She represented the tumultuous province from which her family took its name: Wardak. Fighting and violence is ongoing there, with a large number of Taliban in the region. Wardak neighbors Kabul, and the difference in security between the two provinces is almost incomprehensible.

Dr. Wardak was the province's only female OB/GYN. During the Taliban's reign, most women wore the burqa, but she insisted she could not do her job covered up and simply wore her black head scarf so that her face was covered except for her eyes. She worked throughout those difficult years, and when the Taliban were pushed out and elections held, the people of Wardak encouraged her to run as a candidate for Parliament. With seemingly little effort, she won.

As she sat across from me, her eyes probed mine, silently questioning my interest, my knowledge, and probably my intentions. Her eyes continued to search and probe as we talked, and when silences came, they were not for me to fill. They were there for her to decide if she would continue, and when she did, it was with direct honesty. This was a woman with no time for games. Her mantra, "politics is lying," was repeated often throughout our conversation. She hated politics and said so openly. She was a doctor, and loved her work, and loved her people. "A doctor must be honest and direct at all times," she told me. As a politician, she saw the falsehood and manipulation, and had no patience for it.

We discussed women in politics, gender equality, the political climate, and most important, given her unique insight, the Taliban's role in the future of Afghanistan. Her point of view was unique because she'd had no rights under the Taliban. She'd been forced to cover her face. She'd not have been allowed to vote, much less run as a candidate herself, had the Taliban held elections. Yet, she realized that the Taliban were Afghan, and as such, should be allowed their place in society under the Afghan constitution. Like Hamas and Hezbollah, the Taliban were part of the country and represented a great number of people. Wardak believed that they needed to be part of the process to bring peace, and others like President Karzai and the American government were coming to the same conclusion.

"Let them run candidates if they wish, the same as anyone else. If they win seats, then we must honor that," she said. "But the trick is that they have to abide by the 'rules' and accept women as their counterparts, perhaps even as their new president. Yet, if they are given the chance to run amok, isolated from the political system and peace process, it will be to the destruction of the country and will put Afghanistan in the center of the war on terror."

When I asked about her most important work in Parliament, her answer was immediate and concise. "Security. It is the *only* priority for progress. Achieving it is another story. Yet the Parliament, ministers, and the people of Afghanistan need to work toward a peace process conducted with all of Afghanistan represented as a complete way to end the violent spiral."

Staring back into Wardak's tough gaze, I realized that while she may hate being a politician, she was perhaps the kind of politician this, and every, country needs.

Wazhma Frogh, an Afghan female activist and writer, echoed that sentiment three years later, after ex-president and head of the High Peace Council, Burhanuddin Rabbani, was assassinated in September 2011 by a Taliban emissary. She stated her belief that the High Peace Council needed women involved if the country was ever to truly be at peace, then added: "Women in Afghanistan had to fight to have representation in the High Peace Council. They have been able to make headway where the men could not. For example, some of the women at the High Peace Council were able to make contacts with some of the families of one of the armed opposition groups and were welcomed in their homes. Not one of the men in the High Peace Council has been able to enter the house of an armed opposition group commander."

She then compared the situation to the women in South Africa going door to door, in essence, selling the newly formed Constitution.

"I am sure the world remembers how South African women went around the country uniting every South African in favor of their new Constitution at the end of apartheid. It was actually the South African women who prevented a bloodbath by giving everyone a voice during the Constitution-making process."

Women have an important role in Afghanistan, whether the Afghan men realize it or not. Without the full participation of society, a country cannot be unified. Studies continue to link a society's economic progress and overall stability with gender equality. The viral digital campaign that launched in 2007, the Girl Effect, illustrates simply and powerfully how educating girls directly affects a society's overall progress. The world is beginning to recognize the power women have, and the importance that gender equality and women's rights have in the health of a nation.

As if Najibullah knew that I could use a day off, we spent the next day exploring the older side of Kabul—an outing that could have been scripted for my father.

My father is an architect and loves restoration projects, the preservation of historic buildings in particular. I have fond memories of walks around numerous job sites with him as a young girl, collecting odd bits of wood for my "workshop" at home. I remember the smell of sawdust and the sound of hammers and circular saws, the maze of a framed-out building, and seeing from one room to the next through the two-by-fours.

Tony and I were fortunate to be guided around the oldest preservation project in Kabul, Murad Khane, by the lead engineer. This is a project that falls under the guidance of Turquoise Mountain, a nonprofit focused on restoring traditional Afghan art and culture. Murad Khane is at the heart of old Kabul and was once a bustling commercial center. The area has fallen into disrepair over the last century. It has no sewage, and buildings collapse weekly. We were shown photos of garbage piled eight feet high across this area, the removal of which was an enormous first step toward reconstruction.

Walking through the job site, I felt at home, even if the cessation of work and extensive staring illustrated the point that I was the only woman there. These buildings were all made of clay and mud, and great piles of it were on the ground. Men shoveled it to keep it moist and properly mixed, the smell mingling with that from the open sewers and the sawdust from the woodwork restoration.

Suddenly, my head scarf wasn't a burden as I pulled one end of it across my nose and mouth.

The construction coordinator and project engineer showed me around, up and down narrow stairwells, through rooms and onto balconies. The bazaar's buildings were built around three separate courtyards but were mostly interconnected. Then we ascended one last narrow spiral stone staircase, and I found myself on the roof. All of Kabul stretched out before me, just three stories up. The maze of the bazaar and the restoration project itself became clearer as we walked from rooftop to rooftop, looking down into the courtyards. I was free to watch instead of moving through scenes, trying to take everything in at a brisk pace. Below us, the daily routines of Kabul unfolded. Children fought with a small dog. Women in head scarves hustled through streets. Others in burqas picked their way more slowly as they shopped, occasionally lifting them over their heads to talk or simply to get some oxygen. Men prayed inside an open window. Others pissed in the alley. It was all there to be taken in from above, and I loved being able to watch the scene without disturbing it with my presence.

Najibullah had brought his son, Mustafa, with us, and he'd waited patiently in the car with Shah Mohammad all day during my meetings. The reward? We bought two kites and some string and headed up to Nadir Shah Hill, commonly called Kite Hill, overlooking Kabul.

My father loves kites. He had trick kites and the great big ones that resembled those used for kite boarding and that could drag you along for miles if the wind was strong. I imagined he would be as excited as Mustafa at the prospect of catching some wind. Afghanistan's national pastime is kite flying, and most boys grow up flying them or running them down during kite fights. Every Friday, families come to this spot on the hill where the wind is strong and the space is open. Many will coat their strings with a powdered glass for kite fighting. Kids will duel in the air and aim to cut the other's string with their own. If the string is cut, the kite is lost and "finders keepers." This is where the runners come in, chasing down the kites through the neighborhoods.

Najibullah had introduced us a few days prior to one of Kabul's master kite makers. He'd shown us how he fashioned the delicate and often elaborate kites out of pieces of tissue paper, glue, and thin strips of wood. I'd been surprised that the kites didn't disintegrate upon flight when we tested one in our courtyard.

I watched Najibullah and his son fly the kite from the top of the dusty hill, surrounded by young children, a few horses, and the ongoing reconstruction of King Nadir Shah's tomb, which like everything else, had been damaged during the war. The tomb was an imposing marble structure, topped by a metal dome and covered in scaffolding. The king had been assassinated in 1933, one more in a long line of Afghan leaders removed from office by violence.

I wished Devon could be with me. She was too young to fly a kite by herself, but at four, she would have loved to watch the kites dancing through the sky as much as my father.

On one of my final nights in Afghanistan, I bent the security rules I'd been living under. I upset Tony, and worried Najibullah unnecessarily, but as Katharine Hepburn once put it, "If you obey all the rules, you'll miss all the fun." And seeing Kabul from the back of a motorbike is worth breaking a rule for.

I'd made plans to meet up with Travis at the AINA offices, to talk more about the exhibition and his own experiences living in Kabul. When we set a date and time, he asked if I was "allowed" to go for a motorcycle ride. "Allowed" is such an inflammatory word to me. It immediately puts me on the defensive. *What am I, a child?* In Kabul, though, Travis's question wasn't unusual, as many aid workers and NGO employees must abide by certain security rules involving curfews and drivers. Many are not allowed to go out at night or, if they are, only to certain restaurants on a list that changes based on security reports. One woman I knew was required to carry a GPS tracker in her bag wherever she went. I was under no such restrictions other than the extraordinary care of Najibullah. He and Tony were going to visit the land mine museum while I met with Travis, and we made plans for them to pick me up a few hours later.

Unfortunately for Najibullah's sensibilities, seeing Kabul on the back of a bike was *exactly* what the doctor ordered after three weeks of head scarves, locked car doors, and being home by 6:00 P.M. Not that my trip hadn't been an adventure or that Najibullah hadn't been an amazing guide, but I needed a bit more freedom—a bit more wind in my face. I wanted to see Afghanistan from the perspective of someone who lived there full-time.

The obvious challenge was riding the motorbike with a head scarf. It was difficult to keep it in place when walking down the street and a near impossibility on the back of a motorbike. I attracted second looks in the car, so I'd definitely stand out on the back of a motorbike. Travis told me that women in Afghanistan rode side-saddle, if at all. So when I straddled the seat, I was already clearly a foreigner, regardless of my blond hair blowing out of a billowing head scarf. I tucked the ends into my coat and hoped the Taliban weren't watching.

This was an old bike—more a glorified dirt bike than a motorcycle, dubbed the Super Kabul. Travis revved the engine as I climbed on, and I felt the wave of calmness I always get when I am happy to be exactly where I am. A small burst of adrenaline replaced the calm as the freedom from cars and locked doors and security hit with the first gust of wind.

I quickly realized the head scarf staying put would in fact be an issue, as I couldn't hold on to the bike with just one hand on these streets and I wasn't wearing a helmet. Gutted out, muddy, and worthy of a four-by-four or a full suspension mountain bike, the roads posed serious obstacles: rocks, deep puddles, and enormous potholes, not to mention the traffic. In a car, you see the chaos. On a motorbike, you feel it. So I pulled the side of my head scarf to my face and held the fabric between my teeth. As I did, Travis mentioned casually the rumor that the roads were purposely not fixed to keep traffic slow and give suicide bombers a tougher time. A comforting thought.

There were few, if any, actual traffic rules in this country. There were two stoplights in the entire city. At roundabouts and intersections, people had a general sense of rules, but if you needed to go left and the roundabout traffic flowed to the right, you just weaved between oncoming traffic to make the shortcut. One-way streets? No such thing—often we were the only vehicle going against three lanes of traffic. Lanes were nonexistent. Each road had a varying number of lanes at a given time, from two to four or even five on the same stretch, depending on the time of day. Bikers and pedestrians crossed at will, and at their own risk. On a motorbike you abided by all the non-rules of the road, times ten, plus you had access to the sidewalks.

We climbed a steep dirt road up TV Hill, named for the hundreds of antennae that covered its top. The city of Kabul spread out below us, and the overpowering smell of diesel, dust, and rotting garbage began to fade. Typically, lights dotted Kabul in the early dusk, but that night rolling blackouts had darkened swaths of the city. We stopped briefly to take in the view, allowing a few of the small children chasing us to catch up. One little boy didn't respond when I offered a few words in Dari, but his dirty face lit up with a big, shy smile. He hung around like a sparrow, scrutinizing us while Travis pointed out the landmarks and I finally got my head wrapped around the lay of the land. Travis indicated another large hill directly across from us and said that was stop number two.

Fifteen minutes later, we arrived at the infamous Olympic diving pool, built during the Soviet era but never used for its intended purpose. The pool was a stark rectangular hole in the ground with three concrete diving boards, rusty ladders running up their sides. During the nineties, it was the site of Taliban executions. The accused were pushed from the top diving board into the empty pool. Those who survived were deemed innocent. Most, not surprisingly, were found guilty. Now Afghans used the pool for dog fighting, a popular sport, and impromptu football games. We stood underneath the high dives watching a group playing soccer below us. Voices ricocheted around the inside of the concrete pool along with the ball. A full moon rose behind us, illuminating the men while the dusty air added a strange softness to the scene. I felt as if I were watching a moving painting.

I inwardly cursed my luck as I was used to having my photographer-at-large with me at all times to document these classic moments. I knew Tony would kill to see this as well, and I vowed to ask Najibullah to drive us up here Friday morning before we left.

In the course of our conversation, I told Travis that I raced mountain bikes. As we started back down, he promptly said that he'd been driving cautiously so as not to scare me, but now all bets were off. We tore down the hill, my head scarf gripped tightly between my teeth and the exhilaration of this temporary freedom pulsating in my bones.

When we got back, Tony was upset because he and Najibullah hadn't been sure where I'd been when they showed up at the AINA offices to pick me up. They knew I was meeting Travis, but as I didn't have a phone here and was utterly dependent on Najibullah and others, I couldn't let them know I would be a few minutes late. Tony's outrage was amplified slightly. Maybe he was jealous of the ride—of my temporary freedom—or of Travis's influence, or maybe a little of both. I apologized to Najibullah for any worry I'd caused him, but I was angry at Tony for overreacting, knowing he'd have made the same choice given the opportunity. But the next morning's activities pushed my so-called security infraction to the back of both our minds. On our last day in Afghanistan, Najibullah informed us that there was a buzkashi match near Kabul and we could go.

I'd dreamed of one day seeing a buzkashi game, and had hoped a match would take place near enough for us to watch. Buzkashi was an iconic sport that epitomizes the Afghan spirit, featuring Afghan warriors on horseback. The director of the Buzkashi Federation happened to be a friend of Najibullah, and he invited us to attend the match as his guests, an honor that not only eliminated complicated issues of checkpoints and security, but also provided a few other unexpected perks.

We met Tashili in the dusty field behind Kabul Stadium where the horses for the Kabul team were housed. As we arrived, horses were being loaded into trucks and several were still tethered in the field waiting their turn. Tashili welcomed us warmly and asked me if I liked buzkashi. I replied that it was a great honor to watch a game and a lifelong dream. He showed us the horses, and stopping

Riding my bike past the boys' school in Dashty Rewat in 2009. The first time these boys have ever seen a girl ride a bike. (Photo credit: Travis Beard)

Looking over Kabul's old town from the rooftops of Murad Khane with Najibullah in 2008. (Photo credit: Tony Di Zinno)

Riding the Desert Eagle on my first night ride in Kabul. (Photo credit: Barry Misenheimer)

Q&A at the A4T girls' school in Kabul in 2008. (Photo credit: Tony Di Zinno)

Early morning traffic in Bamiyan. (PHOTO CREDIT: DENI BECHARD)

Riding past a Soviet tank graveyard in the Panjshir Valley. (PHOTO CREDIT: TRAVIS BEARD)

Unloading school supplies in Dashty Rewat. (PHOTO CREDIT: TRAVIS BEARD)

Speaking with village men in the mountains of Panjshir, trying to keep warm under an Afghan sandalee. (PHOTO CREDIT: TRAVIS BEARD)

Woman begging in the street with her child in Kabul—this became the cover photo for the *Streets of Afghanistan* exhibition. (Photo credit: Tony Di Zinno)

Learning to fly kites in my guesthouse courtyard with one of Kabul's master kite makers. (Photo credit: Tony Di Zinno)

Hamid and Travis getting ready to film in the Panjshir Valley, Tour de France style, during one of my first bike rides in 2009. (Photo credit: Shannon Galpin)

Posing with my "prize" after learning to fish with nets in the Panjshir River. (PHOTO CREDIT: TRAVIS BEARD)

Crossing the river, twice, near the turnaround point of the ride across the Panjshir Valley in 2010. (PHOTO CREDIT: TRAVIS BEARD)

Delivering laptop computers to the A4T girls' school in Kabul with Travis in 2009. (Photo credit: Travis Beard)

Standing at the Venue with local graffiti artist, Shamsia, in front of one of her unfinished pieces. (Photo credit: Anna Brones)

in front of a large white one, asked if I would like to get on. I thought he was joking, that there was no way they'd let a woman on one of these treasured animals. There was even an old Afghan wives' tale saying that if a bride rode on a buzkashi horse it would never compete again, and I wondered what would happen if a foreign female rode one. Nonetheless, I was fairly bursting with excitement and told him I would be greatly honored. He smiled broadly and gestured for one of the stable boys to remove the blanket covering the saddle, then allowed me to mount. A crowd materialized, all of the faces with an air of disbelief.

Not waiting to see if Tashili was pulling my leg, I hoisted up my long skirt (I was wearing jeans underneath) so that my foot could reach high enough to slide into the stirrup, and prayed I could make this look graceful. I was thankful for the strength built up in my legs from a summer of mountain bike riding. The crowd grew larger to witness the foreigner accepting the challenge of mounting one of their prized horses. A grin spread across my face as I felt the strength of the animal beneath me. I knew that I would see this horse compete under the skill of one of Kabul's chapandaz, the burly riders that competed in this iconic sport. It was a dream come true.

Regretfully, I dismounted, wishing I could ride it around the field. I handed off the horse to a young man who led it to the trucks. Tashili led me over to meet the president of the Federation, Aji Abdul Rashed. This man could have been a professional wrestler in another life. Heavyset and looking every bit as strong as the horses, he grinned broadly and clapped my hand in both of his with a powerful grip. "You love buzkashi? You must buy some horses, and we will keep them for you," he said in a booming voice that practically echoed through the stables.

"You can help us find sponsorship, and we will make you secretary general of Buzkashi," he continued loudly.

I laughed and said it would be a great honor to own some buzkashi horses, but alas, I was in no position to afford one.

"Not today, maybe in the future," he insisted.

"*Inshallah*," I replied, and with that we shook hands again.

He was obviously enjoying the exchange, and we talked about the state of the sport in Afghanistan, the horses, and of course, the legendary chapandaz themselves. He would be riding himself today and I promised to follow his horse throughout the game.

We watched as the horses got loaded into flatbed trucks, then we all walked back to the cars. Tashili was riding with us for the hour-long drive north of Kabul to an empty field on the Shomali Plain, which was owned by Marshal Fahim, an avid buzkashi supporter who sponsored one of the top buzkashi players Aziz Ahmad.

Marshal Fahim was the vice president of Afghanistan, a former defense minister, a military commander, and overall, a controversial figure. He'd survived many assassination attempts, and when we arrived we were led through tight security. We walked across the muddy field through horses and riders warming up and making adjustments to their mounts. Stone bleachers lined one side, and I realized we would be sitting just inches away from the action.

Guards with guns stood by a private covered seating area slightly above us and separated from the stone bleachers. Najibullah told me that Marshal Fahim would sit there with his friends and heavy security. Shivering slightly, I wondered if they were inside somewhere, staying warm and drinking pots of tea. Then the gates we'd entered reopened and four black Land Cruisers with tinted windows roared across the pitch. Marshal Fahim and his entourage had arrived and now the game could begin.

The riders had been warming up their horses, riding around the field, and talking with one another for the better part of an hour. Slowly, the four teams lined up across the back of the field to introduce themselves to the crowd. Then, suddenly, the game started. As is typical in Central Asian versions of buzkashi played throughout the region, the "object" is a headless sheep, lamb, or calf carcass. In Afghanistan, it was often a small calf. The carcass was tossed onto the field near the winner's circle, and the "rodeo clown" blew the whistle. Riders surged forward to gain position, the members of a team creating a safe pocket for a rider to grab the carcass while on horseback. Leaning over into a crowd of charging horses to pick the carcass off the ground required skill as well as the strength to lift it onto the saddle in one fluid motion. The rider also needed the courage to face getting crushed in the mayhem. He then had to race to the green flag at the end of the field before he could attempt to race back and drop the calf in the circle. But the calf was heavy and difficult to hold on to, and the rider had forty or more riders chasing to steal it, block him, or simply force him off course.

To say that this game was controlled chaos would be an understatement. It was like a rugby scrum with horses surging into the pack, jockeying for position, blocking and maneuvering, until someone, somehow secured the calf and broke free. More chapandaz scored than I would have thought possible and each time the calf was released into the circle, cheers of "Hallal" went round the field. The rider then collected his cash prize from the stands and headed back out to try again.

As a sports photographer, Tony was in his element. He entered the scrum to the delight of the crowd and befriended the "rodeo clown/referee." His new friend encouragingly shoved Tony right into the action and quickly backpedaled out of the melee. Caught up in the spectacle of thundering hooves and acrobatic acts from the riders, Najibullah and I quickly forgot that Tony was in among the players. He emerged periodically to catch his breath and get his bearings, before diving back in.

Three and a half hours later, the third calf was thrown in (the first two had disintegrated under the constant tug-of-war). Tony showed me a frame he'd captured, a portrait of one of the black stallions rearing up. He had the unmistakable cat-that-got-the-canary look. He was pretty sure he'd gotten some good stuff. It was freezing cold as we walked quickly back across the field toward the gate. One of the chapandaz rode over and gestured that I could get on for a ride back to the gate. This drew a few cheers from the crowd, and it was with regret that I declined, as I saw there was no space on top of the horse due to the size of this sturdy chapandaz. He shrugged with a good-natured grin and rode past.

On the way back to Kabul, we had just enough time to detour to the hillside diving pool to show Tony before Najibullah dropped us off at the airport to begin the long journey home. The sky was blue, and several kites dotted the horizon. It was a fitting end to the visit, nostalgic and heartwarming.

Back home, sitting at my kitchen table in a four-in-the-morning jet lag haze, I realized how important the past three weeks had been.

"I found myself in Afghanistan." I said these words to Christiane when I finally got to see her in person. "Does that sound corny?" I was inwardly cringing at the Pollyannaish sound of the statement.

Christiane smiled, wrapped her arms around me, and said, "It would if I hadn't been reading your blogs while you were over there. It's totally obvious you were home."

Tony saw this, too, and understood my fear of being perceived as a so-called do-gooder. "Shannon, you are the anti-Pollyanna."

And he was right. There were no rose-colored glasses when I

looked at Afghanistan. It was simply that it was there, in a war zone, that I stepped up to the plate and accepted that I did, in fact, want to "save the world." Citizen diplomats are needed across the globe, connecting communities and cultures, looking at individuals as agents of change. This was essential if any real change was to be possible in countries like Afghanistan. I needed to be part of something bigger than myself. Devon deserved a mother who was willing to enter the fight. Girls around the world deserved it.

(4)

Turning Point

Colorado 2004

The phone rang and I picked it up to hear my sister's normally boisterous voice quietly say my name. "Hi, Shan." My instincts pricked. Something was wrong.

Holding the cordless phone close to my good ear, my right one being nearly deaf after an accident canyoning in Austria when I was twenty, I paced the wooden floor in my living room as I heard phrases thud my consciousness. *Last night. Walking home. Campus. Attacked. Raped.*

I sat down on the black steamer trunk in front of the windows that looked out the back of my house into the open expanse of beaver ponds. My mind struggled to process what I was hearing. Snow still covered the ground, despite the onset of spring, and I wondered how much longer winter could hold on at ten thousand feet.

Larissa said she hadn't seen a doctor yet but had called the campus police with her roommates. There was a strange twist to her story, something about a man pretending to be a police officer coming to her door and asking for evidence after the episode. All of it confused me, worried me, and I felt a dull ache in the pit of my stomach as I listened. She was scared but safe, and she wanted to finish out the last few weeks of school to get through her finals.

We hung up with a promise I'd call her back after talking with Mom and Dad. Someone needed to go down to the college and be with her. Adams State was in the small town of Alamosa, three hours south of Breckenridge. Immediately, my parents offered to fly down, but I insisted on going instead. I was closer, I could leave in the morning, and I wouldn't try to take over. I was also much too familiar with this story.

I stared mindlessly out the window, my gaze unfocused, my mind blank.

"Shan?"

I refocused and looked around. The phone was still in my hand. Pete was in the kitchen, looking at me from across the counter. "What's going on? Is everything okay?"

"That was Ris." Ris, Rissa, Lis—all pet names used by my family for my younger sister, Larissa. "She's been attacked. She was walking home, across campus. Some guy attacked her."

"Jesus, is she all right?"

"Yeah, no. Not so much. She was attacked. Raped." I stood up and walked over to the brown leather couch and wished the fire was going in the fireplace. It was so cold in this big house. I was always cold, but this was much worse. "I don't understand the details. . . . I don't know if even Ris understands them yet. It doesn't make sense. But she's with her roommates now. I think she's called campus police. Mom and Dad want me to go down. She needs one of us."

"Do you want a cup of tea?" he said, filling the kettle.

"Yeah, sure," I said distractedly. Tea, I thought, the British symbol of comfort. Or perhaps the British proxy for therapy. Right now the warmth and the distraction were welcome. My mind was reeling.

A long pause, then, "Would you be all right with that—if I drove down to Alamosa to see her, I mean? She needs someone to take her to the police station tomorrow, and I should be there."

"Doesn't she have her roommates who could help out?"

"Of course, but she should have family there. Mom and Dad want to check in on her. Make sure she's coping, has everything she needs, you know—how is she dealing? Plus she's got finals coming up and wants to stay to finish the end of the school year. . . ." I trailed off. "But she's pretty freaked out. So am I, frankly."

Pete poured water over two bags of PG Tips. He looked across the room at me, before turning to get the milk out of the fridge. "So what happened exactly?"

I wanted to ask him to say something more than just a series of one-sentence questions. It felt so cold. I wanted him to leave the tea, sit down, and hold me, and have a real conversation about what was going on. Why couldn't he just wrap me up in his arms, ask if there was anything he could do, or just ask how I was? My tolerance of his British reserve was wearing thin. I needed some emotion, some re-action beyond a cup of tea, some love.

"Exactly? I'm not sure. Other than she was attacked walking home across campus. The asshole raped her, and left her there, and she was able to get back to her apartment. The creepy thing is that a fake police officer showed up at her door asking for evidence."

"Fake? What do you mean?"

"Well apparently he showed up in uniform, said he'd been sent over by campus police to collect evidence. She gave him her under-wear in a plastic bag and he asked a few questions and left. Appar-ently, the police never sent anyone to her, and if they had and the officer had collected any evidence on site, then protocol states using a paper bag, not plastic. It means 'he' knows where she lives, or that there are a couple of guys working together. It's beyond creepy."

"So, when are you thinking of going down there?" He set a mug of milky tea on the kitchen counter for me and took a sip of his, still standing in the kitchen, the horrible pink-hued wooden cabinets behind him. Who put pink wooden cabinets in a house like this? I couldn't help my mind from wandering as I digested what I had just heard.

"I was thinking tomorrow morning first thing."

He sighed. "Do you have any money to make the trip?"

I took a sip of tea, my gaze lowered to a familiar pattern of exposed knotholes on the surface of the table. I absently took one hand away from the mug, and with my fingernail I scraped out some of the dust and food particles that always gathered in the deeper crevasses. My heart sank a little with the disappointing turn this conversation was taking. Was this really the priority for every discussion we had? This wasn't the time for logistics or finances. This was the time for emotion, for compassion, empathy, love. I retreated further inside myself.

"No, not really, would you mind helping? My father said he'd cover the costs, but it's a little silly to ask him for something like this. It's just gas, and a night or two at a hotel to get her back on track and give her some support."

This was a recent and ongoing bone of contention: money. More precisely, the disparity of income between the two of us, despite having been married for six years.

I stood up from the table and went to our bedroom to pack a bag, and Pete walked upstairs to finish some work in his office. As I packed, I couldn't help but feel rage building at the injustice of what I was processing. My only sister, nearly ten years younger than me, brutally violated. Deeply buried thoughts clawed at the edges of consciousness, but I refused to acknowledge them. Now was the time to focus on Larissa, but my mind kept wandering backward over a decade earlier.

Eleven years had passed and not once had I talked to Larissa about my own attack. Now here we were. She had just turned twenty. I had been eighteen. The similarity of the situations, our ages, nearly a decade apart, was disturbing. I hadn't talked to anyone about what had happened to me so many years ago, and now it was bubbling just underneath the surface, threatening to boil over. I crawled underneath the covers, exhausted and scared.

The next morning, I awoke feeling as if I had a wicked hangover, despite having drunk nothing but a mug of tea the night before. A glass of whiskey may have been a better choice for once, perhaps deadening my thoughts and allowing a modicum of peace in what was a restless night wrestling with my own nightmares and imagining those of my sister's. The reality was, I was pregnant. We had found out only last month, and I wasn't even showing yet. Pete and my family knew but it was still so new that I hadn't processed it yet.

I made a bowl of oatmeal and boiled the kettle for tea and sat down at the table, my attention focused on the same knothole from the night before while my mind was elsewhere. Pete came in to make some cereal, and after a few strained pleasantries, went upstairs to work. I grabbed my bag from the bedroom and got ready to leave with the weird tension still between us. He didn't think I really needed to go. I knew that I did but was scared to. I looked up at the ceiling as though I could will him to come back down and thaw the ice that was forming. Instead, I sighed and shook my head as though my feelings and thoughts functioned like an Etch A

Sketch. I walked down the stairs to the garage below, still shivering in the chilly house.

Pulling into the small town of Alamosa, I was struck again by how grim this corner of Colorado was. Colorado was known as an outdoor playground. Snowboarders, skiers, mountain bikers, kayakers, and hikers all streamed into the state. Amateur photographers swarmed the trails, inspired by the stunning beauty of the mountains. Yet a few hours south was a flat, barren land of strip malls and alligator farms that made you wonder if there were any architects in the entire forty-mile radius, or zoning codes for that matter. When my father encouraged my sister to attend Adams State in southern Colorado three years prior, thoughts of Durango or Crested Butte came to mind—charmingly rustic mountain towns with a cool college campus vibe mixed in. I was psyched to visit her the first time to see where her formative years would be spent, getting a taste of something different than what she would have experienced had she stayed in the Midwest. But as we drove in, on a lonely road, more akin to rural North Dakota than Colorado, past an alligator farm and numerous forlorn homesteads with rusted-out cars and kitchen appliances in the yards, I gulped and hoped against hope that Alamosa was an oasis, or at least a diamond in the rough.

It wasn't. It was the rough without the diamond. The small campus of Adams State just off Main Street was the only thing that looked encouraging in the entire town. Alamosa was essentially one long main street with a series of hotels and strip malls, and it was immediately obvious that the town was financially dependent on the small college, the students, and their families that came to visit.

Nothing much had changed since that initial visit to watch one of her college soccer games three years prior. I drove through town and past the campus to the Hampton Inn on the edge of town, and I waited for Larissa to get out of class. I paced the room, nervous to see her.

She was quiet when we met up. Her long hair was in its soccer-chic messy bun, her face typically devoid of any makeup. I smiled when I saw her and gathered her up in a big hug. We had always laughed that we were built so differently as sisters. I was five nine, weighed 125, and built like a lanky boy. She was five six and curvaceous, with D cups and hips. She was the powerful soccer player, and I was the ex-ballerina. She looked like Rissa. I didn't know what I'd expected to see. There was no visible damage, thank God, but I knew what lurked beneath the surface. I was at a loss of what to say or do. Act normal? Cry? Rage?

Eat.

"Do you want to get some lunch first?" I asked, thinking a little downtime together would be nice before we headed straight to the police station.

"Sure," she said. She smiled, but her voice was wavering.

We had lunch at the local Chinese restaurant Hunan, and talked a bit about her classes and upcoming finals.

Then I asked the key question that was bothering me. "So what's the situation with the fake police guy at your door? That's just so weird."

"I know. We found out from the campus police that it's apparently been done in a few different college towns. Basically, the person who attacked you, or someone working with him, follows you home and knocks on your door pretending to be the police and collect the evidence. Pretty smart actually."

"Pretty fucking scary. How do you feel about staying there for the rest of the term?"

"My roommates and I made arrangements so no one is ever there alone, and it's only a couple of weeks until we are done for the year."

"But do you feel safe there?"

"No. But I don't know if I'd feel safe anywhere."

I looked down at my plate. I knew exactly how she felt. I paid the bill, and we both stood up, bracing ourselves for the next step. "Okay then, let the fun begin," I said sarcastically. "Where do we need to go?"

"Just head back to the campus and I'll direct you from there. Let's get this over with." We got into the Subaru and rode a few blocks in silence.

We pulled up and stepped out of the car in front of a small police station off a side street. The officer on duty was expecting us, having already talked to Larissa and my father on the phone. He asked us to sit down in his office and went over her report again. He then asked her if she would try to look at a few faces in a book of mug shots. She flipped it blankly. Page after page, she flipped, the faces blurring together, indistinct to the casual observer. Nothing.

The officer then asked if she would work with a police artist to attempt to reconstruct the attacker's face. Larissa agreed, and I watched silently as the artist asked her questions to start the sketch. "Is his nose large or small? Pointed or rounded? Straight or crooked? Did it look like it had been broken?"

Larissa answered in a monotone the best she could.

"Were his eyes close together or set apart? Do you know what color they were? Big or small?"

It was soon apparent that Larissa was overwhelmed and unable to describe her attacker's face in any way that could lead to a picture of him. Sitting there listening, I realized how hard it would be to describe my own mother in such terms, much less a man who attacked me in the dark and who I would much rather forget.

Leaving the police station, I had a feeling of helplessness and déjà vu. There was little to no chance that her attacker would be caught, much less identified. It felt like a useless exercise that kept the policeman informed but did little to bring justice to the situation. Larissa seemed to feel more frustrated than anything else.

In an effort to lighten the mood and create a distraction, we drove to Dairy Queen the next town over. The warm weather and sunshine was a welcome change from the current winter storms in the mountains that I'd just left, and I rolled down the windows, letting the warm breeze breathe new life into the car. I hadn't gone to DQ in years, decades maybe. Memories of walking to Dairy Queen with my father on warm summer nights when I was growing up entered my thoughts. He'd put on his flip-flops and we'd walked the four blocks down Washington Street to get an ice-cream cone dipped in cherry, or a lime slushy, and then walked through the park across the street, mosquitoes buzzing through the evening air around us. It was always warm, and slightly humid, and we could hear crickets and mosquitoes. It was definitely one of my best and strongest memories of him from growing up.

We walked a little on the gravel path past the Dairy Queen, eating our blizzards in quiet thought.

"How's Dad dealing with all of this?"

"I don't know. He doesn't really say much."

"He doesn't really know how, probably. I don't think we've ever talked about my attack."

"I didn't even know you were attacked until last year."

"Really?"

"Well, I was only eight or nine when it happened, right? I remember I heard you guys talking about it at the kitchen table and you were crying, and when I asked what was wrong, they told me you had been mugged in Minneapolis. It wasn't until last year that I found out. I remember I was so mad at them for not telling me."

"Well you could be mad at me, too. . . . It's my fault, too. I just never ever talked about it after it happened, still haven't really, so I never thought to bring it up to you once you were old enough. Not even when you came to visit me last year in Germany. The safe-sex talk, yeah, condoms, college and career, sure. But not the rape. That's just not something I've even thought about sharing."

"'Til now?"

"Well, yeah, 'til now. Makes me kick myself that I didn't tell you about my experience. Like somehow it could have helped prevent it happening to you if you had been more aware. Like you would have had better radar, or been extra-cautious, or some such nonsense. Why didn't you confront me when you found out?"

"I didn't want to bring it up if you didn't want to talk about it, and I think I was just mad I didn't know. Like it was hidden from me. But regardless, it's not an easy topic to bring up when we only see each other once a year."

Larissa came back to my hotel room to hang out and do her homework so that she could be with someone until her roommates were home. We sat on the two queen beds, watching random TV while she studied and I worked. A strange mood hovered over both of us. I worked on my laptop, but was thinking of my parents.

They had two daughters, born nearly ten years apart. No sons. Both daughters were raped. That must have been devastating. The saddest part is I remember my mother being strongly against my move to Minneapolis. She sat on the edge of my bed, and told me how worried she was that something bad would happen. I assured her with all of my seventeen-year-old invincibility that she was being silly—I'd be fine. I was almost embarrassed that she was making such a fuss about it. How much guilt I harbored in the years that followed, that I'd proved her protective instincts right.

I talked with my mother several times throughout the trip. I was having a hard time believing that it had happened to Ris. I was trying to find proof it hadn't happened, because it couldn't have really happened to her. Months later I was so mad at myself for not being more comforting, more mothering. Instead I had felt almost scared to get too close, and kept her at arms' length. The wall that had protected my emotions was becoming a wedge between us, and I felt it and yet couldn't do anything to lower it. I was simply unable to comprehend that my only sister could have been violated in such a way.

A year and a half later, I found myself announcing to my family over Thanksgiving dinner my plans to start an organization to be called Mountain2Mountain. Devon was not quite two years old, my sister graduated college in the spring, and I wanted a change. Haunted by what had happened to my sister and immersed in Devon's development, I felt a pull to change my course. Despite the success I had in my career, I didn't feel challenged or fulfilled as a sports trainer. I didn't care about training individuals or preventing injuries anymore. I was sick of the apathy I saw in the world. I was sick of the violence, some of which had affected both me and my only sister. I was tired of the status quo. What would the world be like for Devon? I could spend the rest of my life ranting about the injustices I saw, or I could step up to the plate and do something about it. How could I raise Devon in a world that I wasn't fighting to make a better place, be it for her, or for her counterparts?

Pete once said after we separated, "Fund-raising for CAI isn't going to be enough is it? You're going to go over there." "There," being Afghanistan. I pooh-poohed him, suppressing the urge to say, "*Yes.* I have had enough of men treating women like they are disposable playthings they can just abuse and leave behind. Why can't you understand that I want to do more? I have to do more. What if this was Devon?" It was bad enough that it was Larissa, but Devon, too? Perhaps I felt I needed to pay some sort of karmic penance to ensure that this couldn't happen to anyone else I cared for. As much as I hated to admit it, Pete knew me better than I knew myself at the time. He saw what I was afraid to voice. I was too afraid he'd say no, or laugh, or worse, try to talk me out of it. I wanted to change the world and nothing was going to stop me from trying. The stakes were too high.

5

Speakeasies and Motorcycles

Afghanistan 2009

"Open this box," the security guard sitting behind the conveyor belt of the X-ray machine demanded. He pointed at a large cardboard box that I just put through, along with my bike box and duffel bag. I inwardly groaned.

"Why?"

"What is inside this box?"

"Computers for a girls' school here in Kabul." I had arrived at the Kabul International Airport's sole terminal and was standing at the final step before clearing the chaos. To be fair, it was a modern-day marvel compared to the old terminal next door where you searched for your luggage among the rest piled up on the concrete floor willy-nilly.

"You must pay tax."

"No—these are old computers, not new. These are donated. For a girls' school, here in Kabul."

"Open the box!" he barked. His colleague stopped gazing blankly at the bags still coming through the conveyor belt and took interest in the exchange, as did several other onlookers.

"With what?" I barked back. I had no intention of paying a tax on old computers and stood my ground. Besides, what's with the X-ray to enter Afghanistan? What could it have possibly picked up that the United States and Dubai X-rays hadn't already?

"*Open!*" People shoved past me gathering their luggage that was continuing to pour out of the X-ray.

"*With what?*" I shouted back. I pointed to the layers of duct tape surrounding every inch of the box, making it impossible to open without a sharp knife. I was making a scene and hardly cared what I looked like. I felt some locks of blond hair escaping from my head scarf, and I shoved them back in. We both waited to see who blinked first.

A middle-aged Afghan, in a gray business suit, standing behind me gathered his luggage from the conveyor belt and asked what was going on. I explained I was bringing these computers over for a girls' school and they wanted me to open the box so they could "tax" me.

He stepped forward, leaned over the conveyor belt, chastised them rapidly in Dari, and then switched to English more slowly. "This woman is bringing computers for our girls, and you are trying to take her money? No, you must let her go. Enough." He grabbed his luggage, nodded at me curtly, and squeezed past the crowd.

The security guard threw his hands up, scowled at me, then waved me out with a brisk, "*Burro burro*," as if I was the one holding up the line.

Working in Afghanistan had forced me to develop an entirely different set of skills: bargaining, patience, and an assertive nature that bordered on rude when I was challenged. Two years ago I was concerned about falling into the "ugly American" stereotype—the one that shouts English slower and louder instead of learning the local language, the one that won't eat suspicious-looking food offered to her, fearing it will cause gastric issues. Afghanistan broke me of that. Don't get me wrong—I was learning the language, and I'd eat anything locals served me, even if it meant I'd be chasing the last bite with Immodium and Cipro for dessert. But when you are in the right, and someone has decided you aren't, no amount of politeness and explanation will change their mind. Often it's only sheer stubbornness and an increase in volume that gets the job done. The blond hair usually catches them off guard as well.

I smiled sweetly at the security guard and gathered my luggage and boxes. "*Tashakur,*" I said, knowing that my sarcastic tone wouldn't be understood but not caring. Having won this round, I stacked the awkward load onto a cart and maneuvered my way through the airport and parking lots to find my driver and Najibullah.

I walked outside alone, pushing my overfull luggage cart across the front of the airport toward the metal gate where my driver was to pick me up. But he wasn't there. Nor was anyone else holding a sign with my name. I wondered what to do. Several taxi drivers walked up and asked if I needed a ride, and I started to wonder if there'd been an accident. He'd never been late before. My phone was dead, so I couldn't call Najibullah to check. I decided to wait and if I needed to, I could double back and grab a taxi driver to take me to my guesthouse. I turned around and, standing right behind the guards, was the short figure of Najibullah, who beamed when he saw me. Relief flooded my veins and I beamed back.

"*Salaam, Najibullah. Hubisti? Chituristi?*"

"*Salaam,* Shannon. Thank you, I am very fine."

Najibullah brought Habibe as a driver. I smiled warmly and

shook their hands heartily while exchanging the litany of greetings to both of them. Habibe smiled at me and then turned his face and said something to Najibullah who nodded in return.

Najibullah smiled and said, "Welcome back, Shannon. We are both very pleased to see you in Afghanistan again."

We headed out into the dusty city in a loaded Toyota Corolla hatchback, down the familiar road that led to my guesthouse. A smile of joy crossed my face as I inhaled the distinctive smell of dust and diesel that, more than anything else, told me I was back in Kabul.

Najibullah and Habibe dropped me off so I could get settled into my guesthouse in the center of town. This one was much more social and accessible than the others I'd stayed at. There were about forty rooms, and at times the breakfast room was packed with men and women from all over: Indians, Pakistanis, Afghans, Canadians, Americans, Germans, French, and Belgians mingling at the buffet each morning. It was much more pleasant than feeling isolated in a building with only one or two other guests. The guesthouse was also located centrally enough that I could walk or call private taxis to get around when I wasn't working with Najibullah. It was a slice of freedom that felt much more normal.

I arrived on a Thursday, so we wouldn't start working until Saturday, as Friday was the Afghan day of rest. This meant that Thursday nights were the new Friday—the big night to go out for the ex-pat community that wasn't on security lockdown. In a dry country where alcohol was forbidden, Thursday nights often meant private house parties or defying security warnings to party at one of the local bars.

Drinking in Kabul invoked the feeling of a 1920's speakeasy, minus the flapper girls. Nondescript unmarked doors with heavily armed security guards greeted us when I pulled up on a motorcycle with Travis. He'd asked if I wanted to join him and the Kabul Knights Motorcycle Club for a motorcycle road trip to Panjshir in the morning. I didn't need to be asked twice. But first we were to drink and mingle with the ex-pat community at L'atmosphere, the infamous Kabul watering hole.

We were let inside door number one. Here, Travis shook hands and hugged the guard who asked us to check our weapons. The guard obviously knew him well and joked with him. We continued down a hallway to door number two. A knock. A peephole slid open at eye level and immediately shut again as the door opened.

We entered a large courtyard with a path that led to a bar and a large open area to drink outside. I took off my scarf and stashed it in my coat pocket for the remainder of the night.

We went inside the crowded bar, filled with foreign aid workers, photographers, journalists, and a few beefy, thick-necked contractors (hired killers, not house builders). All nationalities were represented, including Afghan, and it all felt comfortingly familiar—this ex-pat existence was similar the world over, and after nearly ten years of living in Europe it fit like an old glove. The bar was replete with Heineken, Kronenbourg, wine, and enough generic hard liquor to make one rapidly forget it was illegal here. But at seven dollars a beer, I started to wonder who the real criminals were. To put it into context: two drinks cost me a little more than the equivalent of a hearty multicourse lunch for four at a local *chaikhanna*, or Afghan teahouse.

After introductions to several of Travis's friends and acquaintances, we wandered back outside with Kronenbourgs in hand. We entered the courtyard to gather around a large fire pit with many others who were escaping the noisy crowd inside and taking advantage of a clear night to drink under the stars. It was much the same as ex-pat communities I'd known in Germany and Beirut, where different nationalities bonded over shared work and in common languages. Except that here conversations ranged from local security measures, assignments and projects, and general story sharing from those who'd made this life in a conflict zone their own. Those covering the war here had done so in other conflict zones. People discussed flak jackets and their quality, kidnappings in Colombia, the desire to move to Somalia as the next probable hot spot, and other risky endeavors. Each story led to another, laughed-at retelling of a similar experience in a dodgier locale. A tension-reducing one-up-manship played out over many more drinks.

Eventually, 2:00 A.M. rolled around. The crowd had thinned dramatically, but many were still entrenched, enjoying the last hours of alcohol and flirting before it was back to reality. Travis was talking to a pretty young French photojournalist by the fire pit. Gloria Estefan's "Conga" was playing inside and more than a few inebriated people were making attempts at salsa dancing, which served as entertainment for those of us outside who watched through the floor-to-ceiling windows. I found myself next to a charming conversationalist, a British photojournalist wearing traditional Afghan clothing—a pakol hat and long shalwar kameez—who claimed he was famous for his salsa dancing. I was tempted to ask for proof, but I was too scared he'd drag me along with him.

Two of the thick-necked contractors got into a little scuffle, a signal that it was time to head home. I had an early morning date with a motorcycle gang.

Kabul Knights Motorcycle Club was formed by three friends, including Travis. Members came and went, all brought together by a mutual love of adventure, but no matter who was riding, the core group had the same goal: to experience and explore the real Afghanistan on the back of a bike. They'd ridden many of the main roads, the endless back roads, and hoped to one day ride the ring road that ran the perimeter of the country, but much of it was too dangerous to attempt. The number of Taliban checkpoints and controlled areas continued to increase, making traveling by road more difficult. Overall security had been deteriorating since 2008.

The road north of Kabul into the Panjshir Valley remained relatively safe, as long as you avoided the convoys and heart-stopping traffic on one of the main arteries out of the city.

Travis picked me up at my guesthouse and took me back to his place to meet everyone. Travis's Afghan roommate Hamid was ready to go on Travis's first motorcycle, the Super Kabul. I had met him at AINA the previous fall when Travis and I went for a ride around Kabul. He was speaking with Andreas, a Swede who'd procured a beautiful, albeit old, Triumph from another ex-pat who recently left Kabul. Travis handed me a spare helmet. It was miles too big but allowed plenty of room to arrange my head scarf underneath.

Their friend Jeremy was the last to arrive with Lianne, an English freelance journalist. Lianne had worked with Jeremy previously and knew the crew as part of the extended ex-pat community, although this was her first motorcycle ride with the guys.

Four bikes, six riders headed out of town, stopping only to regroup at a petrol station to do a last-chance health check for the bikes. We had two Chinese motorbikes, one Japanese dirt bike, and the Triumph.

Riders took turns at the lead, making sure that everyone stayed together. One hour into the ride, we had our first breakdown: the Super Kabul. We regrouped by the side of the road, across from a tiny Afghan police outpost. Less than five minutes passed, and we'd attracted quite the crowd. The policemen came over and offered their help tinkering with the bike in between posing happily for photos. Children were soon hanging out around the edges, watching the scene. The riders tried the "Afghan jump-start" while Andreas posed with the Kalashnikovs on his Triumph. Running alongside the bike and leaping onto the seat sideways often jumped the engine to life. This time it did little more than tire out the runners.

After much debate in Dari and English, the decision was made to leave the Super Kabul. Hamid would ride behind Andreas on the Triumph. Surrounding us were snowcapped mountains, mountain bike–worthy hills, and the now–vibrant green Shomali Plain, lush with the spring thaw, stretching out in front of us. It wasn't hard to imagine what it would have been like to travel here in the sixties when it was part of the Hippie Trail. Not for the first time I found my mind wandering to the potential for exploration and adventure here. This could be an adventure travel paradise in more peaceful times: mountain biking, kayaking, hiking, mountaineering, yak trekking to nomad yurts, not to mention the obvious bit of motorcycle touring.

The back roads we rode were deeply rutted, muddy from the recent rains, and they required the drivers to pay close attention to the road. There was no straight line. The bikes wove back and forth, from one side of the road to the other, avoiding obstacles and trying to find the smoothest way through the rubble, much like a mountain biker finding a line through a rock garden. I was riding behind Travis on the dirt bike, but it was not exactly meant for touring with two people. There were two small pegs for my feet but no rail behind the seat to hold on to. I was sitting above the shock, which meant that to keep myself from getting bucked off, I had to hold on to Travis with one hand and use my left to hold the fender behind me, careful not to let my fingers get shredded by the spinning wheel. It proved a serious workout just to stay on.

After twenty minutes of navigating possibly the worst road of the trip, we pulled into Bagram—an Afghan village that also "hosts" Bagram Air Force Base. Makeshift stalls, stores, and repair shops lined streets with the usual chaos of people driving, walking, and biking in multiple directions. We pulled off the side of the road in front of a *bolone* stand, a delicious fried dough stuffed with potatoes and spices. Kids and men gathered to look at the foreigners and their bikes. I took off my helmet, and Hamid laughed when he saw my face. He asked for my camera and took a photo, then showed me a face two shades darker from dust and with a distinct monobrow of dirt between my eyebrows. I laughed and tasted Afghanistan in my mouth thanks to the dust I had ingested and the gritty film coating my teeth. We all shared a few pieces of *bolone*. We dipped the hot, oily dough in a spicy tomato sauce, much like a salsa. I chased it down with a warm can of Pepsi, and I followed Travis and Hamid to the black market. There you can get military knockoffs of all kinds: flak jackets, combat boots, American shampoo, soap, sunglasses, and even iPods. Guns are apparently off limits, but it was hard to believe there wasn't some dark corner in the back of one of the shops where you could purchase a weapon with enough money.

Meanwhile, it seemed that the Triumph's headlight hadn't been working, so we stopped at a stall at the end of the market. As we waited, a swarm of twenty or more people gathered to watch, but unlike in Kabul, when kids surround you here, there was no *baksheesh* plea for money; it was simple curiosity. Fifteen minutes later, though, a policeman came by and threw a few small stones to break up the crowd. The owner of the repair stall showed off his air rifle and fired a few shots for good measure. The Triumph proved a difficult match for parts, and black electrical tape was used to put everything back together as a short-term solution.

Riding again, we hit motorcycle nirvana on a road as smooth as a baby's bottom, courtesy of the American military. Travis opened up the bike and we flew ahead, only to regroup minutes later as the Triumph seemed to be operating on one cylinder now. But after a little more roadside tinkering, Andreas and Hamid turned back to Kabul on the ailing Triumph. Running the bike on one cylinder with two riders was taking its toll. Two bikes down.

Four riders and two bikes continued on toward the narrow river valley entrance that marked the beginning of Panjshir province, where General Dashty regaled me months earlier with tales of Massoud and his own part in blowing up roads to thwart the Taliban's attempts to reach this Northern Alliance stronghold. We were greeted at the guarded checkpoint and waved through with smiles.

The goal was to ride deep into the valley and visit Massoud's tomb, but the multiple bike delays had eaten up a lot of time. We stopped about an hour past the gates and got off the bikes to take a few photos and stretch our legs before turning around. Children streamed out of the fields and houses to watch us. A little boy riding a donkey proved to be a comedian in training. He hammed it up for the camera, and Travis let him try on his helmet. He paraded around on his donkey wearing the helmet and a huge grin, cracking jokes to the rest of the children who laughed at his antics. It was like a sketch out of Monty Python and a fitting end for the ride.

We headed back out of the valley and made our way toward the main road to Kabul with the setting sun casting a golden light as the scenery flashed by. We stopped briefly to fill the tanks with "fresh" petrol, which in Afghanistan typically involved an ancient can of petrol poured into a funnel, sold by an old man at a roadside stall. We purchased bottles of warm Sprite and Fanta at the stall next door. We'd been riding for six hours, and everyone was parched and tired. Travis called Andreas to see if he and Hamid had made it back all right. Men walked over to have a look at the bikes and the foreigners. One man brought out a warhead he'd apparently found somewhere in the fields behind us. When we backed away, he tried to reassure us all was well by showing us that the tip of the dusty warhead was unscrewed, but that was hardly comforting.

Check please!

"Uh, seriously, can we get out of here?" someone said. We were all laughing at the absurdity, and I was torn between the curiosity of wanting to see it closer, and getting as much distance as I could between myself and a possible explosion.

He posed with his prize find for a few photos, and we left, shaking our heads in disbelief and anxious to put some distance between us and the warhead show-and-tell.

Darkness fell as we got close to Kabul, and cars clogged the wide road, but the bikes wove in and out of traffic and along the side of the road, passing neatly through the lines of headlights.

It was late when Travis dropped me off at my guesthouse gate to the surprise and mirth of the security guards who weren't accustomed to seeing foreign women climb off motorcycles. I leaned over to give Travis a hug and thank-you for the incredible day, but as I moved forward he warned me, "Afghanistan." I quickly changed direction mid-lean-in and shook his hand instead. As I walked through the gates and greeted the night guards on the other side, I realized how happy I felt. On each visit, I had the opportunity to experience Afghanistan in a unique way, and to share that back home to those who see this country only as a war zone, destined to remain in the dark ages.

That fall I returned, and I forwent the guesthouse accommodations and accepted Travis's offer to stay at his house with his roommates since they had an empty room at the moment. And so it was that I found myself a temporary resident of the Rock House, named for the sound studio that had been soundproofed in the maid's quarters where the ex-pat band *White City* played. The current incarnation included Travis on guitar, Andreas on drums, and a new lead singer, a British woman named Ruth, who also played bass. Travis and the Afghan "boys"—Hamid, Parweez, and Nabil—all called the Rock House home. English journalist and photographer Gilly rented one of the rooms as an office, and Nabil's grumpy German girlfriend lived there as well, although all I saw of her was the occasional stink-eye in the morning when I went down to make tea and met her in the kitchen on her way to work.

Living at the Rock House brought a whole host of entertaining experiences with the "boys" and a unique insight into living in Afghanistan through the eyes of young Afghan men.

First up was a trip to Chicken Street for a burqa. For a tall girl like me, this caused a bit of humor in the shops and in particular with Hamid and Parweez, who was holding his stomach laughing at the idea of me wearing a burqa that would hit just below my knees, defeating the point of the oppressive garment.

When we got back, we held an impromptu burqa fitting in the living room. My black Dansko clogs were deemed too ugly to be Afghan. The boys decided that I needed to go back shopping for a pair of Afghan shoes—which are completely impractical. In Kabul, women frequently wore high-heeled sandals, deftly negotiating ditches, potholes, open sewers, and speed bumps. Even in the rainy season, they wore heels and open-toed sandals whereas I would choose boots or my clogs. But the shoes were a dead giveaway that I was foreign. The burqa could be lengthened, another panel added to the bottom quite easily to rectify the height issue, but the shoes and my stride were deemed to need some work. We discussed burqa etiquette, and Hamid told me that wearing your hair in a bun under a burqa was a potential sign of a prostitute. Ankle flirting, especially

during Taliban times, was often the only way to judge attractive-
ness. But, let's face it, pretty ankles do not necessarily equate to a
beautiful face. So there was essentially no foolproof way to assess
beauty until the burqa was lifted and the face could be seen. I'd purchased a traditional bluebird burqa, as it was the most common in
Kabul. But there were other colors throughout the country. Mazar-
i-Sharif was known for its dove white burqas, Kandahar for brown,
sage green, and eggplant, and Herat for vibrant purple along with
the neighboring, Iranian-influenced black chadors.

While I was out burqa shopping, the Afghan boys had been
cooking dinner for everyone. Massoud and Parweez were in the
kitchen, and a delicious smell emanated from the pots, but when I
asked what was cooking, Massoud laughed. "We don't have a name
for it. It's an experiment." I went upstairs to tell Travis that dinner
was almost ready, and he laughed too when I told him that I didn't
know what it was. He explained that while he'd been trying to teach
the boys to cook for themselves, and they were starting to try and
were getting better, meals were still a crapshoot. In this case, it was
perfectly edible: a kind of hybrid beef stroganoff with lamb and rice
instead of beef and pasta. Two young women, sisters, joined us for
dinner. They seemed to be sixteen to eighteen years old, were very
pretty, and acted very modern. Both of them were dressed in modern clothes and wore dark kohl eyeliner and bright red lipstick. One
of them was Hamid's girlfriend, and the other seemed to be with
everyone else or no one at all—I wasn't sure yet. It was very unusual
for Afghan women to date, so it was interesting to observe the interactions over dinner and talk to them during their visits. They appeared comfortable with the guys romantically, like American
college-age couples, but in a way that was unusual to see even with
married Afghan couples. They sat close, their familiarity apparent.
While the boys served dinner, the girls poured tea for all of us, and

when dinner was over, they helped the boys clean up. They explained that their families were in Canada and they would be leaving for there soon.

Post dinner, the discussion moved into the territory of Afghan and Western superstitions: Friday the Thirteenth, black cats, ladders, and the like. The Afghan number thirty-nine is the equivalent of our unlucky thirteen, but it had gone beyond unlucky into the realm of taboo in the past few years; it now implied a connection with being a pimp, though no one knew why or how that had developed. Cars with the number thirty-nine on the license plate were to be avoided like the plague, to the point that drivers covered their license plates. Parweez was a lanky, tall Afghan who'd been living part-time with his extended family in Austria. He provided a lot of the household humor, and after dinner he retold hilarious Wardak jokes—hilarious because they weren't funny in the least. The jokes focused on the stereotype of Wardak people being simple and a little stupid. Apparently, you couldn't just substitute a different province into the joke. Kandahar jokes revolved around homosexuality, for example. Parweez swore that the jokes lost a lot in translation. Hamid shook his head and said that they just weren't funny.

I was getting sleepy but couldn't help laughing when the discussion took an unexpected turn to the subject of balls—as in the family jewels, the veg in the meat and two veg. Afghan men apparently couldn't leave their junk alone. They were always fiddling down there, in public, at home—it didn't matter. They loved to move the things around. I assumed this was the result of their loose-fitting shalwar kameez, but apparently they did the same when ensconced in jeans. The discussion "evolved" into the subject of the shaking technique post-piss. Travis stood up to simulate proper shaking technique and soon everyone was rolling on the tashaks. Apparently, toilet humor wasn't reserved for the British. I called it quits and headed up to my room before I fell asleep, leaving them to carry on. I heard occasional bursts of laughter and smiled.

The next day I had a free morning and decided to go for a walk. I hadn't yet gone off exploring on my own, and I kept telling myself as I got ready that the first step was the hardest. I felt this way when I lived briefly in Beirut. The first morning that I walked to work was the hardest. Like diving into a cold pool, you just had to steel yourself, and then *do it.*

Part of the apprehension was the lack of maps or street names. I needed to count streets and focus on landmarks to navigate the city. So, donning my head scarf, I took a deep breath and said good-bye to the chowkidor who "guarded" the Rock House. He was a young man from Logar and looked surprised to see me leaving alone and without a car. I told him I'd be back in a couple of hours, and set off, more nervous than I had thought. The large steel door noisily clanked shut behind me, and my heart jumped a little. The dusty streets in the Taimani neighborhood were quiet and peaceful, and by the time I got to the main road that led into the city center, I was feeling more relaxed and confident. More people were around, and while I still stuck out, I blended more easily than on empty streets. The energy around the main streets and markets distracted most pedestrians from noticing me.

I headed back toward Chicken Street to find a bookstore. I needed a Dari-English dictionary, and that felt like a good goal for the first excursion. As I got closer, the cars, bikes, pedestrians, and kids crisscrossed in a myriad of directions on the main road. The street kids here were ruthless and would follow you for blocks and blocks repeating the same phrase, but you couldn't give them money or twenty more would join the fray. Once, I gave fifty Afs to a little girl who grabbed my hand to walk with me, and I saw her again when I was running errands to buy the burqa and she did the same. This time I smiled and practiced my Dari with her and received the biggest smile in return. Her name was Madina and she was adorable. She was petite, with large brown eyes and the perfect face to encourage people to open their wallets or simply to sweep her up and take her home to feed her a decent meal. Unfortunately, when I gave her a dollar, I was immediately joined by five others. I finally just turned and started walking home toward the empty streets away from the busy center of town. One young boy stuck with me for fifteen minutes, repeating "one dollar miss" over and over. I needed to pick up shampoo so I stopped into a shop. When I came back out, he was waiting and started up again. Losing patience, I shouted "No" and he left. Let's face it—it's heartbreaking to tell any street kid no anywhere in the world. These kids were often working the streets to help support their families. There were lessons to be learned here. One: if you are going to give money to street children, have it ready in a pocket so you can grab it without drawing attention. Two: be firm when you are not going to give money. Avoid eye contact and walk away. Pretending you don't hear them or ignoring them doesn't work; they will hang with you for blocks if they think you'll give in. I watched Najibullah for guidance with this. He always had a stash of twenty-Af bills in his coat pocket to distribute. Twenty Afs was approximately forty cents. Whenever we saw a group of children, he gave something to all of them quickly, and he always bought the gum or pencils that many of them were selling.

Another thing I wanted to pick up was some fresh naan and *mohst*—fresh yogurt. Naan was easy. I could purchase fresh bread from any number of bakers in the area. *Mohst* I had trouble with. A small corner shop had a refrigerator case and some yogurt. I was excited and carried everything home. But when I tore the sealed container open, I saw that it was moldy inside. A few days later, our *chowkidor* pointed me in the right direction. He explained in broken English and Dari that many stands sold fresh *mohst* by weight. A block behind the house, on the corner, there was one with Fanta and Coke stacked outside. Inside, the vendor had a large container of *mohst* in a cooler. When I told him how much I wanted in kilos, he put a plastic bag on the scale and measured it out. Then he tied it and double-bagged it to prevent leaks. I carried my baggie of yogurt home like a prize. The small victories often meant the most.

The decision had been made and now it was time to think about logistics. How did a woman purchase a motorcycle in a country where women didn't ride bikes?

I sent two Afghan housemates to pave the way. Parweez and Hamid went down to the motorcycle shop in Shar-e-nau and talked with the owner. I'd already decided that I wanted a low rider Chinese-made bike called the Desert Eagle. So they were there to haggle and spin the story that the bike was for Hamid, and his "boss"—me—was coming to pay for it. Cue the blond infidel.

I walked in, and they'd already secured the price of $700 for a brand-new Chinese bike—not exactly high quality but perfect for learning the streets of Kabul. Once we handed over the money, the mechanics put some fuel in the tank and checked that everything was working. Immediately, fuel started leaking from the bottom. No worries, they told me—they just hadn't connected the fuel line to the engine. The battery was installed. Twice. Then a variety of tools came out to tighten bolts or simply bang a few things into place.

I stepped into the back of the dark shop to sign some papers and get the registration to show ownership. I had my first experience with using my thumbprint as my signature on official papers. I remembered seeing a document in passing the previous year that had at least twenty thumbprints. The owner was starting to suspect that the bike might be for me rather than Hamid, but he played along since he was making a sale.

Everything checked out. The fuel leak was fixed, and another guy took the bike for a quick test drive. Ironically, the only thing *not* removed was the plastic coverings over the headlights, seat, and handlebars. This was a real Afghan obsession. The plastic stayed on to show that the bike was new. It reminded me of my grandmother's couch when I was a kid. Even the bubble wrap around one turn signal would typically stay. I found it safer to have my headlights and turn signals fully exposed, so I removed it all.

Hamid was driving the bike back to complete the ruse, but before we left, I had to give the customary *chirany*—a bizarre Afghan concept. Hamid told me I had to give a "gift" to a few members of the staff and also bring candy home for the two chowkidors. We stopped at the market to buy several bags of candy and chocolate. Sure enough, when we pulled up with the new bike, the first words out of the chowkidors' mouths were "Where's my *chirany?*" Essentially, custom dictated that if one had the means to buy something like a motorcycle, then that person should share the wealth.

We parked it in the courtyard next to the assortment of other motorcycles. I sat on the Desert Eagle with a glass of smuggled single malt I'd brought for the house from Dubai, and I toasted the boys—grateful for their help, bargaining skills, and guidance. Tomorrow, I would learn to ride!

The boys took me out around 8:00 P.M. It was dark, especially without streetlights, but there was a full moon high in the sky, casting its light and perfect for learning to ride incognito. Hamid tied a men's kaffiyeh scarf around my head and face, and I borrowed Travis's oversized hoodie to disguise my gender. We drove toward the airport, me in the car with Parweez while Hamid rode the Super Kabul. His friend Shams, who worked with Skateistan, rode his motorcycle. We took out the Super Kabul instead of my Desert Eagle, which was bigger, with wider handlebars and a new clutch that was still very tight. The Super Kabul was perfect to learn on. It was a bit smaller, and I felt I could control it without getting too freaked out. The three vehicles played cat and mouse on the nearly empty roads all the way there, driving way too fast considering no one was wearing helmets or seat belts.

We arrived at the long stretch of empty frontage road that paralleled the main road to the airport, and we switched up the riders. The lights were kept off on the bikes to keep our profile as low as possible. Hamid took my scarf and wrapped it like a man's turban, covering the lower half of my face, only my eyes and nose exposed. He rode behind Shams and coached me. After a few runs, back and forth, with the other bike beside me and the car behind us lighting the way, Hamid took over the second bike. He told me to follow him and do what he did: swerving, slowing down, taking on the numerous speed bumps and potholes. My legs were shaking in my motorcycle boots, but following made it easier to relax. It was hard to do something for the first time with an audience—harder still when you are a woman doing something no other woman does in front of a group of men.

Hamid was a surprisingly awesome teacher, patient and relaxed. He didn't say much but told me to do some drills, then let me go. When we decided to leave, he didn't give me the option to ride in the car. He just said, "Follow me. We're going home." We rode the whole way with no problems, even over the muddy, four-by-four demolition-style dirt road by their house that I was dreading. The potholes, deep ruts, and slick mud were less foreboding obstacles than I'd feared. The roaming packs of wild dogs that came out at night proved to be much worse on my nighttime excursions than the road conditions ever were.

Hamid smiled at me when we got back to the house and said, "You're a natural." I couldn't stop grinning and high-fived him. I thanked Parweez and Shams, who smiled good-naturedly.

The next morning, I texted Travis, who was away for a few days working. "I can ride!" He texted back. "Yeahhhhhh!! Bike chicks rock!"

The next morning, I was sitting outside on the balcony in the early morning light, looking at the hillsides and listening to the city come to life. I heard a far off *thump* and a plume of smoke rose in the distance. Something had just gotten bombed. A few minutes later, Hamid knocked on my door.

"Bomber," he said, and walked back out, probably to go back to sleep—completely nonplussed.

Thirty minutes or so later, Hamid knocked on the door again and told me to come down for breakfast. Food was set on the table— eggs cooked the way I adored, with a spicy mixture of cooked tomatoes, onions, and way too much oil. On a plate next to the eggs was Iranian feta, black olives, some seeds I was unfamiliar with, and a stack of fresh naan bread to mop up everything. I'd learned that it was much easier to eat with the bread when you split each piece by peeling off the top layer of bread. This made grabbing food, especially eggs, much easier. Parweez joined us, and I got a better taste of the camaraderie these men share, though I was spared another round of Wardak jokes. I cleared the dishes and announced I was heading into town.

Not yet trusting my bike skills on my own, I walked down the narrow alleyway that led from the house. A few blocks later I reached the main road and heard a loud sound, like a broken horn.

It was a young, black calf tied outside a butcher shop. I realized that if I came back tonight or the next morning, I'd most likely see the head, hide, and entrails in a steaming pile by the curb. The same was true of the goats. When I'd gone for early morning walks, a few streets were quite wet, the blood washed away and a neat pile of "extras" near the road. I assumed they just got washed into the open sewers.

My phone beeped. It was a text from Travis: "Reports of second, roaming suicide bomber and abductions. Lay low."

I was walking toward City Center, so I turned and started home. I texted back: "Shit. Walking into town—heading home now."

He replied immediately: "Get taxi."

I saw on the news later that the morning target was the Indian Embassy. In the end, eighteen were dead and seventy-plus injured, depending on the report. The Taliban took responsibility.

A few days later, after another nighttime practice session, I rode my bike alone to the City Center shopping mall to get a coffee. The basement coffee shop was a great place to people watch. It wasn't like going to Flower Street Cafe or the other ex-pat coffeehouses that were usually filled with foreign NGO and aid workers, contractors, and journalists. I circled the street twice, looking for a place to park that wouldn't involve hoisting the bike onto the sidewalk or leaving it too remote and unattended. I found a spot on the street, on the corner of City Center, and figured it would be fine there. After parking, I did a quick gender change. I let my black skirt down over my jeans, undid my turban and changed its position into a traditional head scarf. Voila! A woman. Once I got a little farther I pulled out my women's head scarf and draped it over the men's, which I then slid out from underneath. My transformation complete, I walked into the City Center for the requisite security check and bag search. Once inside, I went through the mall and into the basement area.

Waiting for my cappuccino, I looked around. There was a unique combination of Afghan businessmen, the occasional ex-pat contractor, and young Afghans. I noticed the last time I'd visited that at a few tables, young men and women were sitting and chatting. This was harmless enough, but in Afghanistan, dating wasn't done. One couple in particular, at the table across from me, caught my attention. Both were dressed in modern attire. He was in black acid-washed jeans with black leather "pimp" shoes and a long-sleeved black T-shirt. She was also dressed all in black, her gauzy head scarf edged with rhinestones, and a large black purse resting on her lap. Her eyes were lined in black kohl, and she was wearing a vibrant rose lipstick. Perhaps they were just brother and sister, or relatives? I gave them the benefit of the doubt, not wanting to assume, until I watched the tension between them develop. They stared into each other's eyes, smiling but never breaking the acceptable distance. There was no hand holding or foot nudging. It was still obvious that they were flirting and very much enamored with each other. The girl began to dab at her eyes with a tissue, her kohl-rimmed eyes turning red. Still, neither closed the distance. She collected herself and smiled, and they resumed their pattern of alternating between chatting and staring endlessly at each other for full minutes at a time.

I drank my cappuccino and got ready to go back to my bike. I did the head scarf shuffle in reverse once I was outside. To my right was a phone card salesman, so I bought a new phone card as I was almost out of credit. Immediately, one of the street children with his pail of spiritual good-luck smoke was on me. I had ten Afs in my side pocket, and I slid it to him, but immediately I had a crowd again. They followed me to my bike, surrounding me as I got on.

They realized I was a woman, and their reactions drew more attention than I liked.

Unfortunately, my bike wouldn't start. Apparently, my good luck smoke karma didn't cover motorcycle issues. I'd conveniently parked near the motorcycle shop where I'd bought it. The kids tried to help, moving the choke switch. But this didn't help at all when they were all trying different buttons. I sat back and sighed. Frustrated, I put the bike in neutral and walked to the shop. I explained to one of the guys there that the bike wouldn't start. He nodded and motioned for me to bring it closer. I did and one of the young kids who worked at the shop jumped on. He moved a button, the red one that I didn't know anything about, and the bike roared to life. Sheepishly I smiled—to which I was sure the guy was thinking, *Dumb woman, what's she doing riding a motorbike anyways?* I gave out the last of my ten-Af bills to the kids that helped, and I hit the road. I reminded myself to ask Trav about the red button.

I made my way into the now-heaving traffic and inched across the four-plus lanes of cars to the Shar-e-nau petrol station. I had some petrol, but without a gauge, I didn't want to run out, especially on my own, so I filled it up. Again, the pump attendants recognized me as a woman as soon as I spoke, and they showed their surprise and curiosity. I thanked them and rejoined the fray. Next stop: Le Bistro for some croissants to bring home to the boys.

I needed to get to the right side of the street again, so I cut my way across and turned right down the bumpy road that ran parallel to the main road and led straight to Le Bistro. I had to get past the security gate, which again meant that my voice gave away my disguise. The guards' eyes went wide when they realized I was a woman, and they laughed good-naturedly, then raised the barrier while smiling. I smiled, nodded, and headed down the road. I parked my steed on the corner. The guard looked at me suspiciously, and I lowered my face scarf and said, "Le Bistro." More surprise and laughter followed, and he waved me to a space catty-corner to where I was to park my bike instead. I dismounted and left the turban on as I went inside the restaurant where I wouldn't need any head covering. The four or five security guards were all smiling and jovial as I walked by. "Nice job," they said in English as I passed. What? Nice job how I parked my bike? Hilarious. I headed inside the two sets of security doors and removed my turban completely.

Fresh fig croissants were piled on a platter. Baked fresh every day, they looked like pain au chocolat but filled with fresh fig. I got the last four for 260 Afs.

I went back outside, turban in place again, a bag of yumminess in my backpack, and the guards were still smiling. They waved me over to chat, and one of the younger ones pointed to his bike; it was a Desert Eagle just like mine. His was all pimped out, Afghan style, with a small Afghan rug on the seat, the *Chips*-style windshield, and some tassels. Proudly, he teased, "You want to trade?" I admired his bike and smiled but shook my head. I turned to get back on mine, very much aware of the many eyes watching to see if I could, in fact, ride. Praying that the damn thing would start, I backed it up and around a UN vehicle whose driver had decided that he should stop right in the middle of the narrow street. I started it up. It roared to life, and the security guards cheered. I smiled and waved and headed off, back down the bumpy road.

6

Motherhood

Colorado 2009

Boarding the plane to DC en route to Kabul, I saw my window seat was next to a mother and child. The little girl beamed up at me, holding a Ziplock bag with sliced star fruit. She happily informed me, "My fruit is shaped like stars and tastes like the Bahamas."

I couldn't help but smile and agree with surprise.

"Is that right? I've never eaten star fruit before or been to the Bahamas. That is *very* cool!"

She beamed wider and put a piece in her mouth.

"How old are you?" I asked.

"I'm five," she said, proudly holding up her right hand to show me her fingers.

"Wow," I replied, "a whole hand?"

"Yup," she responded proudly. Her dark brown eyes twinkled with the spirit of a happy girl excited to be on an adventure. She was the same age as Devon, and she had the tray table folded down with a pile of Tinkerbell valentines spread out. She was putting stickers on them and writing her friends' names on the invites, while her mom spelled out the names to her. It was such a familiar scene I felt my heart ache as I thought of Devon and wished she could be coming with me.

When Devon was born, something shifted. I had been petrified of being a mother. I can remember sitting on the floor of our bedroom, crying to Pete that I didn't have any maternal instincts and "what if they never kicked in?" I didn't want to be a bad mother. To top it off, I was scared of the label "mother." I also hated the labels "husband" and "wife" even though I had been one for nearly a decade. It brought back antiquated images of the 1950s, or worse, that of my parents' relationship when I grew up, which was the traditional model of the father who worked, the mother who stayed home, and the inevitable inequity in the perceived roles. Parents who grew apart and stayed together for the kids, but seemed to make each other miserable in the process didn't set a better example for their children than parents who divorced. It was terrifying and daunting, yet I was seven months' pregnant. Terrifying or not, I was going to be a mother.

When Devon was born, she opened a place in my heart I never knew existed. I wanted nothing more than to make sure she grew up happy, healthy, and full of joy. So why, I am so often asked, when you adore your daughter, when you want to see her grow up—perform in ballet recitals, go camping, meet her first boyfriend, meet her first love, and find out who she is—would you risk your financial and physical security by working in Afghanistan?

What if these Afghan or Cambodian or Pakistani girls were Devon? What if these women's fate was her fate? It's really just a matter of geography, the uncontrollable act of being born in one country versus another that can dictate so much of your future.

Why are their lives worth less than hers, or mine? Someone needs to fight for them. Someone needs to speak for them when they are unable, and someone needs to share their stories. Someone needs to combat the apathy that prevents change. What if that was Devon? I would want someone to fight for her if I couldn't.

It's not an easy decision to leave Devon for periods of time to work in one of the most dangerous places in the world. She was three when I first went to Afghanistan and it was heartbreaking to leave her. It was the first time I'd been apart from her for any length of time, and she was too young to really understand why I was gone for so long or to talk on the phone while I was away. I felt a physical ache throughout the time and distance we were apart, and it made me think long and hard about the path I was embarking on. Luckily, that trip coincided with a trip Pete wanted to take with Devon back to England to see family. So she was having the time of her life with cousins and grandparents and making memories with her father on their first trip alone together. This made my first trip to Afghanistan so much easier.

Now, years later, the trips are easier, as she knows why I am going and understands that I will be coming home. She thinks I am going to "build schools for other kids," and this is safe and easy for a six-year-old to digest. She gives presentations at her preschool and kindergarten, showing the photos from my trips that she likes, as well as Afghan money, burqas, head scarves, and buzkashi hats. She teaches them, "*Salaam Alekum*," a traditional Afghan greeting, and "*Hubisti?*" "How are you?" She's at an age now that she thinks it's pretty cool, but each time I drop her off at Pete's house for a long trip, I feel as if I'm leaving a piece of myself behind. My excitement about the impending trip back to Afghanistan and the next step in project development is tinged with the regret that it is at the expense of being with Devon.

This is the subject that is most difficult for others to understand. How could a mother leave her daughter to work in a war zone?

The controversy really boils down to the fact that I'm leaving my daughter for Afghanistan, not Nebraska. If I was working in California, it probably wouldn't elicit so much commentary. The maddening part is how different that commentary is depending on gender. I look at men in my field, and in adventure sports, like mountaineering, adventure filmmaking, and journalism. I rarely read commentary about a man's responsibility to stay at home and avoid potential risk because he is a father—or that being a father negates his right to follow his passions and build a different future for the next generation if it involves risk. I never see men degraded as parents due to their career choices or risky hobbies. But for women, all of the above are commonplace in media questioning and in online commentary. The most biting critiques of the choices I make are the anonymous comments on news articles. One in particular was a reader's response in my own local paper, *The Summit Daily*, cut deep, even though I knew it was bullshit and cowardly. "Who does this woman think she is, galavanting around Afghanistan in a head scarf, putting our soldiers at risk?"

For weeks, I came back to this comment. It hurt because I knew it wasn't true, and because I knew others might read it, too. This person didn't know me any better than the people who blindly give me their support, or the occasional ones who call me a hero, and yet it's the negative stuff that sticks, challenging my equilibrium and calling into question my choices.

I had this discussion with Christiane, who'd worked with climbers and mountaineers, and Charley, who was the president of the Alpine Rescue Team and had been the executive director of the American Alpine Club for many years. Christiane compared the gender discussion to mountain climbing and the different perceptions of fathers and mothers who choose to climb big mountains. One example she shared was the accomplished British climber Alison Hargreaves, who summited Everest without Sherpas or bottled oxygen, the north face of the Eiger, and Ama Dablam, among other impressive climbs. Alison was also the first climber ever to solo climb all the great north faces of the Alps in one season. She did many of her major climbs while pregnant. She died in a storm while coming down after summiting the infamous K2. The subsequent controversy in the climbing community and press, including many female journalists who publicly questioned the ethics of a mother engaging in such a dangerous sport, was an obvious double standard. Why is the same questioning and post-mortem commentary not done of fathers who climb, take risks, and often perish in their pursuits? Fathers are not pilloried for having left their children fatherless, as mothers typically are. Instead, they are often praised for their intrepid adventurism and lauded for their daring and courage in attempting to break new boundaries and scale new heights.

The chances of dying during an unassisted climb up mountains such as K2 and Everest are around one in four. In an interview with the *Guardian* in 2002, Alison's husband, James Ballard, now a widower and father of two young children, was asked why he'd let her go in the first place. "How could I have stopped her? I loved Alison because she wanted to climb the highest peak her skills would allow her to. That's who she was."

Would that journalist have asked Alison the same question if it had been her husband who'd died on a mountain pursuing what he loved, despite being a husband and father?

Women adventurers and athletes have just as much right to pursue their goals, dreams, passions, and pursuits as men. They should not have to repress who and what they are simply because they become a parent. How many fathers attempt to climb Everest every year? How many skydive, base jump, and freedive? Why, in a country where women have had the right to vote for almost a century, are we still debating gender roles so ignorantly?

Mothers are simply not allowed to take the same risks as fathers according to the public conversation, and those that do are judged harshly. Gender stereotypes continue to skew our perception of the risk equation. Because I am a mother, should I not be working in Afghanistan? That subject is up for debate, with solid arguments on both sides in regards to responsibility, risk, security, and identity. And I welcome it. But we shouldn't be basing it on gender. Unfortunately, we don't debate this in the public forum—we cast judgment based on gender and perceived parenting roles. It's one-sided, and unfair, and frustrating as hell. I know this: Devon is the only one who can judge what kind of mother I am to her. I want her to see her mother fully embracing who she is, and I am setting the example of a woman who followed her path, as I would want her to do. She is the only one whose opinion on this subject matters. The risks I choose to take are measured through the prism of her, and while my level of risk may seem too high for some, it is a personal decision that regards only me and my family.

Being a single parent that coparents can be difficult and frustrating at times. Decisions regarding what's best for the child are mutually shared, but shared with someone you've chosen to break ties with. In my particular case, the fact that I have chosen to make my work in Afghanistan is still a sore point. It probably always will be. But I am grateful for the amicable relationship that Devon's father and I have. It allows great flexibility for both of us and gives Devon the stability of two happy households.

Yet I find myself pondering for the first time in my adult life, "If I were a man, this wouldn't even be an issue." It wouldn't. Fathers travel for work all the time. Fathers often make their careers the priority over family. My ex traveled extensively and for long periods of time from the moment our daughter entered our lives, and still does. He is not criticized or questioned for his choices spent away from Devon.

I look at the example I'm trying to set for Devon. Through my actions, I am showing her that involvement in the global community is important, and that one person can make a difference. I am raising a daughter who will have a strong sense of self. I hope that when she becomes a mother, she will continue to follow her dreams and stick to her ideals rather than give them up when she has her own children; the two are not mutually exclusive.

Part of my preparations for each trip includes writing Devon an "insurance" letter. It's a letter that my sister will give her when she's older if the worst should occur. It's insurance against her not having a written reminder that her mother loved her and how very sorry I am that I'm not there. In some bizarre way, I view that letter as insurance against the worst happening. A karmic token—that if I write the letter, it will never need to be delivered. I also bought two lockets. One is for her and has a photo of me and our old dog, Bergen, in it. It's pink with an elephant riding a bicycle. Her favorite animal is an elephant, and she knows that I love to ride bikes. The second locket is for me. It's green and has a different elephant. It contains two photos of her, and I wear it daily, like a talisman, while we are apart.

Christiane calls her the Elephant Princess, and to this day, if she sees a small item that has elephants on it, she buys it and sends it to Devon, addressing all her letters to the Elephant Princess. Devon has a small drawing that Christiane bought her on the street during a walk the two of us took together in SoHo. Now at age nine, her favorite animal is the snow leopard. She is interested in endangered species, and yet she will always be the Elephant Princess to me and Christiane, even if she has moved on to champion another animal.

I also write her letters on her birthday, each year documenting the year in a few pages of her likes and dislikes, what we did, who her friends are, and the details that make up the amazing little girl she is. Then I seal it and label the front with "Devon—1st birthday," and so on. I've written down why her father and I divorced in words that lay no blame, but simply express my regret that we couldn't stay together for her sake; in the end, my hope is that she would grow up with two loving and happy homes, surrounded by people who love her unconditionally. I've written down her first words, favorite games and toys, and what she likes to eat. When she turns eighteen, I'll give them all to her. Who knows? Maybe I'll continue past then, each year writing a letter to my daughter on paper, hoping she never forgets how amazing she is to me—how she cracked open a place in my heart that I had kept guarded, and how, because of her, I learned to love unconditionally and without expectations.

I don't know what she will think when she grows up. Will she resent the risks I took once she understands them? Will she be proud of me? Will she want to do the same? I hope that she grows up seeing a mother who fought for change. For human rights. For women's rights. That she sees a mother who fought to make the world a better place for her and for girls on the other side of the planet. I hope she understands that you cannot sit on the sidelines of life and wish things were different. It is your responsibility to be involved whether it's in some far-flung corner of the Earth, or in your own backyard: for animals, the environment, human rights—whatever inspires you to take action and enter the fight and contribute in some small, or huge, way.

During a previous visit to Kabul, I'd donated computers for a girls' school. This was a school in Kabul run by Afghans 4 Tomorrow.

The organization had the small guesthouse where Tony and I had stayed during my first visit to Afghanistan, and Najibullah had taken us to visit one of the girls' schools they operated. These were girls who had a real chance to follow their dreams. They were living in the capital, where there was much less resistance to girls' education than in other parts of the country. They had the support of their families and an NGO's commitment to help them finish school. They had the potential to continue on to Kabul University should they choose to. Najibullah continued to work with and help Afghans 4 Tomorrow, and he reached out via e-mail in between my visits to see if I could help with a school computer lab.

I gathered more information about what they needed. Laptops were better than desktops, easier to keep secure and dust-free, and they used less power. I reached out to the Mountain2Mountain community to see if anyone had computer contacts, and eventually a woman with Dell was able to get us six laptops at cost with Microsoft software. A couple of months later, I brought over the laptops for the computer lab, paid for a backup generator, and covered the salary for a teacher for one year. Basic computer skills with Word and Excel would increase the girls' ability to attend university. Many of them, around the age of thirteen, had never turned on a computer. Internet cafés were opening in Kabul, computer programming and business training were important areas of growth, and if any of the girls wanted a chance to study overseas in a student exchange, computer skills were necessary.

After we set up the computers, turned them on, and talked with the teachers, I got the chance to ask the girls some questions. I recognized a few faces from my visit to the classrooms a year prior, and I told them so, not sure if they recognized me. They shyly smiled back and said they remembered. When I asked what they wanted to be when they grew up, they answered, "Doctor, lawyer, engineer, journalist, teacher, and artist"—not any different from the answers you would expect back home. They wanted normalcy and had the desire to go to college, to have a career. They'd grown up with the knowledge that these things were possible in post-Taliban times. Only eight years after the fall of the Taliban, this was a clear sign of progress.

Then the girls asked me, "How did you learn about us over here? Why are you helping us?"

I was momentarily tongue-tied. How could I explain why I wanted to help, even if it was only in some small way? Any answer I could think of sounded inauthentic and trite.

"I have a young daughter back in the United States. Her name is Devon and she is five years old. She can go to school and even to university if she wants, just like most American girls. You deserve to have the same opportunities that she has. I hope that each of you can continue your education and follow your dreams and be an important part of your community."

They smiled shyly, but a small girl who'd told me she wanted to be a doctor had a radiant smile, and said, "Thank you for saying that we are as important as your own daughter."

I gulped hard, not wanting to show how overwhelmed I was. Instead I smiled, put my hand over my heart, and said, "*Hush Amandine, shoma tashakur.*" You're welcome, thank *you*. Another drop in the bucket, but a drop that had the potential to create some ripples.

Past Mother's Days make me think hard about my role as a mother, not because the Hallmark holiday hits me emotionally. It hardly registers as anything to celebrate. The day is typically spent like any other—hanging out with the Elephant Princess, going for a hike if it's not too snowy, making pumpkin pancakes, and squeezing in some work on the laptop. One of my most memorable Mother's Days was spent watching Devon at age four creating her own elephant sign language. This kept me on my toes, considering I was still trying to find time to learn Dari and some basic sign language since I'd been supporting a deaf school in Kabul—having secured a land donation of nearly five acres in a remote, undeveloped area of Kabul for the school's future home.

Where in the "motherhood manual" does one find the rules? Where does it say that I am not allowed to embrace my true path in life? Where does it state that the best role model you can be is to suppress who you are?

Those who know me well see the opposite—that by carving my path I am doing my utmost to raise a daughter who will have the confidence in herself to find her own path and courageously follow it. Her needs remain my priority, and that tempers my choices. Putting her first in the heavy list of priorities doesn't replace my needs, wants, desires; it simply bumps them down the list, not off the list entirely.

As a mother, my daughter comes first. As a woman, I must remain true to myself and the things that are important in my life. Let's not forget that one must work in order to provide. Men continue to work, and oftentimes we view them as heroes because of their sacrifices for their families. My father owned a business, and this required long hours at the office and travel away from us. It wasn't viewed as selfish. It was necessary. It was work.

Why Afghanistan? Why take the risk? Because my daughter is born in a country that ensures her right to choose. She is promised an education. She can ride a bike, ski, or simply walk down the street with little risk other than that which she causes herself with the genetic clumsiness she inherited from me. She can choose when, who, and if she wants to marry. She has every opportunity thanks to the genetic passport she was gifted at birth—that of a U.S. citizen. I had and have those same rights, and I realize how lucky I am. Young girls in Afghanistan shouldn't be afforded less opportunity just because of where they live. I can only hope my daughter feels the same way as she matures into the woman she chooses to become.

7

Road Trips and Prisons

Afghanistan 2009-2010

Sitting in the back of yet another white Toyota Corolla, I looked into the front seat at my driver, Habibe. He was a kind man who practiced his English as I practiced my Dari. He was always smiling, and we shared stilted stories about our children and family. He enthusiastically agreed to drive me to the northern city of Mazar-i-Sharif so that I could visit a women's prison. It had become clear that I couldn't go by plane. Flights were running only once a week, and I didn't have that kind of time to spend in one place. I wanted to visit two women's prisons in the northern provinces to better understand the situation from a women's rights perspective and to look at potential programs that I could create. Habibe's one condition was that his seventy-year-old father-in-law could come along as "protection." Mahmahdoud, aka John, looked as though he weighed a hundred pounds wet and, like many his age, was missing several teeth. His eyesight was also poor. I'm not sure who was protecting whom on this road trip, but having a respected elder in the car couldn't be a bad thing if we found ourselves in trouble.

It would take us eight or nine hours to get to Mazar, assuming that the Salang Pass wasn't snowed in. I became a little apprehensive when Habibe asked me to please pull my scarf further forward, entirely covering my hair and creating a shadowy hood to hide my face—the first of many signs that this road trip was not like a family excursion to the Grand Canyon. There would be no roadside picnics and corny photo ops. My main concern was not bandits, checkpoints, or the Taliban; it was the car. We were traveling in the same car that broke down three times in one day last week while running errands in Kabul. Though Habibe assured me repeatedly that it was travel-worthy, I had my doubts.

We left Kabul on the road toward Panjshir with snow-covered mountains on the left and smaller rolling hills to the right that paralleled the road out onto the Shomali Plain. We went straight through the large roundabout that led to Bagram, and past Charikar. We passed a jeep filled beyond capacity with Afghan men. Three were hanging on the back and one sat on the hood like a comical ornament.

On our left, the river was raging and we followed it for the next twenty miles as we climbed the switchbacks to Salang Pass. These mountains were part of the Hindu Kush, and the road was a major trucking route. Heavily painted and bejeweled trucks clogged the lanes in both directions. As the landscape turned white with snow, we followed the trucks into a series of tunnels built to protect the narrow roadway from avalanches and heavy snowfall. They were all unlit, but many had natural light coming through at regular intervals—all but the last and longest. We entered the dark cavern, the walls and road wet. Enormous potholes spread out across the road, creating obstacles in addition to the complete darkness. To make matters worse, many Afghan cars have very dim lights, and many motorbikes have none. Often you didn't see another car until you were right on top of it. Majority ruled here, much like in the streets of Kabul, and whichever team had more cars spread out side by side across the road, won.

Surprisingly, we emerged unscathed on the other side of the tunnel. The scenery here was among the most spectacular I'd ever seen. As we descended the switchbacks, cars of men and burqa-covered women stopped for impromptu picnics, and I wished I could join them to enjoy the view and be part of the experience. John needed a bathroom break, so we pulled over. He got out slowly, and he drew his brown shawl around himself for a little privacy as he conducted his business in the snow. When he returned, he told Habibe to tell me that if I needed to go, I could borrow his shawl. I considered that he said that to all the young women he played body-guard for. I smiled graciously and said, "*tashakur*" to John. He smiled sweetly at me and nodded in return.

The snow receded as we drove farther, and now the mountains were covered in lush spring grass and wildflowers. Beside us on the left, the river continued to rage with snowmelt. The landscape was dotted with sheepherders, red flowers, and the occasional horse. The game trails that crisscrossed this area screamed for lengthy trail running and mountain biking. I wondered how badly land mined this area was and if I could perhaps arrange a little excursion on fu-ture visits with my bike or even my trail-running shoes. I daydreamed for miles about riding the goat paths, which surely, I decided, must be clear if goat herders and goats walked them regularly.

Hours later, I was sitting with my legs crossed in the backseat, contemplating John's offer of his shawl. The hunt was on for a *tashnab*, a bathroom. Habibe didn't want me to squat on the side of the road, but the one village large enough to have a public bathroom,

Pul e Khumri, Habibe deemed too unsafe for a stop. And so, twenty minutes later, off the side of the smooth road to Samagran, I found myself squatting in the rain behind a crumbling mud wall, in a field of red poppies like the ones Dorothy fell asleep among in the *Wizard of Oz*.

As we got closer to Mazar-i-Sharif, the landscape flattened dramatically into empty plains, reminiscent of my home state of North Dakota. Amazingly, the car had made it nine full hours to Mazar, but as we entered the city, I realized that my phone had stopped working. It had been fully charged that morning, so there was absolutely no reason for this. But here I was, in an unknown corner of Afghanistan for the first time, with no communication link. I fought the urge to panic. *This wasn't a big deal*, I told myself. *You can figure something out.* I explained to Habibe where I was staying and figured I could sort the problem out once I was settled. I sat back and within a few minutes we were driving past the Blue Mosque and my phone worries faded as I marveled at the beautiful aquamarine tilework that decorated the famous structure.

We pulled up to the Mazar Hotel on the other side of the mosque, and at first glance it seemed normal enough, a solid structure of bland concrete Russian architecture and Afghan flags. Once inside, I realized that I'd entered some sort of time warp or perhaps simply a bizarro alternate reality. The hotel staff wasn't sure what to do with me as the only foreigner in the hotel and an unaccompanied female to boot. The reception area was full of Afghan men of varying ages lounging around talking. Eventually, all eyes fixated on me. The staff led me through a maze of hallways and staircases to my room, 206. While I waited for a key to be brought to me, a small group of young men gathered to watch. I groaned. I was hot, dusty, slightly annoyed, and in dire need of my Dari dictionary, which I just then realized I had forgotten in Kabul. I was handed off to the manager, Mohammad Karim. Extremely friendly and perhaps more than a little lonely, Mohammad Karim spent the next forty-eight hours trying to be my new best friend. He was slightly goofy in his appearance, his white shirt tucked into his pants that were belted high above his waist. He had a childlike face, which proved to match his innocent demeanor. He came in to change the sheets on the beds (which perhaps should have been done before I checked in?), fixed my door's lock (a bit worrying), and brought me tea. When I requested a towel so that I could shower—having not realized that I needed to bring my own since the guesthouses I stay at in Kabul typically have at least one thin towel—he scrounged up a ratty orange towel with two holes that seemed relatively clean. The bathroom was down the hall, and when I opened the door, I immediately had the queasy sensation of entering a humid animal den. The musky smell was overpowering. The concrete room was larger than my hotel room and consisted of a bathtub shower with no curtain, a toilet, a sink, and a small mirror. No toilet paper or soap was available. The floor was almost entirely flooded. And the hot water tank was empty. Perhaps I could wait a bit. Perhaps the entire trip?

I peeked into the bathroom directly next door and found a veritable paradise in comparison. The floor was only slightly damp, and it lacked the heady zoo aroma, but when I walked in, I was immediately shooed out by Mohammad Karim. He guided me back to the other door. I was going to have to use commando skills to sneak into the enemy bathroom!

My room had a concrete floor covered with a worn Afghan rug and two twin beds that were basically wood platforms with a sleeping mat—thinner and lumpier than most camping mats. The coatrack stood at such an angle that it looked poised to attack unwary guests. Each time I unlocked my door and peeked out to use the forbidden bathroom, Mohammad Karim came pitter-pattering over to say hello, clasp my hand, or try to rub my cheek and tell me how happy he was to meet me—to which I smiled, said, "*Tashakur, Mohammad,*" and retreated into my room to unpack. Thirty minutes or so later, he knocked and brought in a pot of green tea, then left. I plugged in my phone, hoping against hope that the charge was simply out, but the electricity wasn't working. Mohammad knocked on my door again and delivered a small plate of cookies to go with my tea. I thanked him sweetly and then ushered him back to the door, where he shook my hand longer than necessary. "You are so lovely. I love you." Yikes.

"*Tashakur, xoda al fez.*" Thank you, good-bye.

The saving grace to the comedy unfolding was a balcony overlooking a small garden where I could sit on the end of the concrete ledge and be outside with my head uncovered. I worked on my laptop and watched the swallows chase one another as dusk fell and the evening call to prayer filled the air, content at my own Afghan-styled Hotel California.

Travis arrived that evening, and I couldn't stop laughing when I heard Mohammad Karim accost him in the hallway and follow him inside the room. Travis was on the phone and in a flurry of uncontainable energy. He strode through my room and headed straight onto the balcony to sit outside in the fresh air. I could barely see through my tears of laughter as I shared with him the eccentricities of the hotel and of Mohammad Karim.

The next night, we walked into town toward the Blue Mosque, stopping on the way for a little snack of Afghan burgers, something I'd consciously avoided until now: a small plate filled with soggy French fries cooked in none-too-fresh cooking oil in sidewalk vats, garnished with some shredded cabbage and hot sauce, and rolled up in thin falafel bread. It reminded me of late-night runs to the chippy in England with Pete—greasy chips, doused with malt vinegar and then rolled in several layers of newspaper, the oil leaking through the newsprint as we walked home with a meat pie on top. Ours was topped with a dodgy-looking chicken drumstick that screamed salmonella on a stick. But life was for living, so we took our bounty to the gardens outside the mosque and dug in, daring each other to try the chicken. But seeing as the chicken and the fries were cooked in the same grease, and the chicken had been sitting on the rest of the pile of food, whatever the chicken had, so did the rest of our meal. So down the hatch it went, my fingers crossed that I wouldn't be spending the evening in the toilet-paperless bathroom, swallowing Cipro tablets.

The Blue Mosque was incredibly beautiful, and if this architectural wonder resided in any town other than an Afghan one, it would be the epicenter of tourist activity. In this case, we were the only foreigners among throngs of Afghans. The call to prayer emptied the area of worshippers as they flocked to the open prayer rooms. The bizarre part came as the light began to fade and I realized that the mosque was covered with multicolored neon lights, including a bright neon sign flashing "Allah" in Farsi—turning the centuries-old cultural gem into a 1970s Las Vegas act.

We walked around the mosque until dark, then headed back to the guesthouse, stopping on the way to buy a container of fresh yogurt from a young boy for twenty Afs—about fifty cents. It was covered with a plastic bag so it wouldn't spill. We walked a little farther and bought two fresh round loaves of naan in the traditional Uzbek style Mazar-i-Sharif was famous for. Then we picked a random kebab shop out of the many that lined the street, ordered a few lamb kebabs to go, and took our bounty back to the hotel porch. Mohammad heard us walking up the stairs. He'd probably been waiting the entire time, and he followed us to our rooms. Travis and I went onto the balcony to eat, and within three minutes Mohammad knocked. He brought in some tea. When his cat followed us out to the balcony so did he. I smiled, trying to hide my exasperation, and I shooed both of them out and locked the door. He knocked only once or twice more before bed.

The next morning, Mohammad woke me with a knock on my door. He feigned a look of surprise when I sleepily opened it. In his hand was the key for 207 (I was in room 206), and he explained that he'd made a mistake. I mustered a smile as fake as his excuse and closed the door. Awake, I dressed and walked into town to buy a few supplies as well as breakfast. I was also on the hunt for the fabled Mecca compass to see if it really existed. It was a compass that supposedly always pointed to Mecca instead of north. Thanks to my broken Dari and the wonders of charades, I got shampoo, breakfast, bottled water, and biscuits for emergency snacking, but alas, no toilet paper. I was simply unwilling to play charades for that one.

Again, I was headed off at the stairs by Hotel California's manchild, when I returned from the market. He looked hurt that I hadn't asked him to get me breakfast. I assured him I'd wanted to go for a walk. He said he'd been watching me sleep this morning and wondered if I was okay. Suddenly, the meaning of the 207 key became clear. The room next to mine shared my balcony, and he'd entered it and peered in through my large French door windows. Though this was creepy and more than a little off-putting, I decided he was harmless, as he acted much the same with Travis. He tried to follow me into my room to talk more, but I firmly shook his hand and said bye-bye! But my lock was stuck again, so Mohammad got his tools back out and knelt by my door to "fix" it.

When he was done, I attempted a shower. I entered the still-reeking bathroom, avoided the flood plain, and stripped by the edge of the tub so I could keep all my clothes off the floor. The water heater was plugged in now. The water came out of the faucet hot, but no more than a trickle left the showerhead. So I took the world's wimpiest shower to get the worst of the dust off me. I felt as if I were in an Afghan version of a *Fawlty Towers* episode.

Mohammad must have been waiting outside my door, because when it was time for me to leave for my meeting at the women's prison, he was right there to ask me when I would return.

Security at the women's prison in Mazar-i-Sharif was not much more enforced than the security check at the gates of most Kabul NGO offices. It was completely unlike security at the Kabul prison. I had visited it several times, but the erratic commander had made access and interviewing the women a nightmare. Travis was working in Mazar-i-Sharif for another project, and I'd arranged this trip to coincide with his trip so that he could document some of the stories I wanted to share.

Women and men shared the same prison compound, but the women's section was behind a locked metal door just off the main courtyard. Behind this door were forty women and fourteen young children. Whereas Kabul's women's prison looked like what I expected of a prison block, housing more than a hundred women and children, this prison was nothing more than a small courtyard and two small rooms where the convicted prisoners and their children lived. This multipurpose communal space was all these women saw for the duration of their sentence. It served as their sleeping quarters, daycare, dining hall, and classroom. We walked through a small doorway out of the rain and into the larger of the two rooms where a sea of multicolored head scarves filled the space. Women of all ages and several young children and babies were learning to read and write. The sea of women turned their heads to find out who had arrived and miraculously parted to allow us space to enter.

These women comprised the entire female prison population

for the whole of Balkh province. They'd been convicted of murder, robbery, prostitution, and the ever-ambiguous crime of adultery. Recent studies estimate that nearly 80 percent of the female prison population in Afghanistan have been convicted of morality crimes. Many of the women in jail were trying to escape an arranged marriage or assisted another woman trying to escape one. Many accused of the crime of adultery were actually raped by a male family member—an uncle, brother-in-law, or friend of the family, and they were accused of adultery to save family honor. In Taliban-controlled areas of the country, where prison isn't an option or Sharia law takes precedence, accused women are still stoned to death, beheaded, or—as seen recently in the case of Bibi Aisha whose face graced the cover of *Time* magazine—have their ears and nose cut off to punish them and warn others in the community. This isn't as rare as you'd like to think or relegated to the southern Taliban-controlled provinces of Helmand and Kandahar. In the rural, mostly peaceful province of Parwan, located on the route between Kabul and Panjshir, the Taliban executed eleven women in the district of Shinwari in 2012 alone. Only one execution, that of twenty-two-year-old Najiba—accused of adultery—was covered by the media. An amateur video, posted on YouTube in July 2012, shows her gruesome execution in the street.

The experience of sitting with the women and their children on the concrete floor where the women and children slept and led their entire existence was humbling enough. Two of the women served me tea and offered me a small tin of chocolates, surprisingly gracious—as if I were a guest in their home.

As we began to talk, one woman emerged as the de facto leader of the group. Sitting near the back of the crowd in a thin white head scarf, Maidezel was a fiery woman with an easy laugh and a strong gaze. She freely admitted that she was guilty of murder, and the translator explained to me that Maidezel was accused of murdering her husband's son. But because of the translation, I wasn't sure whether the son was her own or that of another wife, as many Afghan men have multiple wives who all raise their children together. Regardless, Maidezel said she was sentenced to eighteen years. A fellow prisoner nudged her and asked, "Why did you say that? You should have lied!" Maidezel just laughed good-naturedly and got up to sit directly in front of us.

The room was filled to capacity with women sitting cross-legged on the floor facing me, many with children in their laps. Once the children were school age, they would either join their other siblings at home, if that was an option, or become temporary wardens of the government at an orphanage set up for children of prisoners.

These women spent twenty-four hours a day within a few feet of one another, but rather than turn against one another, they'd built a sisterhood, taking care of one another and the children. As if to prove the point, Maidezel was passed one of the younger babies, which she placed in her lap as though the baby were her own.

Several of the women in Afghan prisons were convicted of murdering their husbands. Many of these women were sold or forced into marriages with much older men, beaten, and raped. Divorce was rarely an option for them, because their husbands had to agree to it, and running away wasn't possible. Regardless of the crime the women were accused of, and regardless of the truth behind the accusations, they were often disowned by their families and, as convicted criminals, became outcasts in Afghan society. The social workers helping the prisoners focused on educating their families and creating bonds with them so that the women didn't end up on the street after they were released. At the same time, literacy and vocational programming were one key to giving the women the tools they needed to build a better life for themselves after they'd served their time.

Maidezel grabbed my hand and led me into the other room. There were several sewing machines, and she promptly sat down at one and started making something out of a cream-colored gauze. I sat on the floor to watch, and soon another woman started working on the machine next to her.

Occasionally, Maidezel looked up at me and smiled, clearly proud to show off her handicraft. I was fascinated as I watched a woman so powerful and strong-willed soften as she sewed in front of me, the layers of human nature slowly exposing themselves. Children migrated in from the other room and from the courtyard, and gathered around me. They took turns sitting on my lap, all except for one sweet little girl in a red dress who shyly watched from the lap of her mother. She looked to be two or three years old, but her mother appeared to be in her fifties. I often found it hard to estimate age in Afghanistan. War and poverty coupled with the lack of health care aged faces prematurely. This mother could be as young as me despite her weathered face.

It wasn't any easier to guess the children's ages. They'd had to grow up quicker in this harsh environment, and I often thought they were a couple of years older than they were. Throughout Afghanistan, many kids Devon's age were working instead of attending school, and the kids sitting in my lap, laughing at my silly faces and playing peek-a-boo, were in a tough spot. While the state and culture believed they were best served staying with their mothers, they were deprived of anything related to childhood. Stuck in the same bare courtyard prison as their mothers, they had no playground, no books, no toys, and harldy any stimulation. Even the poverty-stricken street children had daily experiences and a changing environment to stimulate their brains and spur development.

I felt humbled to have been trusted so openly and to get a rare glimpse into their lives. I listened to them talk for hours. The current prison situation for women in Afghanistan would prove tougher to navigate and even tougher to tolerate the more I learned during my various visits. I would find myself becoming more enraged and more determined to do something. Yet I was constantly stonewalled by the whims of the rotating prison commanders. One step forward, two steps back became the two-step the prison system intended for me. I realized over time that it was an arena I needed to leave to human rights and justice organizations with bigger teams and a stronger presence on the ground. I decided to focus on sharing their stories and highlighting the issue so that people understood the difficulties women faced throughout the country.

The next day, Travis and I headed to Sheberghan, the capital of Jowzjan province, eighty miles west of Mazar-i-Sharif. As we drove, camels dotted the fields, and we passed several camel trains on the roadside. We would be staying in a remote area, in a home that housed the organization Travis was working with. I was hitching a ride with him so that we could visit another women's prison a couple of hours past Sheberghan in the neighboring province on his day off.

I spent two days cooling my heels, working on my computer and watching Afghan rural life from the rooftop of the house. One night, the chief of security took us out for a walk around a local park where Afghans picnicked with their families. It had a small swimming pool and was in a beautiful area of walking trails surrounded by trees and flowers. Travis and I posed for pictures on the diving board much to the amusement of our guide. We walked around looking at flowers, a favorite Afghan pastime. I learned a few of their names along with a local history lesson from the security chief.

Sheberghan was once a flourishing city along the Silk Road, and in the thirteenth century, Marco Polo wrote about its honey-sweet melons. Sheberghan is also where Soviet archaeologists discovered the famous Bactrian gold, an enormous treasure cache buried under a hill for two thousand years. The collection of Bactrian gold—a collection of about twenty thousand gold ornaments, including coins, crowns, jeweled necklaces, and medallions—went on exhibit at the National Gallery in D.C. It is a true national treasure of Afghanistan, and a special museum is now being built in Kabul to house the gold so that it can be shared with Afghans.

The region is mostly agricultural and as such is very green. The town itself is now known as the stronghold of the infamous Uzbek warlord General Abdul Rashid Dostum. We drove past his home—a heavily reinforced compound—on the way back from the park. He was currently in exile in Turkey but would be returning to help President Karzai with his reelection bid in the upcoming months.

On the third day, Travis arranged for a driver to take us to neighboring Fayrab province, to the capital city of Maimana, where I was going to visit another women's prison. My alarm was set for 5:30 so we could get an early start. I woke up a few times in the night with my digestive system in chaos. I decided to take a Cipro and kill whatever strain of nastiness I'd ingested. I was lucky to be relatively pain-free, but intestinal liquifaction didn't make for great road tripping. Maimana was a three-hour drive from Sheberghan and not a place to be squatting by the roadside. Rumors of Taliban checkpoints reemerging in the northern provinces had reinforced my dislike for road trips. I had my burqa just in case, as well as toilet paper, and I hoped the Cipro/Immodium cocktail would kick in.

The morning light as we drove was incredible, and even Travis, who wasn't a morning person, commented that once in a while it was worth getting up early for the light. The green landscape remained flat, with numerous camels, donkeys, and goats, and the morning routines of its inhabitants added a timelessness to the scenery. Large, turban-wearing Turkmen sat straight and proud atop tiny donkeys trotting along the roadside. Donkeys and camels alike were loaded with stacks of cloth bags and bundles to transport, while young boys tended to the herds of goats. There were more motorbikes and rickshaws than cars and trucks. The mud houses had a uniquely domed shape that reminded me of desert nomadic tribes. The journey to Maimana was a hundred miles or so, and we both catnapped during the more than two-hour drive. When I opened my eyes again, twenty minutes or so later, the landscape had turned into stunning rolling hills covered in red golala poppies and pale lavender flowers. The colorful carpeted patterns covered the hills, interrupted only by more goat herds. All I wanted was to stop and take photos—all I wanted, that is, until I spied the array of trails winding through the hills and realized that *this* was where I could possibly go mountain biking. No land mines, little traffic, few people to create an audience save for a couple of goat herders. And the area was gorgeous. I broached the subject with Travis, and he thought he could take his motorbike off road on these trails. Perhaps a joint trip would be in order with some dirt bikers and mountain bikers, he joked. I sat back, seriously contemplating it for a future visit.

The beauty continued all the way to Maimana—a thriving Afghan market town. We drove past a bustling goat market, and nearly every woman here wore a white or bluebird burqa. The only ones not wearing burqas were Turkmen women with traditional head coverings in vibrant reds and purples. The men had faces worthy of portraits, and all wore elaborate and colorful turbans. There were no street beggars that I could see, and the only real traffic came from donkeys, motorbikes, and elaborately decorated rickshaws.

Men in traditional emerald-striped coats mingled with the blue-birds and doves everywhere. Even Travis was spellbound. I could easily have stayed here for weeks.

We had plans to meet with the director of a women's organization that works with the prisoners, AWEC, Afghan Women's Education Center. Rashed met us at the corner of a street to guide us. He discussed their programs as we headed over to the women's prison. Security was similar if not even more laid-back than in Mazar. Guards allowed us to duck under the barrier and waved us in. The deputy commander of the prison, Mohammad Akbar, met us at the entrance and led us back with the commander of the women's section. The inside of the compound looked like a small rural farm, and only the telltale barbed wire and men in orange jumpsuits rebuilding a wall revealed that this was a prison. A small blue building to the right of the field was the women's prison. It housed all the female prisoners in the province—currently twelve women and two children (both ten months' old). We entered the building and walked through it, past a tiny courtyard to a large room set up with a loom and sewing machines for the women's vocational training. The freshly painted space doubled as the literacy classroom, but unlike in Mazar, the women slept elsewhere, in pairs in the small rooms across the courtyard. A large bathroom, cleaner and nicer than many I'd used in Afghan guesthouses, was behind the last door in the little compound. The women appeared to be treated well, and their quarters, while still a prison, were less visually depressing than at the Mazar prison. On the surface, the building felt more like a hostel.

We sat down on white plastic chairs that lined the wall in the classroom while the women sat on the floor facing us. The deputy commander, the women's commander, and the teachers joined us. I wondered how open the women would be in the presence of the authority that kept them locked up. We started with an older woman in a pale blue head scarf who seemed interested in speaking and who, as in the Mazar prison, might have been the voice of the group by right of age and time served. At sixty-three, she was two years into a twelve-year sentence for murdering her husband. She had three girls and one son who came to visit once a week. The meeting felt awkward sitting above the women. It was too formal and slightly authoritative. I was acutely aware of the guards' presence on the chairs next to us, as were the women. I asked Rashed if we could sit on the floor with the women, and he nodded and joined me to sit cross-legged among them. I again tried to engage them, this time speaking to a young woman directly in front of me. She wore a black head scarf decorated with silver sequins and held a gorgeous little girl. When I asked Rashed to ask her for her name and story, she smiled shyly and tried to explain her crime. Najilia, age twenty, was originally from Logar province but married a man in Maimana. Her ten-month-old daughter, Basilla, lived with her in prison. Najilia was accused of instigating a plan to help her neighbor and her boyfriend run away. They were caught, and she was jailed for helping, as was the young boy for running away with a girl promised to another. The girl avoided prison but was married off to an uncle. Najilia's husband was supportive of her and knew that she didn't do anything wrong. She said she hoped that when she left she could continue the literacy education she'd begun in prison.

Most disturbing was the story of eighteen-year-old Mahria, a Turkmen woman also living in prison with a ten-month-old son. Mahria had a sweet round face and wore a striking yellow patterned Turkmen-style head scarf. Her husband had gone to Iran for work, and she was left behind at the family home. Her brother-in-law raped her during this time, and—as I was learning happened all too often—instead of the rapist going to jail, Mahria was accused of adultery to save face for the family. She had a two-year prison term with her baby. When I asked if she would have family support when she was released, she replied that she would live with her mother. She added that her husband was still in Iran and had said that when she was released, he would kill her.

This prison was run with the oversight of the Norwegian Provincial Reconstruction Team (PRT). Each province had PRTs related to the local international forces, and they oversaw public projects, reconstruction, and community building. In Fayrab province, this came mainly under the Norwegian directive. Prisons in Norway are radically different from prisons in other countries. Inmates are treated humanely, their living conditions are luxurious by other standards, and they have fewer walls and more space. Norway also has the lowest rate of recidivism in Europe. Here was a prison whose commanders were taught to respect their detainees and treat them with dignity. The prisoners were allowed to go outside, into the courtyard, whenever they chose. They appeared to be treated humanely, and they had female guards. The current commander, Hadj Sadr, came to work here seven years earlier after escaping the Taliban. He had recently returned from Washington, D.C., where he toured American jails and had also visited a prison in Norway. He said he'd been shocked by the level of freedom there in comparison to U.S. or Afghan prisons. He seemed to value the softer, more humane approach. This was refreshing to witness, though I would have liked to have more time to see it in action. Rashed told me that several years ago there were many problems in this and other prisons with the women and the male guards. Guards sexually harassing and raping women was commonplace. This was another example of crimes that were nearly impossible to track, as the women were not likely to speak out and had no incentive to do so because, even if they did, the perpetrator was unlikely to be punished. Since the

Afghan Women's Education Center had begun working there in 2007, there had been fewer, if any, such incidents.

As in the Mazar-i-Sharif prison, the children had no toys or playthings. Sensing the possibility of outside involvement here, I asked Rashed if the commander would allow me to go to the market and buy toys and clothing for the children. The commander agreed. With a smile, he showed us a small brightly painted room with murals that could be used as a kindergarten. He told Rashed that if we returned later today, we could deliver what we bought to the women. Rashed took us to the bazaar, to a shop owned by Afghanistan's most flamboyant Afghan, Humayan. Humayan ran a shop for women, full of sequined dresses, undergarments, and toiletries. He seemed overjoyed to meet us. Rashed explained that he was Humayan's English teacher, and Humayan went to great lengths to make us welcome. He sent for tea next door, and when he found out that we were in the market for toys, he had his assistant run across the street to find some and bring them over. He shared that he had recently vacationed in India, and he pulled out photos of himself at the Taj Mahal—sunglasses, hip jeans, and black pointy boots—looking quite the fashionista.

Locals heard that foreign visitors were at Humayan's, and several came in to say hi and meet us—introductions, more tea, and photos. I picked out some clothes for the children. He wrapped each in plastic, and bundled them into shopping bags. My environmental sensibilities internally battled my awareness of the cultural need to wrap items that were special.

We drove back to the prison, dropped off the bundles and headed to AWEC for lunch. Lunch consisted of Uzbek pilau—basically Kabuli rice, but a bit tastier—or so the Uzbeks claim. I was happy to accept that claim as the dish was by far my favorite in Afghanistan, and I had to restrain myself from moaning happily while I ate—it was so good. The Cipro and Immodium combo I took a few days ago had kicked in, and I was not racing from *tashnab* to *tashnab* anymore. Rashed was surprised to see me eating with my hand rather than with silverware (everyone else was using their hand, but since I was a Western guest, silverware had been brought for me). I explained that as I was in Afghanistan I would happily eat like an Afghan. He seemed pleased, and I worked my way through the bowl of rice and lamb with my right hand, occasionally using the bread to help scoop up the food more neatly. After lunch, we said our good-byes and I thanked Rashed for all his help and hospitality. Wanting to see more of the town before our return to Sherberghan, Travis asked Wahid, our driver, to take the long way around the city.

On the outskirts, Wahid pulled over for gas, and Travis and I got out to walk ahead on the road, surrounded by lush green hills. I saw a herd of donkeys, some motorcycles, and an old Turkmen man riding another donkey converge. It was photography nirvana. Travis and I scoped out potential trails and just when I was considering walking all the way back to Sherberghan, our taxi pulled up. Alternating fields of grass and wildflowers blanketed the hillsides, and we felt content with the short walk and the day's visit.

But sure enough, it was time for a reality check. Two men waved down our car, and Wahid amazingly stopped and got out even as Travis pulled on his arm and shouted at him not to. Focus snapped back to crystalline, and we watched helplessly as he crossed the road. One of the men started slapping and hitting him. Travis jumped into the driver's seat as I rolled up windows and locked the doors.

"If we have to go, we'll have to go. Understand?" he said quietly to me, not taking his eyes off the driver outside.

"Okay, I understand." I pulled the head scarf farther around my face, trying to hide my features without drawing too much attention to the car. It was too late for the burqa. I looked at Travis. How would I feel if we had to leave Wahid behind? *Shit. Shit. Shit.* What in the hell was happening?

Amazingly, the men stopped hitting Wahid and turned to leave. Wahid came back and got in the driver's seat as Travis slid out of the way. I looked out the window to see the men walking back to our car.

"Travis!" I shouted.

Travis looked out and told Wahid to drive away, but for some reason he refused as the men stood at our window and shouted at him. Suddenly, they turned and walked off. Wahid put the car into gear. He tried to make a U-turn to follow them, but Travis grabbed the wheel and told him to drive us home. A little power pull on the steering wheel occurred, and the driver conceded.

We sat in silence while Travis tried to find out from our driver what happened, but he wouldn't talk. Ten minutes later, we were stopped at a police checkpoint. They insisted that the road wasn't safe. No shit. They took Travis's name and asked if I was his wife, he said yes for ease of explanation, and gave them my first name. They didn't question him or bother to look back at me. They said that the Taliban were in the area the day before, and we should be careful. This was relatively unexpected. The north had been essentially void of Taliban for years. Taliban raids and false checkpoints were a recent development and a worrying sign of things to come. The rumors we had been hearing were apparently true. The policeman allowed us to continue on but asked us to send word when we made it back to the guesthouse. I vowed to give our driver a hefty tip.

Exhausted and more than a little freaked out, I curled up in the backseat with my head scarf draped over my face and tried to close my eyes. But not longer after, the taxi screeched to a halt in front of two enormous armored vehicles, their guns pointed at us.

"What the hell?" I shouted loudly.

Travis looked back at me. "It's okay, mate, just a convoy. Looks like they have a mechanical."

"Seriously?" I laughed nervously. "What are the odds?"

Sure enough, a Swedish convoy had broken down and was preventing traffic from passing, keeping its guns trained on the stopped vehicles. I'd have preferred that they scouted the landscape instead of us as they—and we—were sitting ducks if the Taliban was in the area. Within ten or fifteen minutes, they got their vehicle running, and we were all moving. I sighed once we were back up to highway speed. The rest of the trip passed without incident, and when we got back to the guesthouse, Travis asked one of the NGO staff who spoke better Dari than he did to find out what had happened with the driver. They talked with the driver quietly then explained that he'd gotten smacked around for traveling with two *xoragees* (foreigners) in his car—and something about a checkpoint.

Over dinner that night, we recounted the story with the other staff. Travis confessed, " Yeah, it could have been a real problem. I don't know how to drive a stick."

"*What?*" I shouted at him.

"I never learned to drive a stick. Not sure how well that would have worked out had the shit really gone down."

"Are you serious? I know how to drive a stick. I could have jumped over the seat."

"If it came to that, I'm sure I would have figured it out."

"Oh, yeah, because an attack is a *great* time to learn how a clutch works. No pressure."

"Maybe I should put that on the to-do list of life skills?"

"Ya think?" I laughed sarcastically. "Thank God, you didn't have to figure it out today."

While there are pockets of instability even in Afghanistan's so-called safe provinces, such as the ones I visited during my trip to the north, the southern and eastern provinces were simply too dangerous for traveling by car. These are areas that are under Taliban control or being fought over. Commercial airlines travel only to the bigger cities. After the attack on my driver in a relatively calm area of Afghanistan, I was more aware of how I traveled and with whom.

I had been invited for lunch at the home of the female member of Parliament, Sahera Sharif, and her family, to discuss the situation of girls' education in Khost province. She'd then asked me to join her on a visit to Khost City to visit the girls' high school and meet the staff. Visiting Khost was a little trickier than other places. There were no commercial flights, and the road from Kabul was too unsafe. The roads to the southern provinces were notoriously insecure, and businessmen, government officials, and foreigners were kidnapping targets.

Luckily, the Afghan National Army, the ANA, often takes parliamentarians between home provinces on routine helicopter flights for security reasons and timing. Some of the roads weren't just unsafe but remote, and the journey by car could take days. After two attempts to align our schedules, we finally were ready to make the trip together.

Sahera went this route often and arranged the journey with the flight commander. They made plans to confirm the flight one hour before departure, and if it was confirmed, we were to meet at Massoud's square to drive into the ANA flight area together with her security. We would spend the day in Khost City, visiting a girls' high school, a women's group, and another clinic project that Sahera was working on, and then catch the return flight home before dark.

But the trip didn't go as smoothly as we had hoped. Once again, Afghan scheduling wreaked havoc on a simple plan. Sahera, her driver, Travis, and myself all met from different areas of Kabul at the traffic circle near the airport. Several lanes converge and no stopping was allowed due to security—not the easiest of meeting points. Yet I pulled up and sure enough, Sahera was waiting with her driver. I got out of the taxi and jumped in her car to drive onto the airfield. Unfortunately, it became apparent that her driver wasn't sure which entrance to use. Cue some back and forth driving, U-turns, and stopping in the middle of the road to ask directions with random people walking by.

There were two struggles that appeared inherent in Afghan society: timekeeping and information sharing. Afghans will wait and wait when a simple question could solve the situation. Example? We waited outside the security gates of the ANA airfield for nearly half an hour, making us exactly half an hour late for our flight. Neither the driver nor the MP asked the guards for more information or explained who they were. We just waited.

I finally stepped out of the car to get some air. Let's just say we were all a few showers overdue, some of us more than others. The entrance guard saw me and came over to inquire why we were there. Never mind that we'd been parked a few feet in front of him the entire time. I introduced Sahera and explained about our flight to Khost. "Come in, come in," he said. "I didn't realize who you were." *Of course, you didn't. You didn't ask, and we didn't offer.* An Afghan standstill.

The flight hadn't left without us, but it was now not flying directly to Khost. It was flying to Bagram, Ghazni, and *then* Khost. The Afghan flight command had made some changes and that meant that not only had we not missed our flight, but we wouldn't take off for another forty-five minutes. One-and-a-half hours late plus two extra stops? Right on schedule.

There was no point in getting worked up. If I'd learned anything in years of travel, it was the need for patience and the acceptance that things could be frustrating, slow, and inefficient. But plans tended to work out however they were supposed to in the end.

We walked around the airfield to load up. The beast was a MI8, a solid Russian helicopter that rattled a bit, but the crew assured me confidently she was air-worthy. An American copilot joined the Afghan pilot and told me that the Americans were mentoring the Afghan pilots with new flight technology. A large, serious-looking man in a pristine white shalwar kameez and a large black turban arrived with a bodyguard. Both checked their guns with the crew who, finally assembled, passed around earplugs. It was my first flight in a helicopter, and I was excited to get an aerial view of the country. Through the circular windows, I saw the hills that dot Kabul recede as the wide expanse of the Shomali Plain spread out below in muted shades of brown.

At our first stop, in Bagram, Sahera looked nervous. She hadn't heard that we were stopping in Bagram and Ghazni since she'd been on her phone. I couldn't explain the situation to her until the engine was shut down, and when I did, she worried that we wouldn't arrive before the girls were out of school. We had to wait to pick something up in Bagram, and then we traveled another forty minutes to Ghazni. The crew member who'd been sitting by the open door mounted a gun for this leg of the trip. I watched as he loaded ammunition—another reminder that this wasn't a pleasure ride. But fifteen minutes into the flight he was dozing, his forehead on his arm, which rested on the rifle. I relaxed. If the gunner was sleeping, an attack was probably unlikely. But later, when I told a friend the story, she said, "Nah, he'd probably wake up when the first bullet hit."

Bullet-free in Ghazni, we refueled and waited to reboard for another thirty-minute flight to Khost. American soldiers at the base met us. They kindly pointed out a Porta-Potty and brought us food from the mess hall for an impromptu picnic on the airstrip. The man in white pulled out a small rug to pray by the side of the plane. I hoped he was praying that this Russian bird didn't rattle apart in the air—or get shot at. The forty-minute ride from Kabul to Khost was going to end up taking three hours. This would give us just two-and-a-half hours on the ground if we wanted to catch a ride back that day, which I definitely did.

When we landed in Khost City, we quickly piled into a car sent for Sahera and drove to the girls' school. The province is lush, green, and warm. En route, Sahera pointed out the site of the recent Taliban suicide bomber attack that had been all over the news a few days earlier and that had targeted a police checkpoint and killed eleven.

We arrived at the girls' school fifteen minutes later to find everyone had indeed gone home, but a women's group had gathered in the back courtyard to wait for Sahera. Fifty women, many in burqas, swarmed around us in a flurry of introductions, hugs, and a general outpouring of enthusiasm. It was touching to witness, and they were obviously thrilled with their female MP. As she held court in Pashto, I hung back with several young children, trading names in Dari, which amused them greatly. I took photos with my iPhone and showed them, wishing I had a Polaroid, as sharing photos was still the one true barrier breaker the world over. There was nothing quite like being able to take a photo and give it to the person immediately, and I always felt frustrated that I could show people the photos but not give them copies. It would be a powerful connection between photographer and subject in a country where so much was taken and so little given back in human connection. We then passed the time learning how to play Afghan marbles. One of the boys had four marbles: three green and one silver shooter. In the rocks, we huddled and he showed me how to shoot. I was all thumbs, not having played since I was a little girl, and he laughed appreciatively and encouraged me until I started to improve.

One of the women tapped me on the shoulder, and I turned to see that several men had arrived. I stood up and wiped the dust from my hands on my skirt as I smiled and thanked her. The head of school, the director of teachers, and a general gathering of all men interested in the goings-on introduced themselves. We talked about the school, the province, and the state of education while Sahera continued to speak to the assembled women. Tea arrived exactly at the time we needed to be heading back to the helicopter. I groaned inwardly. Sahera joined us, and despite the clock ticking, no one was in a hurry. Not wishing to play the role of the rude American rushing people, I finally interjected that I was incredibly sorry but we really *had to go*. The helicopter wouldn't fly after dark, and we would be left here.

Sahera nodded distractedly as if to say, "Yes, yes, but first another cup of tea," and when someone brought her a plate with bread on it, I stood to gather my things, protocol be damned. I knew that Sahera had family here, and that if we were stranded, we could probably stay with them, but I had no desire to spend an unplanned night here. I started shaking hands with the men who'd gathered and expressed my sincere apology that we had to go and explained that the helicopter was waiting and I would love to stay longer next time. I assured them I wanted to return and see the school with the girls. I walked out to the car. The chopper was leaving at 4:30. It was now 4:25, and we still had to drive through town. Sahera sauntered out with her entourage. As she got in the car, the Afghan police turned up to provide escort, so at least we would have a clear path to the airfield. Women were still saying good-bye and holding her hand as we started to drive off.

We arrived ten minutes late, but the chopper was still there, much to my relief.

"We weren't going to leave without you," the pilot said, and chuckled. "You had five more minutes at least."

"A whole five minutes, eh?"

"Did you get what you needed?" asked the American pilot.

"Not even close," I said, and smiled tiredly.

"Sorry to hear it."

"Me, too . . . Afghanistan, never easy, right?"

We piled into the machine as it was grinding to life. Forty minutes straight back to Kabul should get us there just as night was falling—in time to battle Kabul's epic rush hour. I sighed.

I wasn't sure what had been accomplished on this trip, other than more insight into the workings of the country, the pace of things, and the unexpected turns. At the end of the day, I had my first helicopter ride and made a journey to Khost. It wasn't bad if you looked at the trip as an adventure. It was a chance to see the country in ways others rarely do and a reminder of how lucky I was to get this sort of insight and access. More important, the last few trips illustrated to me that I needed to let go of my initial limited focus on girls' education. My projects over the previous three years—supporting schools and literacy programs, starting computer labs and kindergartens, securing land donations and working to build a deaf school—had taught me an enormous amount about Afghanistan. But there were bigger organizations that could tackle these types of projects more effectively, with large budgets and a team of staff. Trips like this one to Khost, and to the women's prisons around the country, allowed me unparalleled access to a variety of Afghan women. Meeting women in prisons, female members of Parliament, teachers, students, activists—in both urban and rural settings—was giving me a broader understanding than I could have ever imagined of the country and the issues surrounding women's rights.

I was realizing that I needed to keep my focus on the projects that I could support with the limited resources I had, and that inspired me. I was dialing in on projects that worked in nontraditional ways through storytelling, arts, and sports. Projects that were culturally sustainable. Projects that could flourish with limited funds and oversight, engage young Afghans, and that built community in unique ways.

As if to prove the point, about ten minutes into the flight, the pilot called me up to the cockpit and said, "People pay a lot of money to do this in the States. Would you like to sit up here with us? It may help take the sting out of the frustration."

"Seriously? Uh, yes please!" I grinned.

He smiled and gestured to the jump seat between him and Maqsood, the Afghan pilot. I watched the scenery through the curved glass window. We swooped through the mountains southeast of Kabul, everything below us looking peaceful. The details were blurred at this height, snowcapped mountains morphing into green hillsides, with dots of mud houses and crisscrossing roads. Closer to Kabul, Maqsood pointed out the Queen's palace underneath us, tucked into the landscape. I marveled at how easy it was to forget we were in a conflict zone, and that there was a gunner in the helicopter door watching for RPGs below.

8

Financial Fear

Colorado 2010

Several weeks later, I took Devon to get groceries, and for the first time in a long time, I was truly scared. I had $42 in cash and $21 in my bank account. We were out of almost everything, including toilet paper, milk, bread—the necessities. How had I gotten this close to the wire? As we pulled into the City Market parking lot, I told her brightly, "Sweetie, we are only going to grab a few things, okay? So please, let's just get the things we need, and we'll come back later for the other stuff. Okay?"

I opened the back of the Element to get the shopping bags, and she grabbed my hand. "Okay, Mommy. I just want to get my gummy vitamins."

At eighteen bucks a bottle, that would be nearly half our grocery money.

"Sorry, baby, not today, we'll get them next trip okay?"

"But I'm out. We need to get these."

I sighed and grabbed her for a hug. "I know, sweetie. Next trip, okay? Can you just come with and help me get the other stuff for now?"

"Okay," she said, frowning slightly as she took my hand. This was not what I had in mind when I said I wanted to do the best for Devon. My nerves were fried, and I could feel myself becoming short and distracted with her—something I needed to rectify. None of this was her fault.

"Race you?" I challenged her, smiling. We ran across the parking lot, her rain boots stomping through puddles of melting snow, and her infectious giggle made me laugh out loud. My heart pounding, I bent down before we entered the store. I gave her a kiss as I told her, "I love you so so so much."

"All the way to the moon?" she asked.

"All the way to the moon *and* back again!" I assured her. "Now, let's go buy some toilet paper."

As I stood in the checkout line, I went through my mental survival checklist. I had meetings in Denver this week, important ones with potential donors that I couldn't miss. I had several projects ready to launch but as of yet hadn't secured the funding to put them into action. Luckily I had half a tank of gas, so if I conserved, which meant staying close to home this weekend with Devon, I should be good to go.

I'd been here before when I first separated from Pete. I left the marriage with a couple hundred dollars in my bank account. He was not in a mindset to help me with the logistics of separation, and since we had our own accounts, I had no cushion to fall back on to help me break away. He had insisted that if I wanted out, I was free to go, but he wasn't going to support it or make it easier for me to leave.

So I took out a personal loan using the only possession I could take freely from the marriage until our divorce went through—my car. Leveraging it as collateral, I was able to get a loan for $17,000, enough to help me pay rent and supplement the money I earned teaching Pilates. It also allowed me to focus on launching Mountain2Mountain, to get to Afghanistan in the first place, and survive until our joint assets were divvied up nearly a year later.

The settlement we reached over my half of our house was not insubstantial, albeit a fraction of what I could have asked for under the law. I hadn't been willing to battle. Something I, at times, look back on with regret. I felt it was more important to coordinate and focus on Devon's shared schedule than fight over financial issues. I didn't have the stomach for it, and it may have allowed us the understanding that we have today, where we can raise Devon in tandem with very little drama, and share special occasions and the occasional dinner together as an extended family.

Instead of using the money to give me and Devon the stability of a home, savings for vacations together, and the semblance of security, I used it to build our future in a different, some may say riskier, way. I paid off that initial loan, funded multiple trips to Afghanistan, started several of my smaller projects, and more important, worked sixty hours a week solely to build M2M without taking time from Devon. Each night, after she went to bed, I cranked out a solid five hours. The rest of the work was done when she was at preschool or with her dad. The settlement supported us for the past four years while I worked to build our future and create something both she, and I, could be proud of.

On the flip side, I stopped racing because of the time commitment, entry fees, and focus, and I forewent any vacations other than my trips to Afghanistan. I gave up health insurance, occasionally went without car insurance, and often was a month in arrears with rent.

But this day was especially tough. I went to the PO Box, fingers crossed that there would be some checks I could deposit. Nothing.

My eye doctor left me a voice mail that my new contacts were in, but I couldn't afford to go pick them up. My cell phone bill was due. Rent and Dev's ballet class tuition were due in three days. I looked down at the silver ring on my right index finger. It was a gift from my father and sister at the beginning of my M2M journey and was engraved with the words of Longfellow: *The lowest ebb is at the turn of the tide.* My life definitely felt like low tide.

There was only one item in the PO Box: a package from Vail Mountain School, a private school forty-five minutes away. I drove home and once we put the groceries away and Devon was busy building a fort out of our pillows, I opened it. To my surprise, it contained a stack of cards, each of them a thank-you from a child in the fifth grade in a class I'd spoken to a month ago about Afghanistan. They had been reading a book *Parvana's Journey*, by Deborah Ellis, about a young girl in Taliban times who disguised herself as a boy. The children had a lot of good questions. I opened the first card. "Dear Ms. Galpin. Thank you so much for telling us all about Afghanistan. It was really cool to put on a burqa."

I smiled and opened another. "Dear Ms. Galpin. Thank you so much for talking about Afghanistan. I love how so many people like you are trying to change the world one step at a time."

Another had a picture drawn of a globe shaped like a heart. Most of them mentioned the burqas I'd brought to their classroom and wished me good luck in Afghanistan. Many hoped they could go there when they were older. Others wanted me to say hello to Afghan kids for them. I felt my heart swell. This didn't put food in my fridge, but it was a lovely reminder of why I was doing this.

"Who are all these cards from, Mommy?" Devon asked, walking over to the kitchen table and opening the various cards to look at the drawings and pictures.

"These are from a group of kids in Vail that I visited to talk about Afghanistan. They sent me these notes to say thank-you."

"Can you come talk at my school?"

I looked up at her from the pile of cards. "Yes, if you want me to, of course I can. You should help though. What would you like to show the kids in your class?"

"We could show them the Afghan money and the flag!"

"We could do that. . . . How about a burqa and buzkashi hat?"

"Yeah! And can we show them the picture of you riding a horse!"

"If you want to. Why don't you pick out some of your favorite photos. I'll print them, and you can glue them on a piece of foam board. I think I've also got a map we can use. Then you can talk about the photos, and I'll talk about what I do in Afghanistan."

"Okay, but first can I have a snack?"

"Snack first. Afghanistan second. Deal."

That conversation sparked the realization that perhaps I was trying too hard to explain myself and Mountain2Mountain through the lens that others used to view me. I was passionate about working as a woman *for* women in conflict zones where women often didn't have a voice. But I was also interested in how art and storytelling could amplify those voices and challenge the apathy that so often prevented action on the U.S. side of the equation. I didn't want to focus on building schools or clinics or infrastructure or vocational training. These were all necessary and vital steps in a country like Afghanistan, but they weren't my skillset. I didn't have the education, experience, resources, or financial backing to tackle these large sticks-and-bricks projects. Yet time and time again, this was what advisors or board members clung to as though I should model myself on Greg Mortenson. But I wasn't him. I didn't want to be him. I wanted to focus on what women could do *with* an education. I wanted to focus on projects with the next generation that sparked voices, that inspired change, and that could challenge stereotypes. I wanted to transform the way people viewed women and the way Americans viewed Afghans, and the way the public viewed humanitarian work—a goal much less tangible than building a school, and much harder to rally the masses and raise money for. Creating a computer lab or trying to build a school for the deaf was not where I wanted to put my passions going forward. Supporting graffiti and street art projects, working with female activists, and creating other programs that challenged perceptions and empowered voices were.

I was tired of banging my head against a wall. I was tired of living on a tightrope all by myself. I was tired of feeling the weight of the risk of the choices I had made. Yet other than my immediate family, which now included Christiane, I was reminded daily that I was out on that tightrope by choice, and no one else was going to join me willingly.

The area that caused the most conflict from the beginning was the formation of the board of directors and the subsequent incarnations of it that followed. Good people do strange things when they sit on the board of a nonprofit. I've talked to several other founders who led nonprofits and they all say the same thing. Boards are often the most frustrating part of running a nonprofit.

If I could do it all again, I'd consider creating a for-profit entity and steer the profits to the projects I wanted to do. The skewed mentality associated with nonprofits is astounding. Part of the problem is in the name: nonprofit. As if making money is evil. Yet without money, nothing can get done.

I've seen nonprofits, including Mountain2Mountain, which has a tiny budget, barely $100,000 a year on average, held to a completely different set of operating rules than for-profits. For-profits are judged on the work they do. Nonprofits are judged on their frugality. For-profits hire adequate, qualified staff and pay them a competitive salary. Nonprofits often operate on a bare-bones staff, severely underpaid compared to their for-profit counterparts doing the same job. They rely on volunteers and interns to make up the difference. But it's difficult to expect the same level of competence and expertise from staff who aren't paid competitive salaries. For-profits can spend money to make money. They can create innovative marketing campaigns in order to make a much larger profit. Nonprofits are criticized if they spend money on marketing or fundraisers. I see founders of nonprofits get attacked for taking a modest salary, as though running a nonprofit should be a volunteer position done out of goodwill. But that isn't sustainable for building a solid foundation for goals and accountability.

Dan Pallotta gave a great example in a 2013 TED talk about how nonprofits are judged by their frugality rather than their effectiveness. The limitations put on nonprofits create an inability, or unwillingness, to take risks. If you try and fail with a nonprofit project—even if you learn from it to improve other projects, programs, and approaches for the future—you are judged much more harshly than if you have a failure in a for-profit company. If we are trying to shift paradigms of poverty, abuse, and human rights, we can't always play it safe. This is exactly the space where we *need* to think outside the box, where creativity and the ability to take risks are your best assets. Government organizations and large NGOs have too much structure and red tape to be nimble, flexible, and creative with how they tackle issues. But small nonprofits can develop unique and groundbreaking approaches to serious issues. Small organizations, individual risk-takers, and start-ups are in a great position to tackle many of these problems, but the public perceptions and judgments of nonprofit often don't allow it. Getting work done costs money—end of story. It's not evil to have operational costs. It's evil to waste money and not accomplish your goals.

Adding to the dysfunctional nature of nonprofits is the public's obsession with creating heroes out of humanitarians. There is an unrealistic paradigm of the hero's journey, based on the mythology that has developed: a nonprofit is deemed worthy only if its founder has significantly martyred him- or herself with extreme financial and personal sacrifice. Does this unhealthy cycle manifest itself in unrealistic expectations that the public holds toward those trying to do good work? Did I make unhealthy choices in my own life, financially and physically, in order to be more worthy? And does that discourage others from putting their drop in the bucket because it seems too small in comparison? That is not the example I want set.

Did Greg Mortenson feel the need to exaggerate, or perhaps even lie, to sell his story and fund his nonprofit, as writer Jon Krakauer and 60 Minutes have suggested when they accused him of repeatedly lying in his memoir, Three Cups of Tea, and mismanaging donors' funds? Did others feel that need to exaggerate? Would I? Is that the only way to make a small, start-up nonprofit financially viable in today's social media era? Could Mortenson have created such a successful multimillion dollar organization without embellishing the details of his story? Was he just a climber wanting to do something good for a rural Pakistani village and who got frustrated by the lack of support? Was he a man with a hero complex? Or was he something in between—neither the hero as the public wanted him to be, nor the villain portrayed on 60 Minutes and through Jon Krakauer's evisceration?

Who knows? But by insisting on making heroes out of those wanting to do good work, do we create an environment much like the current celebrity culture in which those sacrificing for the greater good drink the Kool Aid and start to believe they *are* heroes—that they are beloved and deserve to be treated as such? A Kardashian in humanitarian clothing? Beyond the ick factor of a celebrity and humanitarian collision, the unholy union creates an unhealthy model for start-ups to base themselves on and for young people to aspire to. You aren't supposed to want to save the world in order to get famous. Yet in a world where people strive to be famous for fame's sake, altruism seems to be getting kicked aside for feature stories.

I often found the constant comparison of my work to that of Greg Mortenson frustrating and misleading. I never wanted to be Greg Mortenson. Yet time and time again, the comparison was applied as though the only way to tell my story was to filter it first through him.

One advisor wanted me to be the next Greg Mortenson, or at least get his endorsement to put on our Web site. "You raised over a hundred thousand dollars and a lot of publicity for his organization."

"I did, and I did that without expecting anything in return. That was a chance to dip my toe in the fund-raising waters and see if we could inspire a community to support another community half the world away."

"Yes, but a note from him on the Web site could really help legitimize what you are doing."

"But he doesn't know what I'm doing. He's doing his thing, and I'm doing mine. I started M2M to develop my own approach. It's not about me replicating what he's doing. It's about tackling the issues that others aren't or won't, or that they are addressing in different ways." The suggestion that I should essentially ride his coattails because he was famous and I had once raised money for his organization seemed absurd and insulting to both of us. Mortenson owed me nothing, nor did he owe anyone else who donated to his organization or spearheaded fund-raisers. That would be like donating money for building a school and insisting to have a plaque with your name on it.

Yet articles, news stories, and magazine features would continue to describe my work with at least one reference to Mortenson, despite my insistence to writers that I shouldn't be compared to him. I wasn't building schools. I wasn't focused solely on girls' education, and I wasn't a climber. There are other humanitarians and activists I was probably more similar to, but *Three Cups of Tea* was a phenomenon and Mortenson was a household name. I worked in Afghanistan; he worked in Afghanistan and Pakistan. I'd raised money for his organization. We both lived in mountain towns. Educating women and girls was at the heart of our organizations, although we had completely different approaches to how we wanted to tackle the issue. My goals were starting to define themselves with artists, activists, and athletes. The more time I spent in Afghanistan, the more I evolved my goals; as my network expanded, I got more exposure to the emerging group of young Afghans. These were young people growing up with Facebook and Twitter, and embracing the opportunities that the post-Taliban era allowed.

At every one of my speaking events, at least one audience member asked me about Mortenson. I fielded the questions diplomatically. I wanted to create a voice, combat apathy, and build a virtual army of women who could tackle the issues of women's rights, gender violence, and inequity *as women* and in culturally sustainable ways. I wanted to focus on changing and inspiring individuals, not just building things. I didn't want to create more international aid dependence. I didn't want to model the "great white hope" approach to aid work that in many ways caused more harm than good. I wanted to use my gender to challenge gender barriers in unique ways, even if it created only a ripple.

The irony was that, years later—when Mortenson's star fell unexpectedly and publicly—I and many others felt the backlash of public distrust. Here I was, having never taken a penny from Mortenson and yet having to answer questions about him and his organization. News reporters called me to ask questions. But neither myself nor Mountain2Mountain had any relationship with him or his organization beyond the initial fund-raiser before we became an independent 501c3 nonprofit. But the public lost a hero. It felt betrayed and foolish, and wanted answers.

It was interesting to look back and see lessons emerging. I learned that nonprofits needed to be as open about mistakes as about successes. Founders had to build strong teams of people smarter and more experienced than they were, and trust them for advice and knowledge. Founders had to let go of control of the organization, especially financial control, to ensure transparency and public trust.

I have always worked for myself, and as an entrepreneur, I have different skills.

I can imagine, conceptualize, and implement projects half a world away, even in a war zone. I am one half of an effective organization, but in order to be successful, I know I need to find the yin to my yang, a business-minded, financially savvy manager to take over the operations for Mountain2Mountain. The trick is to find a person who has a mutual trust in my abilities to continue to create and inspire and evolve without putting a harness on me—and who I can in turn trust to lead my organization onto a solid foundation of financial stability that will allow me to do what I do best.

With the lessons learned and the search begun, I continued to operate my one-woman show and focus on what I believed in. I lived on the tightrope, believing that people would rally behind ideas like mine—behind creativity, activism, risk taking, individual voices, and the changing of perceptions, not just traditional humanitarian models.

It took five years of work and exploration until a lightbulb went off. I was talking to my friend and Mountain2Mountain advisor Heidi Volpe on the phone. She was describing the guilt one can feel after returning from war zones or impoverished countries—paying $4 for a latte at Starbucks after meeting people who earn $1 a day. How do you reconcile that?

Another woman at a fund-raiser had told me how difficult she thought it would be to leave all those orphaned children behind; she'd want to scoop them all up and bring them home.

In both instances, I understood, but I didn't feel that way. I chalked it up to being well suited for the job. I could separate my realities and my emotions, and comfortably cross over time and time again between two worlds. But after the call with Heidi, I realized that I wasn't just right for the job per se; rather, I recognized how lucky I was to be born in this country and era. Through no choice of my own, I was born to a middle-class family in the 1970s in the United States. That gave me more opportunities and basic human rights than women born in Afghanistan. By dumb luck, I'd been issued a geographic passport to a country that allowed me a myriad of expectations and opportunities. This passport shouldn't be wasted. My life shouldn't be spent suffering or sacrificing at the expense of experiencing joy, following my passions, and exploring the world. My desire to create change, to put my drop in the bucket in hopes of starting a ripple, shouldn't overshadow the opportunities I'd received in the lottery of life. That night I wrote these thoughts while I was in bed. I spent days pondering the choices I was making.

Devon showing her support of the #inspirepeace project and her desire to go to Afghanistan. (Photo credit: Shannon Galpin)

My two favorite women in the whole world: My sister, Larissa, goofing around with Devon in Denver. (Photo credit: Shannon Galpin)

The furry addition of the "Bear" to our family, as we bring home a Bernese Mountain puppy. (Photo credit: Mark Wiggins)

Larissa and Devon reading the first copy of the *Streets of Afghanistan* book at our local bookstore, The Next Page. (Photo credit: Shannon Galpin)

Standing in front of the United check-in desk at Denver International Airport with Anna Brones with the entire *Streets of Afghanistan* exhibition ready to transport. (PHOTO CREDIT: MARK WIGGINS)

Setting up the *Streets of Afghanistan* exhibition in the village of Istalif (PHOTO CREDIT: TONY DI ZINNO)

Setting up one of Paula Bronstein's images as part of the *Streets of Afghanistan* exhibition against Soviet tanks at the top of Massoud's tomb in Panjshir. (PHOTO CREDIT: TONY DI ZINNO)

Men walk by the *Streets of Afghanistan* exhibition on the streets in Istalif. (PHOTO CREDIT: TONY DI ZINNO)

Riding a buzkashi horse at Kabul Stadium before loading up the horses for a match in the Shomali Plain. (Photo credit: Tony Di Zinno)

Village life in Bamiyan on two wheels. (Photo credit: Deni Bechard)

Talking bikes and Afghan history with the gardener of Darul Amon Palace in Kabul. (Photo credit: Warren Buttery)

Teaching Coach Seddiq to fist-bump during a training session break on the side of the road. (Photo credit: Sarah Menzies)

Getting permission from and making friends with members of the Afghan National Army at Qargha Lake. (PHOTO CREDIT: DENI BECHARD)

The Afghan Cycles documentary film crew in April 2013 in front of Darul Amon Palace in Kabul. (PHOTO CREDIT: NAJIBULLAH SEDEQE)

Lining up with a few members of the women's national cycling team during a training ride. (Photo credit: Sarah menzies)

Joining Mariam and other members of the Afghan National Team at the end of a long day of filming the Afghan Cycles documentary. (Photo credit: Sarah Menzies)

Why did I feel guilty at the idea of planning a vacation? Why was making no money and working insane hours more important than mountain biking on my lunch break and taking a paycheck as the director of a nonprofit? Why was a bleeding ulcer just an inevitable side effect of the stress and pace I was keeping? How would this affect Devon as she became more aware? Is this the example I wanted to set?

The decade I had spent living in Europe, traveling, exploring, experiencing new tastes, new smells, and new cultures in my twenties had been replaced with sacrifice and guilt. I knew a happy medium was possible. Balance was needed: joy in daily boosts, more laughter, more 7:00 A.M. dance parties with Devon, more midnight hikes, and space for a real relationship with an amazing man. It felt like an insult to the women I met around the world who didn't have the opportunities I did to just throw them away or bury them under a giant to-do list that would never be completed. I am so lucky and blessed to have this life, and I should be setting the example to Devon to make every day count. I can't waste what I was given because I am outraged by the injustices I see in the world. Be outraged. Fight. But don't forget to play. Make time for friends, family, and love. Remember what is important.

The significance of the bike re-emerged. It had been my source of play and of strength, a metaphor for how I lived. With a single-speed, I had to embrace the suffering. There were no gears. I sat, stood, or walked. That was all I got. But I loved its simplicity. I may not love the suffering, but I do love the challenge. I embrace the suffering for the return I get back in spades. Mountain biking requires some blood and skin donation beyond the expected sweat and tears. If I wanted to become a stronger rider, it wasn't just a matter of muscle and lungs. It was about confidence alongside trial and error. I fell, a lot. I bruised. I hoped there was nothing worse, but it was always possible. Yet, despite that knowledge, the expectation even, that I would be hurt, I continued to ride. Why?

Because of the joy I felt on two wheels—dirt in my face, my teeth, mud on my legs, the wind in my face making me feel alive. The exhilaration of bombing down singletrack or the challenge of riding up a steep, rocky climb are the epitome of conquering fear and building mental and physical strength. I couldn't be indecisive. Indecision on a mountain bike—should I go over the rock or around the rock?—would draw blood. I had to let go of the brakes, ride through the rock garden, or I would get stuck. It was all there—life lessons in cheesy, two-wheeled metaphors. The bike was freedom of movement, of individual choice. Nothing was more important than that.

Maria Ward, the author of *Bicycling for Ladies*, published in 1896, stated it best: "Riding the wheel, our powers are revealed to us." That gets to the heart of how I feel every time I ride. It's why I have a ridiculous grin on my face when I ride through mud puddles and why I seek out exploration of new places on dirt trails and back roads. Riding a bike, I'm strong, I'm free, and I'm filled with joy.

What if I could harness that joy and that strength with other women? Could I encourage women who have survived the worst of gender violence—rape, sexual trafficking, and domestic abuse—to get involved in the fight for women worldwide? People seem to put women like this in a box labeled "victim." This label can completely disempower them, as though by being victimized, they are weak. I know different. Survivors are stronger than people think. I believe one woman can make a difference—that one voice matters. I wouldn't have set off on this journey if I didn't believe change was possible with the voice and willpower of a single individual. But I also believe that our strength is in our numbers. If I could inspire more women to use their voice, to stand up for those that are voiceless, I could create more than a ripple. I could create a tsunami of change that couldn't be ignored.

I needed to separate Shannon Galpin, the individual, from Mountain2Mountain, the organization. I had no idea how to accomplish that with zero money in the bank, but I knew that realizing the need for separation and the search for more balance in my life was a first step.

The Barrette

Afghanistan 2010

My first morning back in Afghanistan started off with a bang. Literally. I'd slept fitfully through the night. The heavy spring rain echoed down a drainpipe that emptied noisily outside the door of my room. I awoke to an explosion. I thought it might be thunder because of the rain. As I jumped up to look out the windows, they blew open from the delayed force of the blast. Luckily, the latches were loose so the glass didn't break under the pressure. A telltale plume of smoke and dust rose on the other side of the courtyard perimeter wall, maybe a block away—the same kind I'd seen the previous year when the Indian Embassy was attacked.

Gunfire ricocheted outside, and the guesthouse guards started running past my window. Shocked, I stepped back, my heart banging in my chest. I grabbed my phone and my backpack, and quickly shoved my passport, emergency contacts, and money stash inside. I called my friend Mike who was staying in another room of the guesthouse to see if he was aware of what was going on. He was an American cameraman from Colorado who worked for NBC and freelanced, and was also one of Christiane's closest friends; she'd introduced us when we were both in Kabul at the same time a year prior.

The security guards were standing on the wall that ran the perimeter of the guesthouse. They were shooting down, and gunmen below that I couldn't see were returning fire. Whatever had blown up wasn't the only target.

Mike didn't answer. My clumsy fingers refused to work the phone and figure out the number of his Afghan cell. I called Travis. Amazingly, he was awake, and he answered on the second ring.

"I know all about it. You okay?"

"Yeah, except the gunfight is outside my window."

I could hear gunfire through his phone and outside my window, almost in stereo, except that I'm deaf in one ear. Two guards ran past my window.

"Okay," he said distractedly. "I've got to go." *Click.*

I wasn't sure what to do. I was too antsy to sit still. I had my bag with my passport and money in my hand. The guards had moved from the wall across from me. I opened my door and stepped out. A guard came toward me, motioning me back inside. "Go, go." I ducked back inside.

I was staying in a room that was in a separate building from the main house. I wanted to know what was going on. I turned on the news, but of course nothing had been reported yet. It had just happened—it was happening now! The BBC was talking about the devastation left by the Chilean earthquake. For about twenty minutes, I alternated between watching the news and pacing the small room. Mike still wasn't answering his phone. Finally, I decided to make a run for the main building to check on him and see what the hotel staff were hearing. There was also a safe room there if the situation got really bad.

With my laptop and my backpack, I ran down the narrow outdoor passage toward the main house and through the courtyard. More guards rushed past me in the opposite direction. I bolted through the door of the guesthouse lobby, where the staff was gathered at the desk watching the news unfold on Al Jazeera. I exchanged pleasantries. They looked concerned but calm. I took deep breaths and tried to appear calmer than I felt. I walked down the hall to knock on Mike's door. No answer. I knocked again. Nothing. Had he simply slept through it? Maybe he used earplugs or sleeping pills. My hands were steadier, so I looked for his Afghan number in my phone and called him. I could hear it ringing on the other side of the door. He picked up.

"Where are you?" he said quietly into the phone.

"Outside your door." I replied. The door opened, and I hung up.

He was dressed in a pale cream shalwar kameez, with his curly light brown hair looking a little wild as though he'd been running his hands through it.

"Let's get some tea," he said. We walked across the hall to the breakfast room for a cup of tea and news coverage on Al Jazeera with several other guests already sitting at tables. Gunfire still rang out occasionally, prompting looks around to read the reaction of the staff and each other.

We ate, drank tea, and discussed what was unfolding. The majority of the news on Al Jazeera was still focused on the Chilean earthquake. There was no news yet on the attack.

"Why didn't you answer the door when I knocked?"

"Do you remember the big attack in Mumbai a couple of years ago?"

"Yes."

"Well, there were several coordinated attacks. One of them was at a large hotel."

"I vaguely remember—huge death toll, right?"

"It was big. During that attack on the hotel, the gunmen went door to door, knocking, and when the guests answered, they shot them."

"Oh."

Mike got up for a second cup of tea, and when he sat down, he began to share a few things he'd learned in a security training class for media he'd taken through the news network he worked for.

"Look, the overall goal in situations like this, or in a kidnapping, is to stay alive for as long as possible—not necessarily to get away."

He used a few mistakes I'd made as examples of what he'd learned in the security training.

"The first thing you did wrong is going to the window when the explosion hit. If gunmen had been inside the compound, they would have seen you. Or you could have been injured by glass shattering from the force of the blast. You were lucky that your latches gave way on these weak windows." I gulped and took a sip of tea.

"The second mistake you made was going outside. You heard gunfire, you saw guards, but you were too anxious to wait it out. But outside, you could get hit by a stray bullet, or kidnapped if gunmen had gotten inside."

It was pretty obvious when it's laid out like that.

"I understand wanting to know what's going on and wanting to be near hotel staff or in a public area, so you should make it a point to consider location when you choose your room in the future. You also should always find a hiding place and an escape route from your room whenever you first get settled. Sometimes, the bathroom windows are big enough for someone small like you to squeeze through. Your size is also good for hiding so that if gunmen break into rooms and you can't escape, you can make it look empty so they don't search the room."

Travis called my cell to check in with Mike, who he was supposed to be helping out with some filming. He wanted to know what the plan was with this unexpected turn of events. He was getting footage from the bomb site and was calling me from the motorcycle. He abruptly hung up, and two minutes later he called back.

"Hey, you okay?" I asked.

"Sorry. There was a body in the street and I almost ran it over."

"Seriously? You okay?"

"Yeah, I'm going to get some more footage, and I'll come by the guesthouse after I'm done."

"All right, be careful."

"No worries, mate." Sure, no worries, mate. Except carnage, bodies in the street, and a big-ass explosion.

He joined us for breakfast an hour or so later. The news on the television in the breakfast room was still piecing it together, but the gunfire in the streets had stopped. He showed us some of the footage from the bomb site—essentially a giant crater—and from the gunfight near the City Center. He'd been standing behind a pole, holding his camera out to the side of his face at eye level, when a tracer whizzed by, with a flash of red and an unmistakable sound.

"Holy crap, Trav. That's a little close!"

"Yeah, I know, but I've already got a news agency that wants to buy the footage. I'm glad I went. I don't usually cover bombings. It was really ugly down there. Going to be a lot of casualties. Anything on the news yet?"

"No, it's still mostly the Chilean earthquake. Al Jazeera had a quick update that a car bomb went off. That's it so far. But it's going off on Twitter."

"Yeah, it will take awhile for the news agencies to report."

Travis and Mike drank some tea while they planned the filming schedule. They had only communicated via e-mail until this morning. Mike had needed someone local to be a second cameraman with some street smarts. He remembered meeting Travis on an earlier trip, and I'd reconnected them. They were going to work together for a few days of filming in some rural communities with a nonprofit that had hired Mike to document.

Najibullah came by an hour later to check in with me as we'd originally planned, but we canceled the scheduled meeting he'd made for that afternoon. He said hello to Travis while I made him a cup of tea and introduced him to Mike.

Throughout the afternoon, the city's inhabitants began to emerge to tackle the cleanup. I offered to pick up kebabs for Mike who was getting ready to film an interview at the guesthouse.

"Sure, but take Travis. I'd feel better considering this morning's events. I don't need him right now."

Travis grabbed his jacket and tossed me my keys. "You drive. Your bike's outside."

I caught them nervously. It was the first time back on my bike since I'd arrived and it had been raining all morning. We drove a few blocks through roads flooded by spring rains. The intersections by the guesthouse had notoriously bad drainage. Puddles got so deep that I nearly submerged the tailpipe. There were pools of blood that splashed up on my jeans as we rode through.

I pulled over. "You drive. I'm too sketched out. Please?"

I knew he'd had a rougher morning than I had, literally dodging bullets, but he also rode a motorcycle every day. I hadn't ridden at all since my last visit in the fall, and I felt twitchy from the blood I'd driven through. A month or so later, I would randomly read in a friend's blog that someone had slaughtered a cow there and that was probably the source of the blood.

Travis took over, and we drove the few blocks toward the City Center building. The multilevel tower that housed a hotel and shopping center had its windows blown out. Glass was everywhere, and the police were out in force. On every street, Afghans were sweeping up glass and boarding up blown-out windows. Travis pointed out the pole in the traffic circle he'd been hiding behind during the gunfight he'd filmed.

Throughout the day, news stations pieced together more of the attack. A car bomb had targeted the Park Residence guesthouse, just a few blocks away from my guesthouse. Seventeen were dead and thirty-four injured—a stark reminder not to take anything for granted. My heart went out to all those who hadn't survived. That night, I sat up in bed late, thinking about my choices and the risks I was taking, and how that might affect Devon and my family.

It was cold. The electricity was out, and therefore so was my heat. I got out of bed and put my insulated jacket on over my yoga pants and sweatshirt, kept on my wool socks, and crawled back into bed, burrowing deep under the thin blanket.

A few hours later I was awakened by my bed shaking. My first thought was, *Seriously? Again?* I assumed it was another attack and struggled to figure out why my bed was rocking. The sound of a headboard banging against a wall confused me. *Are my neighbors shagging next door?* But there was no moaning from the other side of the wall, and I was in Kabul; it was unlikely that my guesthouse neighbors were getting it on.

Hmmm . . . What else makes the bed rock?

Oh, yeah, Earthquake.

But I'm not near Chile! My four-in-the-morning mental fog made it difficult for me to tell whether I was awake or having a dream resulting from a stint watching *BBC World News.* Most of the day's news had focused around the Chilean earthquake, and maybe it had infiltrated my subconscious. The shaking stopped, and I reached down in the dark and grabbed my laptop off the floor. I sat up, placing the laptop on my bed, and turned it on. It was too soon for any news, but Twitter revealed in less than five minutes that I hadn't been the only one woken up by a shakefest. Someone posted a link explaining there had been an earthquake with an epicenter in the Hindu Kush.

I'd been back in Kabul only forty-eight hours and my nerves were already fried.

Three days later, I left for Kandahar with the security report update from a friend that my guesthouse was on the Taliban hit list. I wasn't surprised per se. Any foreigner-occupied guesthouse would be a potential target, but the official knowledge unnerved me. I was still a little edgy from my "welcome back." Now came a NDIS report that ten Kandahari suicide bombers had entered Kabul two days ago.

I'd again hired Travis to document this trip though we both knew it was a long shot that he'd be able to video inside the prison. I was glad for the company, although perhaps he'd been living in a war zone for too long—four or five years now—or perhaps he needed a vacation; his mood over the past two trips was increasingly foul. Still, it was easier to hire and work with him rather than searching for someone I didn't know. I also trusted him more than anyone else I knew in Afghanistan. He was the most reliable travel companion and advisor I had, and I was grateful to be able to hire him for projects like this one. His advice and gut instincts were crucial.

After an hour-and-a-half commercial flight out of Kabul, we exited the plane on the Kandahar airfield and walked to the main terminal. The Kandahar airport's architecture was distinctly dated.

Unlike the typical concrete blocks that many public buildings in Afghanistan resembled, this terminal was built in the sixties and suggested a uniquely modernistic view of the future. Sweeping arches framed large windows that looked out on the airfield and beyond, reminding me of Tomorrowland at Disney World. Outside the terminal was a small "garden," a bizarre patch of grass with plastic wood scattered throughout. Images of an Afghan theme park popped into my head. I almost wanted to take a posed photo with Travis as though we were just happy tourists on vacation.

For the rest of our public appearances until we were back on the plane to Kabul, we assumed the attitudes of husband and wife. We went past the plastic garden and down the gravel road to the main security gates. The March chill and rain of Kabul were a distant memory as a warm breeze and full sun greeted us. We walked about a mile down the road to a parking area where our fixer, Sharif, was waiting beside—surprise, surprise—a white Toyota Corolla. Sharif was shorter than me, around five foot five, and had a very traditional Pashtun face with dark skin and large dark brown eyes framed with black lashes. When he greeted us, he exuded a gentleness that put me immediately at ease.

"*Salaam Alekum*, Shannon. It is very nice to meet you. You are most welcome in Kandahar," he said with smiling eyes.

"*Salaam*, Sharif," I replied. "*Tashakur*." Then I realized that my Dari was relatively useless in Kandahar. I knew two words of Pashto.

"Now, for the drive into Kandahar City, it is not far, but I must request you to put on your burqa."

"I understand. Thank you, Sharif," I replied. I pulled the blue-bird burqa out of my backpack.

It was just ten miles from the airport to Kandahar City, but it was one of the most dangerous roads in the province. It connected not just the airport but the U.S. military airfield and base to the city. Because it was the only road into Kandahar City, it was convoy central and thus one hell of a target area to hit both foreigners and military—two birds, one bomb.

Just the previous week, the bridge on the road had been hit with a car bomb when an American military convoy went past. As we drove across the bridge, Sharif pointed to where one entire lane was missing, the gaping expanse showing the ground far below.

As we spoke with Sharif, he quickly moved past formal niceties to the harsher realities and safety precautions he wanted me to take while working with him.

"The burqa for you is a necessity not just for culture, but for preventing a kidnapping. A Taliban attack is not necessarily the biggest danger for you. Kidnapping is. There have been thirty-eight kidnappings in the past thirty days—mostly wealthy businessmen and foreigners kidnapped for a ransom. For money." Kidnappings by both Taliban and criminals were increasing around Afghanistan, but Kandahar was worse simply because security there was far worse. We agreed that I'd wear the burqa anywhere outside the air-port or hotel so that I would go unnoticed in the backseat of the Corolla, like any other invisible woman.

Forty-five minutes later, I was relieved to arrive at our guest-house, not just because of the dangerous drive but because being seated in the backseat of a warm car in a burqa, I was quickly run-ning out of oxygen. I kept lifting the bottom of the front flap and waving it back and forth to circulate some air. Focusing my vision through the mesh also took some getting used to. It was one thing to do so for a short period of time, but quite another when trying to see what was happening outside the window. Men in brown shal-war kameez, large shawls, and turbans whizzed by on motorcycles, the wind billowing their shawls dramatically, like a scene out of

Mad Max. I saw no women until we got closer to the city outskirts. There were women in burqas of all colors—a palette of sage green, pale green, a deep eggplant, and light brown took precedence over the bluebirds and doves I was used to seeing throughout Kabul and the north. The most obvious difference was that there were no female faces anywhere on the street; women wore burqas without exception, their eyes barely visible behind the mesh.

At the guesthouse, the registration desk explained to Sharif that we were the only guests. As we walked to the block of rooms overlooking a garden surrounded by high walls, we discovered that half of the building was completely destroyed. Perhaps this explained the lack of guests? Sharif said that a couple of weeks earlier the guesthouse had been bombed. The Taliban had launched rockets over the wall since it was one of the few foreign guesthouses still operating in Kandahar. It was the only option we'd found. Most foreigners now stayed on the military base or in private NGO compounds. On one side, our set of rooms looked perfectly suitable. On the other, next to the perimeter wall, a similar set of rooms was all but destroyed.

Sharif also said that the road along our guesthouse was regularly attacked because of a girls' school that was behind our building. Locals had found three mines there in one day. Sharif had several nieces going to the school and was visibly concerned as we talked about the violence that the Taliban directed toward it and the Afghan people in general.

I found the juxtaposition of that violence and the current serenity in the guesthouse courtyard hard to comprehend: sunshine, a lush patch of green grass, flowers blooming, and a warm breeze. It didn't feel like one of the most dangerous cities in Afghanistan, even with the bombed-out section.

But this was the province where, in November 2008, during my first visit to Afghanistan with Tony, several girls were attacked with acid as they walked to school. The story had been covered in *The New York Times* by Dexter Filkins, and it had made headlines in Kabul. This was the province where the Afghans believed "he who controls Kandahar, controls Afghanistan." It was the key to the country, and a fierce battle was brewing. Educating anyone, boy or girl, was met with fierce resistance in most of the province. Only in city centers were there schools, accessible health care, and Internet cafés, albeit with great risks. Rural areas were a wasteland of opportunity due to the lack of jobs, resources, and education, as well as the extreme poverty and ongoing battle for territory between the Taliban and international forces. Women had few or no rights, girls couldn't attend school, and boys' education was typically limited to religious studies at madrassas.

It surprised me that the Taliban could retain power and control while putting the lives of their people in the crossfire of their ideology. Sharif talked about the irony of the terrorists calling themselves Taliban. He explained that Taliban were originally religious scholars, and in fact the word Taliban means "student" in Dari. Today the majority of the Taliban community were common people—illiterate, unable to read the holy book they were so vested in. Instead, religious leaders interpreted the original teachings as they liked and instilled that interpretation, however mutated, into the heads of young boys They were polluting already muddy waters, stunting Afghanistan's growth, ensuring that its people remained the helpless victims of their militant countrymen.

Sharif quickly proved himself to be not only a capable fixer and trustworthy advisor, but a wonderful storyteller. Over a pot of milky tea brewed with cardamom in Travis's room, Sharif told us that during Taliban times, he'd been in Pakistan and graduated from the university in Peshawar with a degree in agriculture, though he'd never used it. He returned and worked as an English teacher at a boys' school in his village while the Taliban were still in charge. He showed us a photo ID of himself with a long beard and an elaborate black silk turban—a dead ringer for any one on a Taliban watch list. His solemn expression, long beard, and turban made him nearly unrecognizable from the kind man sitting before me. I asked if I could take a photo of the ID and a portrait of him now. He still wore a thick beard, but much shorter, maybe only an inch long instead of the Taliban's required fist length, and his eyes were kinder than in the ID photo. It was fascinating to see the simple difference a beard, turban, and stern look could make.

Sharif admitted to me that his family didn't know he was working for us. He used to work regularly as a translator and fixer with foreign journalists, but his wife had become increasingly worried about his safety. Sharif explained that he liked the work. It was often interesting, he was exposed to many different nationalities, and it supported his family. He said he also felt he was helping in a small way by making sure others could tell stories of Kandahar to the world. But even though he continued, he took fewer risks than before and didn't tell his wife.

The only family member who knew what he was up to was a nephew. Sharif called the young boy in to do a little shopping for us. Sharif had decided that I needed a new burqa before we visited the prison. He'd deemed my blue burqa from Kabul too "risqué" for the Kandahar scene. Too short? Too blue? Who knew? Sharif couldn't explain exactly, so I simply acquiesced. It's a pretty telling sign of the culture when you can feel whorish in a burqa.

The nephew came to the guesthouse with a brown burqa. It was also too short for me, but it wouldn't be seen other than in a car and inside the prison as I wasn't allowed to walk in the streets or visit the market. He'd also purchased several phone cards for us to give as gifts to the deputy and his guards at the prison. This should allow us more access and hopefully allow Travis to film. He said the cards were better than cash because they gave the appearance of gifts rather than bribes.

Sharif handed me a beautiful cream-colored scarf embroidered with different tones of gold and brown—a perfect complement to the colors of Kandahar.

"A gift from me to you," he said.

"Thank you, Sharif. It's beautiful, I am honored." I immediately swapped my plain black head scarf for it.

He smiled back warmly. "I hope you will wear it and think of Kandahar."

Next, he handed Travis a men's kaffiyeh scarf in local colors. Travis was also visibly touched by the gift and wore it for the rest of the trip.

Sharif got a call that the Canadians were currently doing a routine inspection at the prison. As in Maimana with the Norwegians, here in Kandahar the Canadians were in charge of reconstruction projects and that included the prison. We couldn't show up during their visit, and as the daylight hours were ticking away, I worried that we'd miss our opportunity to meet with the commander. If we did, we'd have to wait a couple of days. I was especially keen not to stay indefinitely in a guesthouse that had already been half destroyed. I requested another pot of milky tea, and we settled into Travis's room to escape the sun. Sharif sat at the desk, I sat cross-legged at the foot of the bed, and Travis sat at its head, propped against the wall with a pillow. Sharif helped us pass the hours by talking about Kandahar, the city, and the Taliban. Sharif was a beautiful storyteller and knowledgeable historian. He shared much about his own life and those of his family alongside the region's history. When we finally got the call that we were clear to go, I was almost sorry to interrupt storytime.

The commander of Kandahar's prison was by far the most accessible and friendly official I'd yet encountered. Not only did he grant us access with nothing more than a cursory glance at my Ministry of Justice introduction papers, he allowed a video camera inside. Travis grinned at me and winked, then started unpacking his equipment. We had yet to get permission to film or take photos in any of the prisons we'd visited. Occasionally, once we were in, we could take some portraits of the women with their permission. We had been kicked out of the Kabul prison before for carrying a camera.

We went into his office for the requisite tea to discuss what we'd like to accomplish by visiting the women. Once seated, he thanked me for wearing the burqa for culture and security, but then said, "I realize this is not your culture, so please, make yourself at home. You do not need to wear this inside."

I was happy to remove the brown burqa, but I was mortified that I'd forgotten to bring a head scarf. I felt naked without it and was self-conscious of going from one extreme to the other, my blond hair messily pulled back in a ponytail. But no one seemed at all concerned, so I tried to relax and focus on what needed to get done.

Travis asked the commander if he could video the meeting. The commander immediately nodded and put on his hat and proceeded to hold court, playing to the camera. He seemed sincerely proud of what he and the Canadian PRT were doing to improve conditions in the prison. He told us he was originally from Wardak, the same province that Parweez made the awful dinner jokes about and where Parliamentarian Dr. Wardak was from. It was another predominantly Pashtun province close to Kabul where the Taliban was reemerging. He'd previously been the deputy commander at Kabul's infamous Pul-e-Charkhi prison, notorious for torture and executions, with frequent prison breaks and riots as recently as 2008. The living conditions of the prison have been criticized by several human rights groups due to overcrowding and subpar living conditions. After forty minutes of tea drinking and questions, the commander stood. "Come, I will show you around now."

Inside the door, I immediately heard the laughter of children. There was a small playground. Two swings and a slide took up a large part of the dirt courtyard. I smiled at the children playing there, and they bashfully came over as I crouched to shake their little hands. They giggled and raced off to find their mothers. The commander gestured for me to sit on a swing, then proceeded to push me as if this were a summer day at the park. I fully expected him to buy me an ice-cream cone next. Surreal didn't begin to cover it.

Travis set his camera and tripod up in an unobtrusive spot to film. Surprised to be able to film, he was incredibly kind with the curious children and women who emerged to talk with me, fully aware that some may not want to be on film. He filmed so discreetly that soon even I forgot he was there.

Beyond the playground was a small building that contained the women's rooms where they ate, slept, and studied. It felt more like the Mazar-i-Sharif prison—communal rooms and dirt courtyards but in slightly better condition. I realized that I'd expected it to be much worse simply because it was in Kandahar. I'd expected this visit to be one of the most depressing in terms of conditions and commanders, and yet it was well run, at least on the surface.

The commander told us he'd recently completed a training exchange at a prison in South Carolina, courtesy of the American Embassy—just as the commander we'd met in Maimana had done an exchange in the United States and Norway. Such exchanges appeared to be extremely beneficial to the prisoners under their care.

Afghan women's prisons in particular had been infamous for the high rate of rape by male prison guards. Most women's prisons now had female guards, which lessened the level of abuse, though there were still babies born in prison. When I asked about this in front of guards or commanders around the country, they often replied simply, "You should not ask such difficult questions."

It was hard enough to imagine being raped and then thrown in jail for it, charged with adultery while the attacker lived out his life freely, with no repercussions. But to then face systematic rape from your jailers? Only an estimated 6 percent of rapists faced jail time in the United States, but at least the victims weren't subject to the double atrocity of being jailed.

As we walked to the back courtyard, women gathered and several pulled on my sleeve to tell me their stories. They clustered around me and described escaping arranged marriages, murdering their husbands, rape by male family members, and on and on. All of these stories were similar to those I'd heard in other prisons—the women incarcerated with little knowledge of their sentence. Many didn't know how long they would be there. Few had received legal representation to plead their case in court. When facing an accuser in front of a male judge, what chance did any of them have if a woman's voice was worth only two-thirds or in other cases, only half of a man's? Examples of this abound throughout Islamic law, or Sharia law, which states that two women would need to testify against one man. Sharia is the basis for personal status laws in most Islamic majority nations. These personal status laws determine rights of women in matters of marriage, divorce, and child custody. A 2011 UNICEF report concluded that Sharia law provisions were discriminatory against women from a human rights perspective. In legal proceedings under Sharia law, a woman's testimony is worth half of a man's before a court. Pakistani scholar Javed Ahmad Ghamidi has written that Islam asks for two women witnesses against one male because this responsibility is not very suited to their temperament, sphere of interest, and usual environment.

I'd met with a deputy minister of justice in Kabul six months prior and asked him about the judicial system in regards to women's rights. He spoke openly about the rights technically afforded to women in the current constitution. His opinion was that the issue was not in the affordance of their rights under the judicial system but in the implementation of the justice system—not enough lawyers, too many corrupt officials, and longstanding cultural norms. Most of the women were illiterate, lacked access to money to afford a lawyer or pay necessary bribes, and most lacked even the knowledge of their rights or of what to ask for.

Rape most often fell under the crime of adultery and landed women in jail—that is, if anyone actually learned about it. Many women, especially those in conservative provinces, were simply dealt with through Sharia law or "cultural courts" within families and communities: shot, beheaded, stoned to death, or simply beaten and disowned by their family. On the helicopter ride to Khost with Sahera Sharif, I'd asked if Khost City had a women's prison. She smiled wryly and replied, "We are Pashtun. Our women do not need prisons. We deal with our crimes ourselves." Irony was heavy in her voice—frustration and defeat apparent even through the helicopter noise.

Kandahar prison was where I met Nooria, a woman who has become a symbol of everything I strive for. Nooria was accused of killing the son of her husband's other wife. He blamed her, she denied it—a game of he said, she said. Regardless, she was the fifth wife of her husband. He was sixty-five and she was twenty, and she'd been his wife for four years—married off to him when she was sixteen.

She told me that his first three wives were dead—all killed by his beatings and fond use of knives. She shyly pulled up her sleeves and showed me multiple slash scars, as if someone had used her arms as a knife sharpener.

She told me that she felt safer in prison, away from her husband. The women, like in many of the prisons I'd visited, seemed to have formed a sisterhood. They slept, ate, and, when allowed, studied together, and they raised their children communally. I'd asked several women if they felt safer in prison, and many replied that they did. While I couldn't imagine the oppressive loss of freedom as anything less than a death sentence, these women often had very few freedoms outside of prison, so the loss of freedom perhaps wasn't much of a loss when compared to the protection from their husbands. The hardest part of prison for many women was the separation from their children, as only very young children typically remained with the mothers. That, too, I keenly felt, the notion of not being able to see Devon because I'd been raped was mind blowing.

After I'd spoken with the women for a couple of hours, dusk settled in. I knew the commander and his team were waiting to have dinner. I asked Sharif to please tell the women I wished them all the best, that I was grateful for their willingness to speak with me, and that my heart was with them. Then I moved through the crowd, clasping their hands in mine and thanking them individually in Pashto and occasionally in my scant Dari. Nooria pressed a silvery jeweled hair barrette into my hand. She'd taken it from her hair to give to me. I smiled and gently refused, not wanting to take anything from these women, but she insisted. The commander took the barrette from her and tried to put it in my hair but couldn't figure out the clasp. The women laughed at his clumsy fingers, and

Nooria took it back with a small smile and the women turned me around, their hands lightly on my shoulders. I could feel one of the women slide the rubber band out of my long ponytail, then another combing my dirty blond hair roughly with a small plastic comb. A third clipped it neatly together again with the silver barrette. They handed me back my black rubber band, laughing and smiling while Nooria smoothed back a few loose strands from my face and kissed me on the cheek.

I was glad for the cover of darkness as I felt tears building. I smiled, holding back the wave of emotion, and turned to leave with the commander. I paused once to wave and say good-bye again. At the door, Nooria was there waiting for me alone. She clasped my hands tightly, speaking softly in Pashto and not letting go— thanking me for taking the time to visit them, for listening, and for giving them a chance to talk and share. No translation was needed. Sharif recognized the moment and held back, waiting for me to ask for his help. I held her hand for as long as she let me, squeezing lightly, hoping she could sense how much emotion I felt for her. As I turned away from her, the tears released and coursed down my dusty cheeks unchecked.

As we left, I put my burqa back on, seeing for the first and only time its benefit by covering up my overflowing emotions. The commander walked us out and invited us to stay for dinner. We politely declined as it was already late, and we wanted to get back to the guesthouse. He was worried for our safety and insisted on sending us away with a heavily armed escort. A pickup with four armed men in the back followed us to the hotel. Their spotlight shone into the car, illuminating us like a high-profile target in the backseat. I was lost in my thoughts as we drove, hidden under the brown burqa, bouncing along the otherwise dark and empty roads. As we arrived at the hotel and parked in the empty lot, I raised the front of the burqa from my face and thanked Sharif for all he'd done for us that day.

Travis and I walked through the quiet lobby and through the inner courtyard to the back of the hotel. I tried to ignore the bombed-out section that reminded me how risky it was to be there. I went straight to the intact section of the guesthouse rooms.

Travis looked over. "Are you okay?"

I kept facing the door, looking down at my key. "Yeah. Well, no. But I'll be fine." While it was great working with Travis on trips like these, having him document and give advice, his cynicism could be tough at times. I knew he'd think I was ridiculous for getting so upset over a silly barrette. I walked back to my room, dropped my bag, and curled up on my bed. I bawled, uncontrollably, for ten minutes.

Spent, I felt released. I went outside to sit on the concrete stoop outside my door that overlooked the garden in the cool night air. The clear evening sky was filled with the sound of the last call to prayer. I stared into the garden, my mind empty. This place would be beautiful if only it wasn't so damn dangerous.

Dinner arrived ten minutes later and was served in Travis's room. I sat at the bottom of his bed cross-legged, my face blotchy and my eyes red. He appeared to notice but didn't ask any questions, and I didn't offer, but his tone for the rest of the trip was gentler than usual. I stared at the bizarre meat on my plate that looked like lamb with some sort of rubbery skin and fat. At first, I thought it might be the eggplant from lunch until I realized it was all attached. I was hungry enough to dissect it and not think twice about it until my mind wandered to our friend Gilly's recent run-in with dodgy meat in Kandahar. He'd had a rare case of botulism, something I'd actually had to Google the day before to learn its symptoms and how it was contracted. Tainted meat and contaminated canned food was the leading cause apparently. Botulism contained the same toxin used in botox—a poison women spent large amounts of money to inject into their faces to get rid of wrinkles. I crossed my fingers with each bite, though maybe the silver lining would be a reduction of my newly formed crow's feet from the inside out?

To get my mind off the botulism and other such thoughts, I asked Travis what time we were leaving with Sharif to go back to the airport. The road was so dangerous that Sharif wasn't keen to do it again, so he charged an extra $100 just for the drive. I was happy to pay it considering the risk for him and us, and I was more than a little concerned. The feeling that I was tempting fate had been with me this whole trip, ever since the Kabul explosion woke me up a week prior.

With thoughts of botulism and convoy bombers dancing around in my head, I said good night and headed back to my room. My nerves were on edge but I was exhausted—a bit as if I'd had a Red Bull and vodka—and I fell asleep with the lights on, fully dressed. I used my eye mask to create darkness, as though the light would keep the boogeyman away like it did when I was a kid.

Thankfully, it was a peaceful night. I awoke to the call to prayer. The muezzin sounded as if right outside the window, and birds chirped madly. I washed my face. As I was drying it, Sharif knocked. He announced his arrival and that of breakfast, again served in Travis's room.

Travis had just woken, and Sharif and I poured the wonderful milky tea from a brown thermos. It was so much more comforting than the ever-present weak green tea served elsewhere in the country. He took his previous seat at the desk, and I again placed myself cross-legged at the foot of the bed for some fresh naan and fried eggs. Sharif was a bit distracted. I could tell he was not looking forward to the drive since the heaviest convoy traffic took place throughout the morning.

After a tense drive to the airport, skirting around the missing chunk of bridge and pulling off the road when a convoy drove past in the opposite direction, we arrived back at the parking lot where Sharif had picked us up two days prior.

We said good-bye, and I tried to tell Sharif how much I appreciated the risk he'd taken by working with me and asked him to text us later to let us know he'd gotten back safely. I was worried about him, knowing that the Americans had declared the recent offensive in Marjah a success and that an upcoming offensive in Kandahar would be next, increasing the daily risk to him and his family.

Security at the Kandahar airport was much more thorough than in Kabul for its domestic flights. Sniffer dogs walked throughout the men's bags, the main security checks taking place when passengers got inside the terminal.

As soon as we were seated on the plane, Travis was asleep with his headphones in his ears. The desert morphed into snowcapped mountains outside my window while I considered the past few days and wondered what awaited me back in Kabul.

My guesthouse was still standing when I got out of my taxi. At the gate, I smiled at the guards. Sandbagging efforts out front revealed increased security. I grabbed my key at the front desk and asked the new guy working how everyone was.

"Everyone is fine—not to worry. We are fine. No problem," he replied.

I dropped my bags in my room, grabbed my messenger bag and helmet, and took my motorcycle out for a spin to clear the cobwebs and get a coffee and a botox-free lunch.

An hour later, a fig croissant was in my belly, and I was slowly sipping a second cappuccino while sitting in a red plastic chair. My table on the stone patio overlooked the garden at Le Bistro. My thoughts kept returning to Nooria and my reaction to her gift. Why had I reacted so emotionally when we left? I'd visited many prisons in Afghanistan, all of them heartbreaking in their own way. All of them tugged at my soul, threatening to harden it with cynicism so that I could keep the strength to continue hearing these stories without losing myself in them. I couldn't remember the last time I'd cried about anything. Had my heart already hardened? If it had, it was long before Afghanistan.

10

Whore

New York and Afghanistan 2009

My skeleton finally came out of the closet in a very public way one sunny spring day in 2009, before an audience of millions. I was tapping an interview with NBC's Ann Curry for *Dateline*. We were sitting in a small darkened office in Rockefeller Center, spotlights illuminating us and blinding me to everything in my periphery. I'd presented to Ann a key point about the backbone of my work and efforts with Mountain2Mountain. I was telling her that I believed we needed to transform the perception of victimhood, both as individuals and globally if we were ever to combat the apathy that prevented action.

I'd met Ann two weeks prior to this interview at a women's heroin rehab clinic on the outskirts of Kabul. I was doing initial research with the staff and founder to see if I could do some work with the women there—literacy classes or establish safe houses for those who had no home to go back to. I was also considering what could be done for the children living on site with them. I'd brought toys and supplies for a kindergarten and discussed what could be done post-rehab with the women to ensure they had options. Like those in prisons, many here were disowned by their families. The stigma of drugs and prison was such that even when I'd talked to educated women in the government, they spoke as if these women were beyond help and would forever be victims relegated to the streets.

Ann's cameraman was my friend Mike, and he invited me for a drink to the Serena Hotel, where many of the major news teams holed up in Kabul. I arrived at the gates of the country's only five-star hotel on the back of Travis's motorcycle. I'd just ridden to the other side of town to visit an orphanage run by an Australian woman who Travis thought I might like to meet. I invited him to come with me to the Serena since we were running late. Given that he was a freelance photographer and insider, I also considered that he and Mike should meet.

As I walked through the glass doors into the opulent lobby covered in dust from head to toe, I became aware that I was, as usual, a complete mess. My long pale blue skirt that I wore over my jeans and motorcycle boots was more brown than blue. My head scarf was dusty, and I caught a waft of gasoline as I pulled it back. I smoothed my hair that had escaped its ponytail. My face, it seemed, had absorbed the brunt of the dusty ride, and when I removed my sunglasses, Mike laughed loudly.

"Would you like to use the bathroom to clean up a bit?" he asked quietly.

I glanced at Travis, and he said in his ever-cool Melbourne accent, "Um, yeah, you'd best get cleaned up a little, dahling." I raised my eyebrow questioning.

I walked down the hallway to a bathroom. I barely recognized myself. I had a dark monobrow, dust having covered the empty space around my sunglasses. My face was a different color altogether, and my two front teeth had a smudge of gritty dust across them.

"Good lord!" I exclaimed, grabbing a towel and turning on the faucet.

Mike had forwarded on a couple of my blog posts to Ann's producer, who would also be on the trip. Unbeknownst to me, I was having dinner with the entire production crew. Mike had figured if we were to meet in Kabul, the crew may as well meet me, too, in case there was any interest in what I was doing. They'd arrived several days ahead of Ann to research and chase down potential stories. Over a buffet dinner that could rival Vegas, I shared what I was working on in Afghanistan. We discussed how my approach to working there was different from that of many NGO's: my lack of professional security, my friendship and trust with the Afghans I worked with, my interest in projects that focused on individuals over sticks-and-bricks projects, and my focus on youth activists and female leaders. We also discussed my desire to travel the country and really see it in unique ways, although I hardly needed to explain that as they were all privy to my motorcycle entrance.

Having Travis there proved useful as he was one of many freelance journalists who'd lived in Afghanistan long-term, without security, among the Afghans. He traveled mostly by motorcycle, for freedom and fun, and because it cut through Kabul's crippling traffic. He shared his own view of the country from the perspective of one who lived a real life there outside of a compound. His inside views of Afghanistan gave weight to how I presented my own work there, minimizing the risk of having a cynical news crew label me a Pollyanna or a stereotypical do-gooder.

Talk moved to my work in the women's prisons and the women's heroin rehab center. They were intrigued, and by the time coffee rolled around, they asked if they could tag along.

It soon became apparent after a couple of meetings the next day that the crew wouldn't be allowed to accompany me into the Kabul prison. No filming was allowed, and news crews weren't generally welcomed. But the rehab center had no such restrictions, and they came along to my first meeting with the director who ran the center out of passion for the women and their plight, and with very little funding. They filmed me interviewing several of the women and followed me later to the market where I bought toys and supplies for the children in the kindergarten and brought them back to distribute. I also discussed plans for a playground and a part-time preschool teacher with the director.

A few days later, when Ann arrived in Kabul, the team developed the footage into a story about children addicted to heroin for the Today Show. Ann met with several street children and addicts, and followed the story to the clinic. She asked to interview me briefly at the rehab center about my work with women and children and my views on drug addiction.

We met outside the clinic in the front garden on a particularly beautiful spring day before the heat and the dust really kicked in. Mike wired me for sound and told me to stay relaxed and have a conversation with Ann. After some small talk, we got into the interview, and I got my first taste of Ann's penetrating gaze. Her black eyes searched deeply, and I found it a little destabilizing at first to be speaking with someone so intensely focused on what I was saying.

When we finished, I got on my motorcycle, and they got into their two-vehicle convoy with security guards, and we parted.

A week later, I was sitting at my desk at the Park Palace, listening to Al Jazeera English and wondering why the bathroom drains always smelled so toxic, when I got a call from Justin Balding, Ann Curry's producer who I'd met at the Serena.

"Hi, Shannon, this is Justin Balding from NBC."

"Hi, Justin, how you? Are you guys still in Kabul?"

"No, we are back in New York. How are things?"

"Pretty good, considering. What's going on?"

"Well, the reason I called is I wondered, is there any chance you could fly home via New York? We would like to interview you in the studio with Ann."

"Seriously?"

"Seriously. We would like to do a story on your efforts. It's a good story."

"Wow. Thank you, Justin. I'd be thrilled for the opportunity. Thank you."

"No worries. I'll call you in a few days to check in, and I'll get our production assistant to figure out flights with you. She'll handle all the logistics for you. Be safe."

So eight days later, there I was, in this small darkened office, sitting on a chair across from Ann with bright spotlights illuminating us and making it impossible to see Justin and the rest of the crew watching on the couch and in the doorway.

Ann started getting personal. She wanted answers. She wanted to know why—why did I risk my life in Afghanistan when back home I was a single mother to a young daughter? Why at the age of thirty-two had I given up financial stability to work in a war zone? And why did I work in such an unorthodox and potentially dangerous way for a woman, traveling around Afghanistan alone, without security, often by motorcycle?

"Because," I said. "Because I have to." I paused, waiting for Ann to jump in, but she didn't. Her eyes searched mine. "Because if I don't, who will?"

Ann's dark eyes held my own and made it difficult to concentrate. Softly but firmly, she said, "That's not good enough."

It's not good enough? I thought frustrated. Well, shit, what was "good enough?" I had no idea *why*. I was just doing what I was doing.

I laughed nervously, trying to buy time, not sure *what* to say, worried about what was going to come out of my mouth.

"Is this going to be a Barbara Walters moment?" I joked, suddenly more aware that the cameras were rolling.

"No," she said, still holding my gaze intently, "but if you're saying that we have to be transformed, then we have to be honest about what transformed you."

Something shifted inside me. She was right. It wasn't good enough. Not anymore. My closest friends didn't know the truth, and my family didn't know the details. For more than a decade, I hadn't spoken about what happened to me that dark, frigid Minneapolis night. I had rarely even thought about it. And yet now, on national television, it came to me in a rush that my own personal catastrophe, my own victimization, defined everything I had become and was motivating everything I was doing in life. An epiphany caught on camera.

"Okay," I said, looking straight back into her gaze. I'd avoided the real answers for so long I'd nearly forgotten what they were.

I closed my eyes, took a deep breath, and remembered a saying I'd heard many times in the past—the truth will set you free.

"Okay," I said again, and again looked into her eyes. "When I was eighteen, I was raped and nearly killed."

It was late Spring of 1993, and I had come to Minneapolis to pursue my dream as a modern dancer. I had taken the wrong bus home late from work, which meant I had to walk the darkly lit paths through Loring Park to reach my apartment on the other side. I was lost in my thoughts, hunkered down in the cold with my hands in my pockets, considering my chosen path as a modern dancer and whether it was the correct decision for me after all. Suddenly, a hand reached from behind me and clasped me around my mouth. Another powerful hand grabbed me around the chest and forced me backward along the path to uneven dirt and grass, my feet tripping over themselves. I struggled until I felt the cold, sharp edge of a knife against my throat.

I fell face first as my attacker shoved me into the dirt. He applied his boot to my head, pinning me in place, the pressure threatening to crush my skull. Dirt filled my nostrils and mouth, making it hard to breathe. "Don't move," he said in a low, menacing voice.

I heard his belt buckle clank and his zipper being undone, and I panicked, struggling under the pressure from his boot. *He's going to have to take his foot off my head to do anything,* I thought, so I would lash out when the pressure let up, and then I would roll away, scream, and run for help. I felt for all my limbs so as to get my bearings, and I tried to brace myself on the ground. I waited for what felt like an eternity, tense, like a sprinter listening for the starting gun.

I felt him remove his boot and I thought, *Go! Go now!* Yet with the same foot that he had just used to pin my head, he kicked me hard in my ribs, causing me to instead curl into the fetal position. Again the boot made contact. And again. And again. I lay there pathetically in the dirt wincing at each kick, trying to protect myself. Thoughts of bolting evaporated as I struggled to simply breathe. Then he grabbed me and forced me onto my back. Before I could uncurl, kick back, or even take a breath, the knife was at my throat again. I froze and looked up to see his eyes boring into me through his ski mask. "I told you, don't move!"

He pinned my legs with his knees and applied his full weight to my body, crushing me. His free hand punched me again and again, the force of his punches causing him to inadvertently dig the knife into my skin with his other hand. He grabbed my hair and slammed my head back into the dirt. The knife remained, pressing in hard, but he let go of my hair and fumbled with my pants. The knife made small cuts along my throat as his hand bounced around, his body weight cutting off circulation in my limbs. I tried to say no, but it came out as more of a whimper. Hot tears coursed down my cheeks as he punched me again in the face. I felt his knife slice a new cut, warm blood running down the side of my neck.

His hand was inside my underwear now. Taking off his glove with his teeth, he pulled and tore my underwear, his nails goring my skin, ripping at the most sensitive parts of me. He plunged into me and it felt like he was ripping me in two from the inside. He grunted and the knife cut into my throat, and then he put his bare hand on my mouth and nose, nearly suffocating me and pressing my head into the ground again. I nearly passed out from the pain. As he thrust inside me, his hand pressing harder into my face, I could feel myself drifting away. More grunting and a sharp cut across my lower abdomen brought me back. He would thrust a few times and then cut me, thrust a few times and then cut me again—as though to keep me alert, or because he liked the sight of my blood, or because he could.

Eventually, he stopped the cutting and sped up his thrusting. I felt my head sliding back and forth in the dirt. *Stupid, stupid, stupid,* I thought hazily. It became a sort of mantra. *Stupid, stupid, stupid.* How could I have let this happen? Why had I cut through the park? Why hadn't I taken the right bus? Why hadn't I walked with my head up and my hands out of my pockets?

Three slow deep thrusts, and he mercifully groaned, shuddered, and stopped. Blood dripped down my belly and my neck, mixing with the stream of hot tears into the dirt below. Warm liquid stung my insides and dripped to the ground as he pulled out of me. I closed my eyes, unable to move, my tears and blood intermingling in the dirt beneath me. Was he going to slit my throat?

Keeping his hand over my nose and mouth, he pushed himself up to his feet. He bent over, kicked me twice again, and replaced his hand with his boot. He needn't have bothered; I didn't have the lung power to breathe, much less scream. He pulled up his pants and looked down at me, his eyes dark behind the ski mask. "Whore," he said, practically spitting the word. And then he left.

I lay there. I waited for whatever was coming next, not believing he was gone. But nothing happened. I listened to the sound of the leaves rustling in the wind. Keeping my eyes closed, I tried bending my knees, placing my feet on the ground, and rolling onto my side. The pain coupled with the realization of what had just happened caused me to vomit violently. The heaving wracked my bruised abdomen and possibly broken ribs, and I started crying again. My hair was matted with dirt and blood, and when I gently touched the back of my head to inspect the damage, I nearly passed out.

Somehow I eventually staggered to my feet, pulled up my pants, and rearranged my clothes as best I could. I stumbled onto the path and looked around. I squinted under the glare of the street lamp, my head swimming. I willed myself to put one foot in front of the other, just wanting to get home, but the path never seemed to get any closer to the sidewalk on the other side of the park.

I had been praying that someone would find me, see me, hear something. Now, finally, someone turned up. A man in a suit and overcoat walked toward me and, upon seeing what a state I was in, tried to grab me to help.

I recoiled, and he stepped back.

"Miss," he asked, "what happened? Are you okay? What can I do?"

I shook my head and tears began to pour anew. He tried to touch me and again I backed away like a frightened animal. He removed his overcoat and held it out.

"Please," he said, "take it."

I shook my head, just wanting to get home.

"Where are you going?" he asked. "Can I help you?"

I nodded and pointed down the street.

"You live down here?"

I nodded again.

"Can I take you to the hospital? Please. Can I call the police?"

I shook my head. "Please, I just want to go home."

He seemed unsure. Watching my face for signs of fear or resistance, he gently put the coat around my shoulders. It covered me down to my calves and felt like a warm blanket. He walked me to the door of my brownstone a block away. When I reached the door, it occurred to me that I might not have my keys or money. By a small miracle, I had my keys. I felt a wave of relief wash over me to not have to return to the park.

The man waited as I unlocked the main door. He made no move to step closer.

"Please, miss, can I call someone? Anyone?"

I shook my head again and took off his coat. Handing it back to him, I felt sorry that I had probably gotten blood and dirt on it.

"Thank you. Thank you," I mouthed softly as I turned to go inside the lobby.

Upstairs in my apartment, I pushed the bookcase in front of my door and turned on the shower. I spent hours sitting on the bottom of my bathtub under a warm shower, soap and water stinging my cuts and wounds. I tried to clean myself but found everything was just too painful, and I simply plugged the drain and let the water course over me from above and fill up underneath me. When the bath was full, I sat there until the water went cold. The depth of the old clawfoot tub allowed me to stay nearly completely submerged. At some point, I got out and crawled into bed. I stayed there for days. Blood stained through my clothes and the bedclothes. The cuts on my throat and abdomen were too crisscrossed and long to cover with Band-Aids and they were shallow enough that I didn't worry about them. The wound and swelling on the back of my head, my bruised ribs, and my torn up insides were the worst. I lay in bed for several days, in the dark, in a blessed state of fog.

I often think back to that man. Not *that* man. But the one who gave me his coat. That act of kindness. I wonder if our paths have or will cross again. If he knows how much that kindness he showed me has resonated with me, even if I could do little more than grunt and point at the time. How many others would have seen me coming and crossed the road, avoided my gaze as I was avoiding theirs, and just walked past, shaking their heads and wondering what trouble I had gotten into, not wanting to get involved, or not be late for an appointment? But this man saw me, tried to help and tried to comfort me. I will always be grateful for that. It was a welcome contrast to the injustice just done to me by another.

When I made my first call, after coming out of my self-imposed cave, it was to my aunt and uncle in nearby Shakopee, south of Minneapolis. Upon hearing I had been attacked, they drove into the city to get me and take me home with them. I don't remember much about the period that followed. I do know that after several days in Shakopee under their watchful eyes, I moved back home for several months with my family in Bismarck, North Dakota. I told everyone that I had been attacked, not raped. My mother, who'd initially battled my decision to move to Minneapolis, was the first person, and for a while the only one, to know the truth. She figured it out when I made an appointment to visit my OB/GYN to get tested for STDs. I had been too upset and disoriented to go immediately after the rape, but I needed to get an all-clear for my sanity. I was so scared at the doctor's office that I passed out in the chair when the nurses took my blood for the AIDS test.

I dealt with the trauma by trying to push it back into the farthest reaches of my mind. I did whatever I could to act as though nothing had happened. When a close family friend found out I had been raped, she commented to my mother that I "wasn't acting like a rape victim." I briefly started up again with my boyfriend from high school. It felt safe and normal, and yet I pushed him away when things got too familiar, scared he'd never look at me the same if he knew everything. I was afraid to show any vulnerability, yet I also failed to bury what happened so deeply that it wouldn't spill out.

I worked that summer as a maid at a Days Inn, and briefly as a flagger on a road construction crew. I didn't dance once. Not anywhere. Not at a studio. Not at a bar. Not even in my head. I dated. Superficial flirtations that allowed me to pretend to be normal. When autumn came, I moved back to Minneapolis. My mother accompanied me. We stayed together at my aunt and uncle's house in Shakopee.

The first day there, I asked my mom if I could borrow the car to drive into the city.

"I want to drive to the park," I said.

She knew immediately which park I meant, and she simply nodded and gave me the keys. "Take care of you."

I almost cried when she didn't question me or ask to come along. She understood that I needed this and that I needed to do it alone. It was one of the most sensitive things I could remember her doing. I drove to my old apartment and looked for a parking spot. The park was just ahead. I walked to a bench on the outskirts of the park. The sun was high in the sky, and people were bustling around the sidewalks, going about their day. I sat at the edge of the bench, ready to bolt at the slightest hint of a threat. After a minute or two, I took a deep breath and sat back against the bench, willing myself to stay. I sat there for an hour or more in the sunlight, unfocused, just being present in the place that tried to break me. Then I stood up, determined to leave this place behind.

And for most of my entire adult life I did leave it behind. It bubbled to the surface for the first time when I tried to help Larissa. But the pace and juggle of my life, the distance between Pete and me that was leading toward divorce, and my focus on raising Devon, ensured that it was a passing thought, nothing more. But looking back, the guilt of Larissa's attack and my fear of the same happening to Devon allowed what I had repressed to bubble up, slowly, one bubble at a time, over a decade, as though it was an oil slick.

But it was Ann Curry's insistence on voicing the truth to better understand my motivations that broke through the final barriers. I realized that I was not ashamed of what happened. What had happened to me had also happened to my sister. We were two strong, independent women. We were not victims. It happened to women around the world daily. In the United States alone, a woman is raped every two minutes. Why wasn't I talking about it? Why wasn't everyone talking about it?

But it wasn't until I met Nooria that the dam broke—the personal connection we made, the barrette, the unique situation of talking alone with the women, without security guards listening in. I saw myself in her. In all of them. I could be any of them. Because I was born to two American parents in the Midwest, in the 1970s, my life was very different than the ones these women led. As a rape victim, if I had been born in Afghanistan instead of the United States, I might be in jail under the crime of adultery or prostitution.

The injustice felt all the more sharp knowing we were interchangeable if not for geography.

The question I am most often asked is "Why?" Strangely, it's the simplest but the hardest question to answer. I wrestle with words to find a simple explanation.

Afghanistan is a country that begs for understanding and for compassion. It's a country where women have been routinely stoned to death for morality crimes where the Taliban took hold, but the people prove their resilience daily, fighting tooth and nail to regain their land, their freedom, and their future.

It's a place I'm inexplicably drawn to—wanting to understand it in hopes that I may understand myself. It's a place most Americans view through a very narrow lens because terrorism, poverty, and oppression are all the media tend to focus on. When the media do focus on the individual stories, they often do so through a skewed lens of victimhood that encourages Americans to think that these horrors are limited to "those" people: Those poor women, those poor victims. What about myself, would I be considered one of those poor women? Someone to be pitied? Someone forever defined as a victim and thereby limited by all that it implied?

Getty photographer Paula Bronstein took a powerful portrait of a self-immolation victim that I chose for the photography exhibition I'd created with the Afghan photographers, *Streets of Afghanistan*. I printed up the portrait seven-feet-tall so that viewers would be confronted with her face, larger than life. Heartbreaking and difficult though the subject is, her beautiful face is revealed underneath a drawn-back burqa and her burnt hands crossed in front of her reveal the beauty in the heartbreak that I see throughout Afghanistan. She has been victimized, but her resilience and her soul come through in her eyes. She is more than someone to be pitied.

I believe a large part of my "why" is my desire to understand the misunderstood. To see the beauty in the heartbreak. To see beyond the guns and bloodshed, the fear and apathy, and to connect with the underlying spirit of a people. To see the beauty that resides in all of us and share that back to others as a way to change perceptions and inspire action by connecting our stories through our common humanity.

11

Panjshir Valley

Afghanistan 2010.

The eve of my attempt to ride across the Panjshir Valley served as a reminder that what I was attempting wasn't a bike ride across Kansas.

Mike Simon and I had again been staying at the same guesthouse near the center of Kabul, but he was evacuated the previous night at 10:30 P.M. by the UN, prompting him to inform me that he wouldn't ever stay there again and neither should I. Two stays, in two years, and two major security situations. Mike was in the country to film the author Khalid Hosseini who was a spokesperson for the United Nation's Refugee Council. This meant that Mike fell under UN security protocols that are among the highest of any organization working in Afghanistan. He was given three minutes to pack and leave, and as he did, he tried to call me to get me out as well.

I didn't get his repeated calls because I was at a rock concert at

L'Atmosphere and couldn't hear the phone ring. Travis's band White City was playing with two other ex-pat bands, one of them supposedly made up of British spies. The night felt akin to a college party, long lines for $8 warm cans of Kronenbourg beer and no-name hard liquor, which ran out within a couple of hours. The entertainment-starved crowd cheered and danced, while the low-quality speakers and amps crackled. It was a great night out in Kabul, and it wasn't until after midnight that I took my phone out to call a private taxi and saw all the missed calls.

My friend Kate called about the UN report first thing in the morning, confirming what Mike had been told. She worked for a large Australian NGO and had better access to security reports than I did. There was a security warning about another imminent threat against our guesthouse during the next forty-eight hours.

Throughout the day, it appeared that it was a false threat. The UN was understandably hypersensitive to any perceived threats after the attack that killed eight a year before at a UN guesthouse not far away. Mike said he told the UN security who collected him that he wanted me to come with him, but when he couldn't get hold of me, the security team told him, "Look, she's not our responsibility." He sounded shaken and was going to be staying at a UN guesthouse for the remainder of the trip. I was scheduled to leave early in the morning for Panjshir but, depending on the situation, we considered staying elsewhere just for the night. Travis and Kate had both offered up floor space at their places if I needed a safe place to crash.

This was complicated by my shadow. Nick Heil, a freelance writer, author, and former editor for *Outside* magazine, was with me on this trip. For three weeks, Nick had been following me, observing, interviewing, and documenting what I did, and hopefully bringing clarity to the "why" for a feature in *Outside*. He was also a biker and the backbone of this story was a ride I was planning across the Panjshir Valley. From a mutual friend, he'd heard about my previous rides in Panjshir the year before, when I'd gone with Travis and Hamid, as well as about my plans for this adventure. After talking with me at length and gaining my trust, he pitched the story to *Outside*, and it was accepted.

Unfortunately I found out that some of Nick's colleagues felt that what I was doing was controversial simply because I'm a woman, because I'm a mother, and that the ride was some sort of ego trip to get *Outside* magazine to write about me. It hurt deeply hearing that and put me on the defensive. I had thought that *Outside* would get it—that they would understand what I was doing more than anyone else. They wrote about Greg Mortenson multiple times with glowing accolades, as well as numerous adventurers and humanitarians, but mostly they featured men. Was it as simple as that? Gender? Or was it something else?

After my first ride in Panjshir a year earlier—testing the waters in villages and on goat paths to gauge reactions and open conversations—the people's curiosity and openness gave me the idea and the confidence to try something more ambitious. I wanted to ride across the province and attempt to summit the 14,000-foot Anjuman Pass that marked the border with Badakhshan. Travis, Hamid, and Jeremy had ridden this stretch on their motorcycles, and it had taken them two attempts. They'd completed the ride, summited, and circled around the back side into the neighboring province to make a big loop. On both occasions, they'd spent the night at Idi Mohammad's home in Dashty Rewat. I'd asked Travis if he thought the climb would be possible by bike. He said he doubted it but it would be a hell of an adventure. As always, his was the perfect blend of cynicism and adventurous spirit. I hired him right there and then to come with me and document the trip.

At the same time, I thought about connecting a series of community rides back home to my ride in Afghanistan. Since girls couldn't ride bikes in Afghanistan, I would ride my bike across the Panjshir Valley one year from the date that I became the first woman to mountain bike in Afghanistan. At the same time, communities back home would ride their bikes and raise money for our projects that benefited women and girls. I dubbed it the Panjshir Tour.

A few months later, after numerous e-mails and phone calls, Nick and I met face-to-face for the first time in Dubai. As I'd requested, he'd let his hair and beard grow in. When I'd initially asked him to start growing a beard for the trip, he'd replied, "Okay, I'll try," in a voice that sounded like he seriously doubted his face's ability to sprout more than a few stray hairs. But the beard appeared to be filling in nicely except for two small round patches on either cheek.

We arrived in Kabul the day before the latest parliamentary elections. There was scattered violence throughout the country, targeting election officials and candidates, particularly female candidates. That day, two candidates and eighteen election officials and campaign workers had reportedly been kidnapped in three separate incidents. Election violence was notorious in Afghanistan. Intimidation, kidnapping, and murder of candidates, campaign workers, and election officials made campaigning nearly impossible in Taliban-controlled provinces.

Election-related violence had started back in July when a shopkeeper in Logar province was killed when he put up a campaign poster in his window. This was a warning to local residents not to participate in the upcoming elections. In nearby Khost province, Sayedullah Sayed, a candidate for Parliament, was fatally wounded—losing both his legs—when a bomb planted in the mosque he was attending exploded.

The past few weeks had seen more of the same across the country, with the worst still focused in Taliban-controlled Pashtun provinces in the south and east. That particular morning, fifteen districts had declared their polling stations would be closed due to an inability to secure them.

Al Jazeera English had posted an interactive map to track electoral violence. It broke down threats into three categories related to their sources. The map also contained blue markers for each of Afghanistan's thirty-four provinces, indicating whether the number of female candidates had increased or decreased since the last parliamentary election in 2005. Though the total number of female candidates had risen from 335 to 413, this gain had been largely limited to Kabul province where security was strongest.

Under President Karzai's amendments to the electoral law made earlier that year, sixty-eight seats were reserved for female candidates. That would suggest that there would be little point in intimidating women for running as they would be technically running against one another for guaranteed seats. Yet the reserved seats in provinces that did not have female candidates would not sit empty. They would go to male candidates under electoral law, thereby increasing the risk to women running for office; intimidation or assassination could equal an extra male seat.

Female candidates were accused of being prostitutes and un-Islamic, their campaign workers kidnapped, and their families threatened. This increased risk hadn't deterred women like Naheed Ahmadi Farid, a twenty-four-year-old in Herat. "I want to be a voice for women," she said when an ABC reporter asked why she was running for office. "Because there was about thirty years, thirty-one years that women didn't have any voice. I think we have to change the situation for women, and I want to be a member for that reason."

Journalist Alexander Lobov wrote, "At this point, hopes aren't high and all parties are concerned with maintaining the status quo. As long as both corruption and violence are kept in relative check, the elections will still serve as a moderate PR victory and the country will continue on its present course."

It was a lot of risk to take for a so-called moderate PR victory, but in Afghanistan, continuing on the present course was actually a step forward, especially for women's rights. Countrywide security had deteriorated over the past five years, and yet more female candidates were taking part in this election than the one in 2005. People were coming out to vote, and there was the feeling that the elections, however flawed, had to continue if Afghanistan was to survive.

Around midnight on our first night in Kabul, the walls started shaking. I hadn't been able to sleep, so I was sitting in bed writing. I'd just e-mailed Nick the election map link I'd found on Al Jazeera's Web site.

Nick was awake, too, and replied, "Hey, thanks. Um, did I just feel the building shake?"

"Yup, earthquake. I wasn't sure if you were sleeping through it. :)"

"Well, I was sleeping, but not through it! I got up to check it out and the dude in the hall with a gun just reassured me and waved me back into my room, saying, 'Everything ok. Relax. I have six men on patrol.'"

We woke up to the news of a rocket attack in Kabul around seven o'clock. Earthquakes and rockets—a great start to Nick's first experience in Afghanistan. It was nothing unusual, but what I hadn't accounted for when planning this trip was the heightened levels of violence and protests across the country resulting from one ignorant man in Florida, a minister who'd threatened to burn the Koran on 9/11. The threat of a 9/11 Koran burning wasn't just ignorant from the perspective of tolerance, religious freedom, and respect. It wasn't just tasteless to take the focus on 9/11 off those who'd lost loved ones and turn it into a sideshow, making a day of mourning and remembrance into a twisted Islamaphobic protest. It wasn't just dangerous to fan the fire between Christians and Muslims worldwide. It was also bigoted, reckless, and nauseating. Our country is great because of the freedoms we have. People of all religions and races and nationalities have traveled from afar to call America home because of these freedoms. This is not something anyone, of any faith, should take lightly. *All* beliefs deserve respect and are afforded the freedom to be practiced under our constitution. That's the beauty of it.

The Florida minister had the freedom to burn the Koran should he wish, as others had the freedom to destroy the Bible or Torah under the same laws. But actions have consequences. Proof in point? Another anti-American riot exploded in Kabul in protest to his publicized plan.

Threats degrading Islam, like Koran burning, play into the hands of the Taliban by fueling the belief that this is a war against Islam and not a war against terrorism. Fueling this fire puts our troops and international forces further at risk. It also puts journalists, humanitarian organizations, and development aid workers in greater danger. Those like me, who choose to work in Afghanistan to help rebuild, educate, and create stability, get thrown into the fire as well. I watched the news before flying into Afghanistan, with growing anger at what a small-minded bigot with some media attention could do to rock an already unstable boat.

Luckily, the elections took place with limited violence, and Kabul escaped mostly unscathed this time around.

Meanwhile, once we made our decision to stay at the guesthouse, we got to work. The bikes needed to be assembled, and we met in my room to do the assembly and talk about the ride logistics. We chattered on about single-speeds. This would be Nick's first time riding one, also at my request, so that we would be riding similar bikes and would, in theory, have a similar experience on the journey. I made piles of clothes, food, and bike tools that I would reduce to the bare essentials so that Nick and I didn't carry more than we needed. I had a bag of easy-to-eat snacks, power gels, bars, and packets of honey almond butter for quick fuel on the bike, as well as my café latte-flavored hydration powder and water filter. Most importantly, I added the key item for the ride—the silver barrette Nooria had given to me in the Kandahar prison. I opened one of the small pockets in my hydration pack and placed the barrette inside next to the locket with Devon's photo. A piece of Nooria would be with me on this ride, a piece of her free, and a reminder to myself of why I was doing this and who I was doing this for.

On the news that evening, we heard updates on other provinces as we were packing—two attacks in northern Afghanistan: one in Balkh province where I was headed after the Panjshir trip to revisit the women's prison, and the other on a military base.

It would be a relief to ride in the remote mountains of Panjshir for a few days.

Neither Nick nor I slept particularly well. He said he'd had dreams about a ship getting attacked.

Our driver picked us up at the guesthouse—a sweet man named Najibullah, recommended by my fixer and translator, Najibullah. He was a small, plump, smiling man from Panjshir, since it was always key to have someone local with us. I was often amazed at how many Afghan men I'd met named Najibullah or Mohammad, or both! Najibullah was actually Najibullah Mohammad. The driver Najibullah—Najibullah 2—as I thought of him, showed up in a rented Toyota four-by-four whose back door didn't open, so we had to load the bikes over the backseats, which didn't fold down. This was a complete pain in the ass and made me long for Shah Mohammad's Toyota Corolla hatchback, though not his driving skills. Amazingly, our Panjshiri translator for this journey was yet another Najibullah who'd also been recommended by "my" Najibullah. I referred to him in my head as Najibullah 3. It was a warped version of the old "Who's-on-third" comedy routine.

Najibullah 3 was dressed in a freshly pressed suit and shiny black leather shoes. He was friendly, but quiet, and extremely formal considering we were on a three-day trip to the mountains. Unfortunately, his English wasn't very strong. He looked a little overwhelmed when I laid out our plans and asked more than once if I could speak more slowly. I wondered if he was overwhelmed by the speed at which I was speaking or petrified by the idea of what I was proposing. I considered dialing up Najibullah just to make sure he knew what we were up to and could, if necessary, explain it to Najibullah 3.

Our first stop was to pick up Travis as well as a few supplies I'd left there. He let me keep my motorcycle and a storage trunk at his house between visits. The trunk was stocked with a few clothes and extra bike gear from the ride the year before so that I didn't have to schlep it back and forth each time I came to Afghanistan. The trunk sat in the corner of his courtyard alongside the collection of motorcycles. It was coated in dust, but when I lifted the lid, I felt as if I was receiving a little Christmas surprise. Inside were my bike shoes, gloves, and a number of things I'd forgotten about, like my extra helmet inside my favorite Osprey backpack and other road trip necessities: toilet paper, duct tape, tampons, industrial military-grade wet-wipes I'd picked up at the Bagram black market on the last trip. At the bottom of the bag was my first aid kit stocked with

Cipro, Immodium, Vicoden, Band-Aids, saline spray, and Neosporin. Game on. What more could a girl need to venture on a mountain bike across the Panjshir Valley?

Travis had obviously just woken up and looked haggard. No big surprise there. He'd probably had a late night after the rock concert. I suspected there would be a lot of napping behind sunglasses en route. There was also a new girl wandering around—Travis's latest conquest or one of the boys', or simply a temporary roommate crashing in the living room. I didn't ask.

"You ready?"

"Rock on, mate," he replied hoarsely.

Travis blearily grabbed his stuff, and we loaded it into the back. I noticed that the four-by-four was already packed to the gills and we still needed to pick up more supplies, including bottled water and snacks. As we were driving to the shop, Travis asked, "Hey, do you still want a female translator?"

I nearly punched him. I'd been searching for a decent translator for this trip for the past month and just secured Najibullah 3 two days before, in the nick of time thanks to the help of Najibullah 1.

"Well, we could pick up Fatima. She'd be great. Her English is perfect, and you wouldn't have to pay her. I told her about what you are doing, and she'd love to come with us."

I searched his face and something clicked.

"There isn't going to be any drama if she comes, is there?" I looked directly at him, trying to read his features. He probably didn't have a strictly professional relationship with her.

"Nah. She's cool." He smiled, an evil twinkle in his eye.

"I'm sure she is," I replied, smiling and rolling my eyes.

I was torn, as I'd be thrilled to have a female translator for the first time. It was hard to find female translators who were able to travel and stay overnight with a group of foreigners. Most of their families wouldn't approve. With her, we could sit with the wives in Dashty Rewat and really converse instead of using broken English-Dari exchanges brokered by the elder sons. At the same time, I felt bad about letting Najibullah go, despite his poor English. Travis suggested I simply offer to pay him a full day's fee. No harm, no foul.

I explained to Najibullah, slowly, that we'd found a female translator who was going to join us unexpectedly, and I asked if he would mind if we didn't use him after all. I apologized for the change of plans. He nodded, not really understanding, and I called the original Najibullah 1 to explain properly, then passed the phone over. Najibullah was happy with a full day's salary and no need to road-trip in an overpacked four-by-four of foreigners planning to ride bikes in the mountains.

Najibullah stepped out of the car to grab a taxi, and within five minutes, Fatima joined our motley crew. She smiled widely and introduced herself, then excitedly jumped in back next to Nick and me while Travis moved up to the front. We were off!

Our four-by-four was a right-hand drive, like a British car. Travis sat on the left side, and as soon as we were out of Kabul, heading north on the highway, he became Najibullah's eyes for passing. The highway was notorious for high speeds and bad drivers, and though it was one of the safest in Afghanistan in terms of IEDs and kidnappings, it was one of the most dangerous in terms of car crashes. As Najibullah was on the right-hand side, he couldn't see if he could pass until the car was almost entirely in the lane of oncoming traffic. This put Travis directly in the line of fire of the trucks coming at us at full speed. The result was a wild game of chicken, a comedy act that the three of us in the backseat enjoyed immensely. Tears were rolling down my face until Travis and Najibullah settled into a comfortable rhythm for traffic navigation.

We stopped at our highway bolone stand as per Panjshir road trip tradition. It was my fifth or sixth time there, but Nick's first. It felt different without Hamid along. He and Travis had a brotherly banter that I missed.

I was desperate to go to the bathroom, and while the bolone was cooking in the dark, murky vat of reused oil that most likely hadn't been changed in months, if ever, I snuck out back to find a discreet place in the surrounding fields. But every time I thought I was in the clear, a solitary Afghan would emerge from one direction or the other. Eventually, I went back to the stand and grabbed my bag. Inside was a Go Girl, a vibrant pink flexible funnel that was created for women to pee standing up. I had it for emergencies like this, and so I undid my jeans and simply turned my back and peed like a man. No need to bare my ass and squat, attracting attention. In fact, no one was the wiser, and I considered how lucky men were. The world was literally their urinal.

When I rejoined the group, Nick's eyes were wide, taking everything in as we made ourselves at home. We were seated on green plastic chairs at a table with a red-and-white checkered plastic tablecloth, on the side of the dusty highway. Market stalls lined both sides, and we were the only foreigners here. Bags of fresh *mohst* hung from the sides of stalls, along with stacks of Coca-Cola bottles and the requisite piles of red plastic jugs used for collecting water. Piles of bolone and a pot of green tea arrived at the table, served by one of the owner's sons. We dabbed the freshly fried dough with the newspaper to absorb the artery-clogging amounts of dirty oil while Fatima rinsed out the teacups with hot tea before pouring a full cup for each of us.

Full of fried dough and potato, we finished our tea and loaded back up for the best part of the drive, leaving the flat landscape of the Shomali Plain outside of Kabul for the mountains of Panjshir.

Travis continued to direct traffic for Najibullah, but the chaos of the first two hours abated.

Jeremy called Travis to check if we were en route. Jeremy and Travis had a $500 bet that Jeremy couldn't stop smoking for six months and Jeremy was due to collect it. He told Travis he'd donate it to Mountain2Mountain if we made it to the top of Anjuman Pass. He was extremely doubtful that we could, and was confident his money was safe. I felt the familiar thrill of a challenge and a strong desire to prove him wrong.

We arrived at the Gates of Panjshir, and for the first time since I'd been going there, Massoud's seventy-year-old red-haired guard was not at his self-appointed post. I wondered if he was okay and if I would see him again. We checked with the guards at the official entrance and drove around the corner to set up the bikes out of their view to avoid questioning or delays.

We unpacked by the side of the road, just past the bridge where I first mountain biked the previous year. The Panjshir River was raging alongside us, and there couldn't have been a more stunning scene to start this ride.

Nick and I assembled the bikes and put on our shoes and gloves as Najibullah watched amusedly. He, like Jeremy, was doubtful of this endeavor's success.

We took off together on the newly paved asphalt road, and immediately, the ride was harder than I thought it would be. I'd only traveled here by car or motorcycle in the past, and after two weeks in Afghanistan with little exercise, my legs felt leaden. The road would be a gradual climb along the entire valley floor until we reached the Anjuman Pass and took on the mountain itself. It was a beautiful sunny day but a bit too warm for my conservative riding outfit. This was hardly the place to wear racing lycra or bare my legs. I had on a variation of my outfit from the year before—padded bike shorts under a long pair of loose, black Prana yoga pants, my ever-present black Patagonia halter dress, and a blue long-sleeved tunic over that. I'd tied a men's black-and-white checkered head scarf around my head and another around my neck. The outfit was topped off with my Osprey hydration pack, biking gloves, and my well-broken-in Sidi bike shoes. Though they had holes, they fit like gloves. A rubber band around my right pant leg kept it out of my chain, and I skipped the helmet entirely. I thought about the barrette and locket inside my pack, and my Longfellow ring under my gloves, and I remembered how lucky I was to be doing this no matter how uncomfortable it would be and already was.

I soon realized that the worst part about the ride wasn't the climbing or the security concerns, but not being able to get enough air to keep my body cool. Nick had rolled up his khaki pants and his shirt sleeves, which was at least something. Big sweat patches appeared under his arms and on his chest, his blue button-up hiking shirt not quite up to the job of absorbing the amount of sweat he was generating. This was not a scenic excursion, as much as I wished it was, so I was trying to drive a fast pace so we could complete this safely and quickly.

The initial climbs weren't particularly extended other than Nick's aptly named L'Alpe D'Huez climb that kicked both of our asses. Most were short and punchy, and I stood and easily outpaced Nick on each one. While I pretended not to notice, my inner pride was beaming just a little.

Nick pulled up beside me after an hour or so. "This isn't flat!"

I looked over at him, smiling. "Who said it was flat?"

"Well, Panjshir Valley. Valley floor—flat. This isn't flat."

"I told you it was a steady incline the whole ride until we reached Anjuman Pass, and then it's a climb, most likely on foot pushing the bikes."

"I don't remember you saying that."

"Oh, well, it's too late now. Let's ride!" I laughed. It didn't matter what the terrain was or would be. We were biking across an insanely beautiful corner of the world. What more did we need?

The reaction of those who saw us was apparent in the first few miles: surprise, curiosity, and a lot of double-takes. Periodically, boys and men joined us, riding alongside, asking questions, and occasionally challenging us to a race. One man in traditional shalwar kameez and a pakol hat rode along for a couple of miles. He was commuting to the neighboring village, from his day job as a teacher at a boys' school to an office job in the afternoon. As we rode together, we talked in my basic Dari about his work and his family.

An hour or so later, Nick and I were alone again, and I saw the hill in front of us that housed Massoud's now-completed tomb. When we reached the top, we stopped to allow the four-by-four to catch up. I sat on top of "our" barrier, and as Travis got out of the car, I smiled, pointing at my seat—the barrier Shah Mohammad almost took out exactly one year ago on my first attempt to mountain bike here. It was easy to spot, as it was the only one whose concrete had been distinctly redone. We looked down the cliff into the green valley, and I shared the story with Nick, laughing at the memory of Travis's abrupt awakening from one of his many road trip naps to see us careening toward certain death.

We enjoyed the cruise from the hilltop into the village below and headed toward the capital of Bazarak, a small village that served as the seat of the provincial government. I waved down the four-by-four and asked if Najibullah could stop in Dashtak or another village before we were too far back into the valley, and get us some extra cases of bottled water for the ride tomorrow as well as some meat for our family in Dashty Rewat.

Nick was obviously stunned by the beauty of the landscape, and more than once we discussed how many people would pay large amounts of money to have this experience, to ride through this unexplored region. It was wonderful to see this region I'd visited many times now through his eyes for the first time. He was a mountain man at heart, based on what I knew of him, and it was obvious he connected with the rugged landscape surrounding us, and perhaps understood for the first time one part of why I was doing what I was doing.

Occasionally, a motorcycle or carload of young men tailed us for a while, and it unnerved me a bit. But Nick and I soon discovered that it dissuaded them when I rode inside of Nick, side-by-side. Nick effectively took a protective stance as a blocker. A firm *"xoda al fez"* made our intention clear. *Bye-bye!* Move along. Nothing to see here.

We pulled into Bazarak, and I was disappointed that we didn't have time to stop in to say hello to some of the public officials I had visited on previous visits, or to eat lamb kebabs at my favorite *chai-hanna*. We wanted to get to Dashty Rewat by nightfall, so we kept pushing through after refilling our water bottles from the four-by-four. Fatima told me that Najibullah also doubted we could get to the Anjuman Pass. "But," she said, smiling broadly, "he also thinks Dashty Rewat is too far for you and that you will have to get in the car to get there by nightfall."

I laughed appreciatively at the extra goading from our good-natured driver. He'd proved accommodating with this crazy expedition, even allowing Travis to climb through the sunroof to film from the top of the four-by-four as Nick and I pedaled along.

Despite the extra incentive to prove Najibullah wrong and take Jeremy's money, I could feel myself getting tired. The roads became dirt, and we spent more time navigating ruts and bumps. Before long, though, I recognized the sweeping road that overlooked the river basin, and the construction crews below signaled to me that

Dashty Rewat wasn't far around the next bend. We would make it before nightfall—a relief, as dusk was settling in.

We rounded the final turn. On the edge of town, the new building and security gate of Idi Mohammad's family was in stark contrast to the dilapidated mud houses and corrugated steel stalls that made up most of these villages. Idi wasn't home. He was in Kabul and since cell phones didn't work this far into the mountains, we couldn't let him know we were arriving. As usual, we were showing up unannounced.

His brother, Fardin, greeted us in his stead and welcomed us inside. I gratefully got off the bike and noticed the fatigue on Nick's face. His beard was dusty, but it had filled in much more since I'd first seen him three weeks ago in the Dubai airport. While he didn't look Afghan, he also didn't look American. We'd been riding hard for five or six hours, and when we climbed the stairs to the guesthouse's upper level, my knees ached with each step. This was the first time I'd climbed these stairs in the guesthouse that I'd paid to help decorate a year and a half ago as thanks for the family's ongoing hospitality. There was also now a porcelain squat toilet inside, a welcome addition to the outhouse.

We were dirty and sweaty. Nick's cotton button-down shirt was soaked through, but we sat on the toshaks on the floor to wait for tea. We rifled through our supplies to eat biscuits, chips, almond butter— anything to get fuel into our bodies. I offered the various bags around to the kids who'd followed us in, and to Fardin. The Prince biscuits I'd brought from Kabul—chocolate paste sandwiched between two pale biscuits—were the winner. Both Nick and I stretched out our tired legs. My usual respectful pose of sitting cross-legged was too uncomfortable and caused my hips to cramp. We quietly and methodically shoved food into our mouths, and I noticed two of Idi's brothers were looking curiously at Fatima.

Fardin asked Fatima questions in Dari, and after her long exchange, I asked her to explain.

Fatima looked Hazara, from the Pul-e-Charkhi area, but she'd been raised in Iran after her father died. She had a more modern and global view of her birthplace. She was also brutally honest and frank, a trait that I took a shine to immediately. Her mannerisms and demeanor were decidedly Western, as most of her social group in Afghanistan was the ex-pat community.

She explained in English, "They probably think I'm a prostitute."

"What? Did he say that? Why? Because you aren't married?"

"They know Travis isn't married, and as an Afghan woman traveling alone, and with my looks, they think I'm maybe Uzbek, not Afghan at all. The real question is the propriety of a single woman traveling with a group of foreigners without a male escort."

"Shit, we should have said you and Nick were married." I laughed. Nick looked over with a blank stare. Fatigue had been settling in around him like a cloud until he heard his name.

Fatima laughed and said, "Or Travis."

"No way, not Travis. They may see him a few more times in the future, and we'll have to maintain that lie. But they'll never see Nick again."

At that moment, the door opened and one of the younger boys came in with a tray bearing the tea and glasses. He clearly took pride in being the one to serve us.

Nick perked up after our bellies were full, and he downed a second cup of tea. Talking through Fatima, he asked Fardin some questions.

"What do you think about Shannon riding a bike through the valley?"

I smiled at Fardin and interjected, "I can leave the room if you would like to talk openly without offending me."

As Fatima translated, I watched Fardin wave his hands and shake his head at me. "No, no, no, you should stay. It's no problem." To Nick, he said, "I respect Shannon and the work she is trying to do. I have no problem with her riding a bike. She is very sporty and strong. When she came last time with a bike to the boys' school, she walked up a narrow path with her bike and rode down behind the school. The boys were all amazed a woman could do this."

Nick grinned. "Do you think there is any man in Panjshir faster than Shannon?" I wondered if the "joke" would translate.

Fardin laughed with a big smile, getting the joke. "No, there is no man in the valley as fast as Shannon." I laughed loudly when Fatima translated this and smiled at Fardin. He had a twinkle in his eye as he smiled back, acknowledging the banter.

"We are going to try to ride to the top of the Anjuman Pass," Nick said. "Do you think we will make it to Anjuman?"

Fardin replied, and all the men started laughing. There was a flurry of words back and forth between Fardin and Fatima.

"We think that yes, Shannon can do it," Fatima translated to Nick in a deadpan voice, "but that you will not. You are too fat."

I burst out laughing despite myself and looked at Nick, who was hardly fat. I wondered how he'd respond. "It's true, it's true." He sighed and nodded self-deprecatingly. He nodded some more and shrugged at the men as if to say, "What can I do? You are right."

The children laughed uproariously.

Changing the tone, Nick asked, "Can Afghan women ride bikes?"

Fardin responded seriously. "No, it's not part of our culture."

I sat back and wondered once again why it was that foreign women and Afghan women were treated so differently. A woman was a woman. Why was I allowed to get away with this? In Saudi Arabia, for example, being a foreign woman didn't give you any more leeway. Rules and customs were to be observed by everyone, regardless of nationality.

I excused myself to go to the bathroom. I took off my bike chamois and dressed again with a clean tunic and pants. I'd be sleeping in this, too, and in the morning, would simply put on my clean chamois under the pants. I used the wet wipes to remove the layers of dirt and grime and sweat as best I could. I felt tired but strong, and more confident than ever that we could do this.

Soon, one of the other children came in with the red plastic tablecloth to unfold across the space between the toshaks, signaling that dinner was on the way. A large flat naan was thrown down in front of each of us and plates of mysterious and slightly gray meat covered in suspicious-looking sauce on beds of rice arrived, along with tomato and onion salads. I looked sideways at Travis, who'd gotten dysentery after every meal we'd had here, and winked. He groaned quietly in response but took a hunk of naan to scoop up some rice and meat, knowing what he was in for.

Nick had yet to eat in true Afghan style. Seated on the toshaks across from me, he'd crossed his long legs and was watching me scoop food into my hand to eat or use hunks of naan as a food-to-mouth utensil.

The men and children watched Nick with amusement as he scooped some food with his hand and rice spilled everywhere.

"I have the same skills as a five-year-old," he lamented.

After dinner, Fardin took a tin of naswar from his pocket. He smiled at me, a twinkle in his eye again as he offered it to me. I laughed but declined. I told Nick the story of the first time I'd tried naswar with Fardin, encouraged by Travis and Hamid, and that it had led to flu-like chills, me turning a dark shade of green, and a rapid run to vomit in the outhouse.

Fardin now poured some into his hand and pressed it into a little ball. Once he had it wedged against his gum, he asked about Devon. I pulled out my iPhone. I had a folder of photos just of her for these occasions. Most of the family now knew to use their fingers to slide each photo to the next, and as usual, the phone went around the room. I wondered if Steve Jobs realized how innate his technology really was.

A couple of villagers joined us, but my "betrothed"—the Afghan comedian with the stereo we met on our first visit to Dashty Rewat— was fishing at a lake on Anjuman Pass. I laughed when I heard this. Great, we would make it to the top of the pass just in time to run into him. He'd probably interpret this as a huge gesture on my part that I was willing to climb a mountain just to be with him.

Things quieted down, and I took my cue to have tea with the women in the other part of the compound. Fatima came with me, and I was again grateful she was along to translate. We entered, stooping through the half door that divided the compound from the new building and courtyard. The wives and grandmas were excited to see me and ushered us into a room I hadn't yet visited. They gathered around, along with all the children, but for the first time, the older boys weren't in attendance since they weren't needed to translate. There were women only, a girls' night in, so to speak.

Immediately, the questions started as Fatima and I sat drinking tea in front of ten or more faces.

I asked how they were. The last time I was there, Idi Mohammad's gorgeous wife, Huma, had a new baby, and I got to meet him. Adorable, he was now one year old and had been named Mohammad. I was thrilled to see he'd survived his initial harsh winter. I also met the newest member of the family. This time, Fardin's wife, Massouda, had the newborn. I saw that she'd lost two of her teeth to malnutrition and the stresses of multiple pregnancies so close together.

The women asked about Devon, and again the iPhone made

the rounds, starting with my favorite member of the family, Idi Mohammad's mother. She asked, for what seemed the twentieth time, "Why don't you have more children? Don't you want a son?"

I smiled and nodded, and for perhaps the twentieth time responded, "No, I still only have my daughter, Devon, and I love her as much as any son. I'm very lucky to have her."

Grandma smiled knowingly at me, assuming I was barren, and said, "I'll pray for you that Allah grants you a strong baby boy."

Great, I thought. *You do that, and I'm going to double up my protection.*

The talk immediately turned to birth control when one of the wives asked me directly, "Do you use birth control?" The iPhone was still circulating around the room, and I was so surprised that I had to ask Fatima if she'd translated correctly. She had, and so the first topic of conversation at the girls' night in was about birth control. I turned the question of whether I was on birth control around and asked if any of them were and what they knew about it.

Massouda replied that she was now on birth control, a form of the pill, that the local doctor gave her after her most recent baby. She'd been told that she could be on it safely only for one year. Clearly, the campaign to convince men to give their wives space between babies for the health of the mother and the child was being heard in some form. She pointed to where her teeth had fallen out and said she hoped that it would prevent more tooth loss.

I couldn't speak to that but was intrigued at the direction of the conversation. They asked why I never came back to train midwives—something I'd discussed with the men a couple of years ago. I explained that a training in Dashty Rewat wasn't possible because there were no women who were literate. The new midwife now working with the doctor at the village clinic was a welcome addition, and I was relieved to hear that some maternal care had finally arrived.

Idi's oldest daughter, Ariana, was to be married in a few months. The women talked about this proudly, and Ariana smiled softly. It would be a big celebration for the family—the first of the children to be married.

Then the women shared that they couldn't leave the house except under a burqa at night or on special family occasions. I was shocked. I knew I shouldn't have been. But this region of Afghanistan, and this family in particular, had always struck me as more progressive or simply less conservative than other rural provinces. Panjshir was the bastion of Massoud, the Lion of Panjshir, who'd been a proponent of girls' education and the iconic leader of a free Afghanistan.

I asked if they knew about the girls' school I'd discussed building here with Idi Mohammad. Huma said that the village had laughed at Idi when he'd proposed it. The local mullah was against it. Even though there was a school in a neighboring village, the girls here weren't allowed to attend.

Speechless, I decided not to broach the subject with the men tonight about progress on the village land donation for a future girls' school in Dashty Rewat. I was devastated, but this explained the delays and suspicions I'd had during prior visits. I swallowed the lump of disappointment and frustration building in my throat.

After a few more questions, Fatima and I said good night and wished them all good health and for the babies to grow up big and strong. Nick and Travis had been hanging out with the locals, and both appeared mellow and sleepy. Tomorrow was going to be another long day in the saddle, so I got ready for the ritual tuck-in. The young boys pulled down the blankets and pillows from the corner stack, and Fardin came around to tuck us all in, Nick, Travis, Fatima, and me at one end of the room around the toshaks. Najibullah slept at the other end, next to the entrance, along with Idi's oldest son and a few of the youngest—our protectors perhaps.

I slept so hard that I wasn't sure I'd even moved. I opened my eyes, stretched my legs, and woke to several of the younger boys watching me. I sat up and smiled at them, then searched for the little bag I kept beside me with my contact lenses. Nick and Fatima were stirring as well. Travis just groaned and rolled over, trying to avoid the daylight. Once we were upright and had rubbed the sleep out of our eyes, the room was filled with tea and our hosts.

The red tablecloth came back in, and a breakfast of naan, fresh cream, and a cherry preserve was served along with plates of fried eggs. It was the perfect way to fuel up for the day, and I was grateful for something solid to put in my belly as I'd discovered the Dashty Rewat curse got me yet again and had already liquefied last night's dinner. Needless to say, I was even more grateful for the squat toilet and the pink toilet paper they now stocked for special visitors.

After breakfast, we discussed the logistics for completing the pass. Beyond Parion, there would be no more villages. We'd have to ride for a few more hours before we got to the start of the arduous climb. This could take a few more hours, and we'd possibly have to walk our bikes a good portion of the way. We couldn't ride to the pass and get up and down before nightfall. I suggested sleeping in the car, but that was met with dubious looks. Frankly, I couldn't see any other option unless we rode as far as we could, doubled back to Parion in the car, and restarted the next morning. Safety was a huge issue. This wasn't like bike touring across the United States or Europe. We couldn't just set up camp by the roadside or in the hills because of land mines, kidnapping, or assassination. Ten medical aid workers had been killed a few weeks before on the other side of the pass. It was a lawless area back there. We didn't even know if the four-by-four would make it all the way, as it had to be turned off several times the day before so the radiator could cool down. We agreed that we'd make a run for the pass as best we could and leave Parion open as our potential option to do a double-back if we needed to.

The fact was we really didn't know what to expect beyond Dashty Rewat. When Travis, Jeremy, and Hamid did this trip on motorcycles the year before, it took them all day from Dashty Rewat to get over the pass by nightfall. We would be about three times slower than the motorcycles. We didn't even fully know what the road condition would be as construction crews had been working on sections of it for the past few years. Stretches that had been dirt in the spring were now smooth pavement, interspersed with boulder-ridden, rocky areas that were so torn up we had to pick our way through. It could be faster riding or much slower than we anticipated.

The other concern that unexpectedly greeted us that morning was water. We couldn't buy bottled water here, and Travis and Najibullah hadn't bought any in Bazarak as I'd asked. Travis had of course assured me it would be "no problem, mate," but I should have known better and stocked up with more than we needed in Kabul. This was a major problem. He suggested river water as an option, and Nick and I looked at each other incredulously, knowing it could literally kill us. Travis seemingly had no concept of these kinds of things. Livestock and human waste as well as mining pollution were all dumped into the river. I wouldn't eat the fish caught in this river without a Cipro chaser, much less drink the water. I wasn't even willing to put my water purifier to that challenge. Nick was seriously not amused and wrongly assumed that I was considering the river solution as a viable option. I tried to assure him I was not.

We headed downstairs and brainstormed. I asked the family to boil enough water to fill all the empty water and Sprite bottles we could dig out of the truck. Meanwhile, I walked across the street to check out Fardin's little shop and see if there was something that would work. I bought a full case of individual juice boxes on the bottom shelf, covered in dust, but still within the sell-by date. I also bought several Afghan prepackaged cakes, biscuits, and tea. They might be stale, but they never seemed to expire. Idi's brother had also packaged the remaining naan from breakfast for us and loaned us four blankets, a tea kettle, and a little fuel tank (which was empty) for our potential overnight in the car, if it came to that.

A crowd gathered outside when we finally got our show on the road. We waved good-bye, and several kids chased us as we started riding. My ass felt sore, but my spirit was happy. Nick and I eased into a gentle pace to coax the legs back into what was going to be a long, tough day in the saddle.

Thirty minutes or so out of Dashty Rewat we came across a Kuchi camp off the side of the road. The Kuchis are Afghanistan's nomadic people. Kuchi literally means "nomad" in Dari, but they are typically Pashtun in ethnicity. Camel caravans, brightly colored tents and clothing in vibrant purples, fuchsias, and emerald greens made me feel as though I'd stepped back in time. Every view was postcard perfect, and Nick was also visibly blown away. My awe quickly took another course a few miles later as we encountered a gnarly set of switchbacks—steep, loosely graveled, and seemingly unending. After grinding our way up a couple of them, we started walking to conserve energy. I considered switching out my rear cog for an easier gearing if this was how the rest of the day was going to play out. Travis and crew pulled up in the four-by-four. He had a huge grin. "Don't worry. It levels off in a bit, and you'll be able to ride again."

"Thank God for that," I said, gasping. My calves were cramping from walking on my toes in bike cleats up the incline.

When we got to the top, we pulled over next to the four-by-four and had an impromptu snack and chat. Fatima sat down beside me.

"I'm so proud of you," she said. "You are really doing this. This is really great."

I smiled broadly, feeling and tasting the grit in my teeth, and I leaned over to give her a hug. I was touched and so glad she was with us. I only wished she knew how to ride a bike as I was certain she'd join us in a heartbeat. Having another female presence along, especially an Afghan, made this ride resonate all the more deeply for me. I offered to teach her how to ride when we got back to Kabul and she nodded enthusiastically.

At each hill, I left Nick in the dust—a good feeling, as I'd worried before we left that he might find the pace too slow. I had the advantage of riding my single-speed in the mountains of Breckenridge, which sits at 9,600 feet, so the long climbs that forced us out of the saddle didn't faze me. Nick was used to gears, although the altitude in his home of Santa Fe almost identically matched the elevation in the Panjshir Valley—around 6,000 feet. As we rode, we were steadily climbing and would continue until we reached the summit of the Anjuman at 14,534 feet.

I vacillated between tiredness and feeling the pain, to euphoria at the beauty back here and the positive reaction from the locals. Nick seemed to be trudging through in survival mode.

Before we arrived at the last outpost of Parion, Travis pulled up next to us and said to just ride past, ignore the checkpoint, and see if we could evade the police who'd delayed him, Hamid, and Jeremy on their first attempt with motorcycles. They pulled ahead and went through, and we followed. It only took about ten minutes before a police jeep pulled up beside us. The four-by-four was long gone ahead with my translator. The police were insistent that we return with them to check in. I tried to explain that our papers were in the truck with the driver—the familiar duel of broken English and broken Dari as we tried to communicate. They finally understood and told us to wait while they went ahead to find our crew. We sat on the roadside and before long, the police returned with Travis and Fatima, who offered to go back to register us.

Travis said, "They will allow you to wait here and rest, but as soon as we're gone, start pedaling and we'll catch up with you when we're all clear."

Once they were out of sight, we pedaled off to make up some miles and keep on schedule. An hour or so later, we stopped. The road was getting very desolate, and we didn't want to go much farther in case they didn't turn up and we had to ride back to Parion.

Soon Najibullah pulled up with a note from Travis to sit tight and that they were just waiting for the commander to arrive and sign the papers. We unloaded some food and supplies from the truck for an impromptu picnic and wrote a reply to Travis and Fatima. Our personal Pony Express turned the four-by-four around and headed back to Parion.

One $250 "donation" later, the crew arrived at our picnic area with an all-clear. I'd never paid a bribe and certainly didn't want to start now, but we were in the clear, along with a proposal from the commander to Fatima. The police had warned Travis about Nooristanis with guns up by Anjuman, and they wanted to send a police escort with us—hence the bribe. We got off easy, as the previous year Travis and his friends had to pay $500 for permission to continue *and* each took a police officer with them on the backs of their motorcycles. Fatima was a little worried about the proposal. The commander was very insistent and had taken a serious liking to her. Travis said it was worrying enough that he would advise against staying in Parion for the night for Fatima's safety.

At this point, several elderly men walking down the road offered us tea and food should we need it. This was incredibly kind, and I wished I could take them up on the offer, but we needed to press on.

We came across a small bridge construction and a road crew. As we rode close, they practically swarmed up to stop us and chat and ask what we were doing. We were probably the most interesting thing they'd seen all week, and several asked if they could ride our bikes. For fifteen minutes or more we watched and laughed as the men took turns on our bikes. They wished us luck and strength as we set off again.

As we continued, the roads became steeper, rougher, and more remote. The mountains that surrounded us on all sides started to feel like the badlands from an old Western movie. I imagined Afghan snipers on the mountaintops above. There was a noticeable energetic shift in the atmosphere, the sense of being watched and the awareness of the vast emptiness around us made my skin tingle. As Nick and I biked through a couple of small river runoffs that crossed the dirt road, he commented on the shift as well.

When we were walking our bikes up a major incline, an old man in a white turban came down with two donkeys and stopped us. He asked where we were going, and when we replied "Anjuman," he started shaking his head and mimed a rifle. He kept saying we shouldn't go up there—men with guns, not good. Dari and sign language made everything pretty clear, but we explained that our driver and translator were in the truck coming up behind us— would he explain more to them?

We continued on as the old man spoke with the crew. Nick expressed his unease, and soon Najibullah pulled up and Travis got out. Travis pointed ahead, and we had our first clear view of the Anjuman itself. The mountain's jagged silhouette was in full view, with a few small snow fields tucked into the saddle that dipped between two peaks.

"Nooristani gunrunners," Travis confirmed. "The old man is talking about Nooristani gunrunners around the pass. Apparently it's been an issue for a while now. It's not Taliban, just criminals. Drugs and guns."

"Well, shit." Defeat was heavy in my voice. "That's a definite no for staying the night up there." And I had to face it—a strong argument against even venturing up there at all. "Could we maybe just ride a bit farther while we think? Maybe ask someone else?" I was grasping at straws.

We decided to ride a bit farther as I preferred to think about this while I pedaled. The others drove ahead to see if they could find anyone else to speak with. Nick and I discussed the palpable change in atmosphere, tension, and risk.

"It's starting to feel like a rigged game of Russian roulette, don't you think?" he said. I had to agree. I knew he wanted to turn around, and while my head was in agreement, my heart needed a few more pedal strokes to come to terms with the news.

I was disappointed. Seeing the pass in front of us made it all the more tempting. So close. I understood why mountain climbers talk about the descent from a climb being more dangerous than the ascent. You can push through and get there, but you still need to survive in the danger zone long enough to get down. Our danger zone wasn't extreme elevation and lack of oxygen, but men with guns.

We were both riding at a steady pace, feeling the tiredness but pedaling strong. I didn't want to turn back because of this sort of stuff, but it *was* Afghanistan after all. Gunrunners of any sort were to be avoided, no matter the country, but in the remote, desolate badlands of Panjshir, their presence was an unfortunate reality. The trip had just turned from a challenge and exploration to potential suicide. This wasn't even a real choice, especially when I had Devon to think about.

I had to remember that the goal was not the summit—this was simply a logical end point. We'd already achieved the real goal: riding for two days across the entire valley as a woman, challenging perceptions, asking questions, racing young boys and men on their bikes, and connecting this ride to a series of rides back home to raise money for projects in one of the few countries in the world where women couldn't ride bikes. Even in the sixties when Afghanistan was a tourist destination—and Afghan women in urban areas like Kabul attended university alongside men and wore short skirts and no head scarves—biking was still a deep-seated taboo.

I knew we couldn't use the backup option and double back and stay in Parion with the police chief taking such a shine to Fatima. It wasn't safe, and I wouldn't put her life at risk just to do a third day of riding, which was already feeling too dangerous even in the daylight. We couldn't do the pass safely regardless of where we spent the night, so the decision was made for us.

Travis suggested that we ride up to the major river crossing, cross it if we could and ride the little incline for a proper look again at the Anjuman. He said that there was a large grassy field with a stunning view of the surroundings. It would be a nice place to sit and contemplate what we'd done before we turned around.

The river crossing was knee-deep and freezing cold, with a strong current that threatened to push me over. Staying upright on the slippery rocks was nearly impossible in bike cleats. We would get to do it twice, of course. But on the other side was one of the most incredible spots I'd seen in Afghanistan. We sat in the field with our bikes, my legs wet up to my knees, and I quietly cried for the second time in Afghanistan. I took out the barrette and held it in my hand while I digested my disappointment and my elation that we'd gotten this far.

The afternoon sun was fading, and Nick and I decided to enjoy a little of the incline in reverse. We got back on our bikes and cruised toward home, the light golden and soft with all the dust in the air.

We kept riding for an hour or so, enjoying the "free miles" of pedal-free descents.

Coming up to a lengthy incline, legs tired, and the cold air of nightfall settling in, I stopped. I waved the truck up and said, "Okay."

"Enough?" Travis asked.

"Yup, it's time to go home."

He smiled gently.

"Come on then, let's get you in."

Najibullah pulled over to the roadside, and we gingerly stepped off our bikes. Fatima got out of the car to give me a hug.

"I'm so proud of you, Shannon. This is really amazing," she said as she squeezed me harder.

We took the wheels off the bikes, stuffed them in the back, which was now strewn with empty Sprite bottles, snacks, and Travis's camera equipment. We piled into the car and headed back to Dashty Rewat to return the stuff we'd borrowed. I was quiet in the back, tired, hungry, and disappointed, my legs cramping. Nick joked that the way to do this ride would be to drive up the Anju-man Pass, jump out with the bikes, and ride the entire pass and valley downhill—totally doable in two days and way easier, though the symbolism of climbing the mountain would be lost. Either way, I was in no mood to talk about a redux, yet.

A couple of hours later, we arrived at Dashty Rewat in the dark and despite the offer of warm food and a bed where we could stretch out, we made the unwise decision to press on. The consensus was that we might as well get back to Kabul tonight, Travis's dysentery and my mood being deciding factors.

Travis, Fatima, and I were in the backseat so that Nick, the tall-est, could stretch his legs next to Najibullah in the front. We were all bouncing around with the bumps and Najibullah's increased speed to get us home. It was a four- or five-hour drive, and Nick got the ride of his life. In the front seat, Najibullah played "dodge the trucks" from the right-hand drive position, which left Nick staring wide-eyed at oncoming truck traffic. He decided it would be a money-making video game: Afghan Highway. Travis ran with it and created a spontaneous game from the backseat that assigned Nick five points for calling out the correct passing intervals for Najibullah.

"Zero points if you get dead, mate," he said dryly.

The drive led to several high-pitched screams from Nick, who was gripping the dashboard. This inspired raucous, slap-happy laughter from the three of us in the backseat, and certainly kept us entertained for an hour or so despite the increasingly uncomfortable ride.

When we stopped to get some fresh naan at a late-night bakery, I took my head scarves off and tied them around the "oh shit" handle in an effort to traction up my legs. I leaned back, slipped both feet through, and let my legs swing free as we went over the bumps. My ass was falling asleep, but getting my legs up helped enormously. *I could be stretched out on a toshak right now,* I thought more than once. It had been a rash decision to press on. We should have stayed, spent more time with the family, then taken Nick to see Massoud's tomb on the way home.

We got back after ten o'clock and drove straight to the guesthouse, which again—like it was after the Kandahar trip—was still standing despite the threat warnings. We unloaded our gear, said good night to Fatima and Travis, and thanked Najibullah for his help and phenomenal support.

When we got inside, we realized that all the restaurants were already closed. We hadn't had anything solid to eat since breakfast other than a piece of plain naan when we'd stopped in Panjshir. I was ravenous for some real food. I explained to the front desk staff the situation, and they kindly fixed us a plate of reheated leftovers from dinner that we could take back to my room to eat. Nick and I devoured everything, still in our filthy clothes. I took out my little two-shot bottle of single malt that Mike, another Scotch drinker, had given me—not nearly adequate to mark the occasion, but still, it was something. We each took a swig and then, exhausted, we said good night.

Alone, I took off my Longfellow ring, pausing to read the inscription for the thousandth time: "The lowest ebb is at the turn of the tide." I walked into the bathroom and turned on the shower. As I let the lukewarm water wash over me, I watched the dirt and dust turn the water around my feet a muddy brown. My mind empty of thoughts, I stayed there until the water became cold. Then I dried myself off and layered myself up in the warmest clothes I could find. I took out the silver barrette and Devon's locket from my hydration pack, and placed them beside the Longfellow ring. My talismans and spirits with me, I climbed into bed with an exhausted smile.

(12)

Strength in Numbers

London, Colorado, Afghanistan 2010–2012

Three days later, I was a world away in London Heathrow's brand-new Terminal 5. After searching high and low for an outlet to charge my laptop, I was sitting in a quiet area of the terminal checking e-mails.

My thoughts were heavy, as if the culmination of the ride, the three weeks of interviews, conversations, and probing from Nick, and the relief of the trip being completed had stirred all sorts of emotions and memories up. Sitting there, I realized I wanted to share a thought that had been revolving in my head on the plane from Dubai, where Nick and I parted ways on different flights back home.

He was the first person I'd talked to about my rape in any detail, ever. Talks over cups of tea each night in Kabul, specific conversations about my work, and my motivations became more and more intimate as the trip wore on. At one point, Nick said, "You know,

I'm really surprised at how much you've shared with me throughout this trip. I anticipated you being more guarded from our initial phone conversations."

"I guess I realized at some point that once I made the leap to allow you to join me, I'd better be okay with sharing. I don't have any control over what you write. You can write whatever you want, and I can't do a thing about it. The only control I have is to be completely open. The way I see it, if I'm open about everything, then it gives you a better chance of understanding how I think and how I feel and why I do what I do."

So for some reason, I felt I wanted to share what was going through my head with him. Maybe he'd understand what I was feeling; maybe he'd understand me better and therefore tell a more accurate and honest story.

Nick sent me an e-mail while I was in transit. In it was a quote from the book he'd been reading on the trip, Ernest Hemingway's *A Call to Arms*: "The world breaks everyone and afterward many are strong in the broken places." I sat there, my eyes focused on the words, reading and rereading the quote for a full ten minutes. My world narrowed into focus. A chill ran down my spine, and a heaviness of realization settled in my heart.

Could the rape have a silver lining? Was that even acceptable to consider? Could it be the root of my courage and drive? If so, then I would be saying that the rape was what allowed me to have the courage to work in Afghanistan the way I did. If that was indeed the case, then I had to realize the irony that I had a rapist to thank for my courage and passion and bullheadedness. And that was potentially the way I could forgive him. If that was even possible.

For a girl who didn't want the rape to define her, it defined me more than I ever thought was possible.

I am stronger in the places that were broken. Sometimes to a fault.

I remembered how the last guy I'd dated had said on more than one occasion, "Why do you have to be *so* strong?" Perhaps more his own feelings of weakness than my strength were at fault. My previous boyfriend, Mark, who remains a dear friend, hadn't complained about my strength per se, but had commented after we broke up that I wasn't particularly "soft." Lord knows Pete would agree that my strength was front and center in our relationship. Was it an overcompensation?

Perhaps my real strength was in my vulnerability . . . and if that were true, I was much weaker than I wanted to admit. Perhaps my strength was less about my inner strength but more like an armor, worn to protect myself but impenetrable to those who wanted to get closer to me.

My mind racing, I called Christiane, international charges be damned.

She answered on the first ring. "Hi, sweetie! Where are you?"

"I'm in London."

I could hear the relief in her voice. "I'm so glad. How are you?"

"I'm good. Safe. Confused, though. I need to talk."

"Is it about Nick? You sounded tired and overwhelmed in your e-mails. Emotionally spent."

"Oh man, you have no idea. It was tough—him being there, me feeling like I was under a microscope half the time, and then becoming friends as we were spending so much time together—then remembering that everything I said was 'on record' and up to his interpretation and his editor's direction."

"Do you think he'll do a good job?"

"I think so, but that's subjective, isn't it? It was hard knowing that some of his colleagues were unsupportive of this story and thought I was a narcissist, like I was a little girl playing dress up as an activist. My work shouldn't be controversial. It wouldn't be if they were writing about a man. If I hadn't known, it would have been easier to relax and be myself. Instead, I felt on the defensive for most of the trip."

I took a deep breath. This wasn't why I'd called.

"So, here's the deal. What if my rape had a silver lining?"

I paused, not sure how that sounded.

"I'm listening."

"I am who I am because of all the things that have happened to me, right? So that means that the good and the bad define me. Would I be the woman I am today if he hadn't attacked me? If I hadn't thought I was going to be killed, would I see the world the way I do today? Is my strength, in part, due to him? And if so . . . then in a really fucked up way, I have him to thank for who I am today. I like who I am. But I wouldn't be here, wouldn't be doing what I do, wouldn't think the way I think, wouldn't fight for what I believe is right, in the same way."

I paused, thinking, and Christiane let the silence wait.

"I will never forgive 'him.' Never. Fuck him. But perhaps I can come to terms with this in a different way. Maybe by admitting that that night *did* define me, then it no longer does. Does that even make sense?"

"It does, sweetie. It does. You are the woman you are because of all that you have endured, but you aren't broken—you are strong, but you are also compassionate, and loving, and beautiful. I am so sad that you had to go through this. You didn't deserve it. No one does. But maybe you are letting go of the final hold that experience has over you. Maybe this makes you whole in a way you never knew you weren't."

"I don't have the right words. It comes out all wrong, saying my rape has a silver lining. That's insulting to everyone who's ever been raped. But I don't know how else to say it."

"Don't worry about saying the wrong thing to me. You have been through so much on this trip. Much more than you ever anticipated. And following the last trip to Kandahar, it's a lot to begin to process, and you haven't taken the time to do that."

"How can I? I'm too busy trying to survive day by day. Pay my bills, keep a roof over my head and Devon's. Feed her. I don't know how much longer I can keep this up, Christiane. Why am I doing this? I'm sacrificing everything to make this work, and now I'm sacrificing my personal life to an audience that is already judging me before they know me. I'm not sure I'm strong enough for this. I'm exhausted. I'm broke. This trip was *so* hard. Seriously, enough. I don't need to be processing this decades later on top of everything else."

"I know, I know," she said softly. "But right now isn't the time. You just need to get home. Cuddle up with your Elephant Princess, and just rest. You need to find some time for yourself."

That Hemingway quote integrated itself into my life, and the life of Mountain2Mountain, in the years that followed. It became something I periodically pondered, until eventually it became the heart of my first TEDx talk with TEDxMileHigh in January 2012, which highlighted the backbone of everything I believed and wanted Mountain2Mountain to represent—*The Perception of Victimhood and the Power of Voice.*

I took the stage, standing on the infamous red dot, and looked out at the crowd. I took a deep breath, and the first image came up on the screens on either side of me. "What do you see when you look at this photo?" It was from my first visit to Afghanistan—the photo Tony had taken of the woman in the burqa sitting in the middle of the road, begging with her young child.

"Do you see potential? Possibility? A change-maker?"

During the talk, I challenged the audience to think about how they viewed victims, individuals, and countries, and how difficult it was not to become apathetic to the injustices we were assaulted with daily in the media.

Then I put up a photo of me riding a buzkashi horse in Kabul.

"Now, what do you see when you see this photo? Do you see an adventurer? An athlete? An activist, a fighter, a mother, a daughter?"

I looked out into the crowd, voicing my biggest fear.

"Or do you see a victim?

"You see, many years ago when I was walking home from work, I was brutally attacked, raped, and left for dead. A victim at eighteen.

"But I was only one of over two hundred thousand women raped in the United States every year. That's one woman every two minutes. Had I believed I was a victim, had my friends and family treated me as one, had I been born in a country like Afghanistan, perhaps things would have turned out differently. But in fact I was petrified of that label . . . victim. The finality of it."

In a matter of minutes, I was through the hardest part, and my voice got stronger as I reached the heart of my talk, what I had come to realize since I'd first spoken to Ann Curry, and what had become the backbone of all Mountain2Mountain's work going forward.

"It starts with *voice*. Yours, Ours, and *theirs*. I would start with looking at a different model of philanthropy altogether, where the victims we want to 'fix' are instead the solutions to the problem itself. Giving victims a voice creates a much more powerful ripple than a handout. Empowering them to use their voice can change their lives, their communities, and their countries from within— organically and sustainably creating change with the individual, which acts as a catalytic spark through the entire community.

"So as we leave here tonight, I implore you to change your perception not only of victimhood but of risk. Risk doesn't mean you have to start your own organization in a war zone. It's a risk to use your voice to stand up for someone who doesn't have one. It's a risk to say no. It's a risk to say yes. But that is life—life is a series of risks, of opportunities, and if we want to see a world without oppression, without conflict, without victimization, we have to take risks. Change doesn't happen by playing safe.

"So leave here, use your voice, implore others to use theirs, and assess the risks of doing nothing in your own life. Then look outside yourself into your community, and look at how you can speak for children, for abused women, for refugees, for the homeless, because you can see them as more than victims. You can see them as catalysts for a better world."

Thus a few months later, Strength in Numbers was born, although I didn't realize the full extent to which it would emerge and allow me to evolve into my truest self—an activist, not an aid worker. I was on the verge of creating a sustainable global program, using the bike as a vehicle for social justice with women who'd previously been labeled victims. I would build an army of women who could change the world, stronger in the places that were broken and therefore more capable of taking on the challenges ahead.

In a blink, I was done. The audience was applauding, and I walked off the stage, for the first time aware that Afghanistan may have changed me more than I could ever hope to change Afghanistan. Afghanistan allowed me to be fearless and to be vulnerable and to realize that both were sources of my strength. Now it was time to use my voice and encourage other women to use theirs. One woman can create change, yes. But I also realized that our strength was in our numbers, and together, as individuals, we could pedal a revolution. I knew what I wanted to do. Now it was time to get to work.

But first I had one last big project in Afghanistan.

In November 2012, I returned to Afghanistan with a photography exhibition, exactly four years after meeting the Afghan photographers at AINA. The *Streets of Afghanistan* photo exhibition had launched in the United States at an event at the Denver Art Museum. Five Western and five of the original AINA-trained Afghan photographers had contributed images, and I had blown them up ten feet tall by seventeen feet wide on collapsible frames. The images could be set up anywhere, in any configuration, to allow the viewer a unique interaction in a variety of locations. My goal was to take photography off the walls of a gallery and surround the viewer. Instead of viewers staring at a wall, they had to walk among the images, contemplate the face—larger than life—of a young girl. They imagined themselves in the streets of Kabul, the rolling green hills of Badakshan, or contemplated the empty caves in Bamiyan where the giant Buddhas had once stood before the Taliban blew them up.

I had also created a series of black-and-white photography from Afghanistan in the 1960s and displayed it on easels to showcase Kabul as a progressive and peaceful city: women in miniskirts at a record store in Kabul; women and men studying side by side at Kabul University. This series showed that Afghanistan was much more than what Americans saw in the news and media today. It gave a sense of hope for what could be based on what had been. Too often I heard people talk of countries like Afghanistan as deep dark holes of terrorism, poverty, and oppression that had never escaped the fourth century. Looking back just a few generations to see that Afghanistan *had* been a modern Islamic country shocked many who saw the photographs. Sometimes we have to look back in order to know what is possible in the future. If men and women went to school side by side, if women walked freely in the streets of Kabul without head scarves, perhaps they could do so again. Forty years of occupation, civil war, and unrest changes a society for the worse, but this doesn't mean that it can't right itself given the opportunity.

While I'd originally wanted to use the exhibition to challenge perceptions of Afghanistan, I realized that it would be even more powerful in the literal streets of Afghanistan.

I had funded a graffiti art project in Kabul created by Travis and Gilly under their moniker of Combat Communications. They'd brought in the street artist Chu from England and gathered artists from Kabul University to learn about the history, culture, and techniques of street art and graffiti. This was a statement on the power of public art and the power of art as activism. One young woman in particular took what she learned in the workshop and embraced it wholeheartedly. Shamsia developed into a talented graffiti artist who focused on the bluebird burqas as her trademark. Images of fish and bubbles intertwined throughout her images as though the burqas were underwater, representing the words that Afghan women say but that no one hears. The community engagement of public art inspired and created conversation, which was what made street art so powerful. Art as activism, not just through its subject but through the very nature of its application and audience.

I wanted to take the entire exhibit to Afghanistan and set it up as a series of public art installations for Afghans. Unlike the art exhibitions that reside in embassies or secure locations, I wanted to explore the idea of making the exhibition accessible to everyone. Public art doesn't belong only in secure environments; it belongs on the streets. If art is voice, then voice needs to be public. Furthermore, of the photos taken from Afghanistan every day by journalists, photographers, and travelers, how many are seen by Afghans? How often are these taken images returned?

I launched a Kickstarter campaign to raise the funds to take the exhibition over to Kabul. Knowing I couldn't execute this endeavor solo, I enlisted the help of good friend and writer Anna Brones. In the spirit of her "say yes to everything" policy she'd adopted for the upcoming year, she gulped and said, "Hell, yes." Tony was a no-brainer. I knew he wanted to return to Afghanistan, and it felt synergistic to have him along to document the finished exhibition, which included several of his prints from our first trip together.

We departed Denver International Airport with thirty-one black duffel bags containing the *Streets of Afghanistan* exhibition, thanks to the three-truck convoy of friends who dropped us and our gear outside of United Airlines. Miraculously, all thirty-one bags, twenty-nine photographs, and two bags of luggage arrived in Kabul after three flights, two delays, and forty-nine hours of travel. It took five porters to help maneuver our luggage through Kabul International Airport and one confrontation with the customs agents.

"What is in the bags?"

"It's a photo exhibition." They looked at the bags, then at me, not comprehending.

"Do you have a letter?"

I sighed. *Here we go again.*

"No, I don't have a letter. This is a photo exhibition we are setting up in villages around Afghanistan."

I understood the confusion. What photo exhibition fits into thirty-one duffel bags? I could imagine how the aluminum collapsible frames looked on the screens of the X-rays they'd just gone through.

"These are photos taken by Afghan photographers to show Afghans."

"You need a letter."

"I don't have a letter."

"You must have a letter."

"I don't have one."

"These are not photos."

Aha, the problem is the bags.

"Okay, fine." I raised my voice slightly with frustration and exhaustion. I walked over to one of the porters and grabbed a bag. I hoisted it onto the metal desk and unzipped it. The agent's eyes went wide, and he backed up. I pulled a photo out and put it upright on the desk and started to open it like an accordion, the image expanding across the desk, all ten by seventeen feet of it.

"See? It's a photograph."

"Okay, okay. You go now."

I looked down as I pushed the enormous image back together so the agents couldn't see my triumphant smile. I put it back in the bag, zipped it up halfway, and dragged it to the porter who helped lift it on top of his cart.

Anna's face was aghast.

"All right," I said, "let's roll." I grinned as I circled my finger in the air. The porters grinned back, and off we rolled to find my friend and fixer Najibullah, who would be waiting outside as he was nearly every time I arrived.

"What about low profile?" she asked, thinking back to the conversations we'd had about security and such.

"This is different. Gotta surprise them. We got over forty bags in total to Kabul. I'm not getting stopped by customs in the final stage!"

We walked outside into the dusty air of Kabul. Najibullah was at the exterior gate to meet us with a minivan and a smile to welcome us back to Afghanistan.

"*Salaam*, Shannon."

"*Salaam*, Najibullah. *Hubisti?*"

"Thank you. I am very well."

He looked over at Tony, his smile widening. "*Salaam*, Tony. It is very good to see you again." For four years, Najibullah had asked how Tony was, and he was clearly pleased to see him again.

Smiling, Tony grasped Najibullah's small hand in both of his. "*Salaam*, Najib, I am very happy to be back."

"Najibullah, this is my dear friend Anna. She is going to help us with the project."

Najibullah looked at the bags and the porters, and smiled at all of us. "That is very good. I think we have a lot of work to do."

I laughed and nodded. "Yup, you're going to love this, Najib."

"Do you like our vehicle?" Najibullah pointed to a blue and white minibus. Standing in the doorway was a small man with Uzbek features, in a cream shalwar kameez and light brown vest. "This is Mohammad. This is his minibus."

"Najibullah, it's perfect. Thank you for arranging everything."

I shook Mohammad's hand, and he smiled in return. We'd gone back and forth via e-mail about how big of a vehicle we'd need for transporting the exhibition, and us, around Afghanistan. I'd eventually told him to imagine thirty to forty large duffel bags plus people, and I left the logistics to him.

Once in our guesthouse, we stacked the bags by the security gate so that the guards could search them. While we unzipped them, and as if on cue, one of the guards asked me where my motorcycle was. Home away from home—it was good to see some familiar faces. As storage for the exhibition, the staff gave us an empty room on the second level, overlooking the street and the security bunker that was sometimes used for banquets. Every day, we had to carry the heavy images—each an awkward forty pounds— up and down narrow staircases, avoiding barbed wire, and loading them into the awaiting minibus. Anna and I were going to get as strong as bulls.

I let Anna and Tony hang at the guesthouse to get settled while Najibullah and I made a visit to the Kabul police commander, General Salangi. This wasn't required, but it was recommended to let him know what we were planning, as the exhibition would be in public places under his jurisdiction. Sitting behind an enormous desk at the far end of the room, the general was an imposing figure, built like a bear. His enormous frame made it easy to imagine him bare-knuckle fighting. We sat on the chairs that lined the wall near his desk while he spoke into his cell phone. He was watching a television that allowed him to view security cameras at street level around Kabul. A traffic accident was getting cleared, and he was advising the police on the ground where to go. He hung up, handed the phone back to his colleague, then turned to us. Najibullah had met him many times before, and after greetings, he introduced me and explained what I would be doing in Afghanistan on this trip.

After some discussion, General Salangi thanked us for informing him. Najibullah told him that in a couple of days we planned to set up the exhibition north of Kabul in the village of Istalif and asked if there was anything we should be aware of. The general said things had been quiet and that he would alert the Istalif police that we were coming and that we should be treated as guests.

"They will allow us to set up the exhibition without any trouble," Najibullah informed me.

The next day, we loaded up the minibus and headed to Kabul's historic Darul Aman Palace ten miles south of the city center for our first test run.

As we drove toward the palace, its solemn structure emerged, residing stoically on top of one of the many small hills that dot Kabul. Najibullah explained to Anna and Tony that decades of war had not been kind to the palace. It had been set on fire twice and had sustained heavy gunfire and shelling from rival mujahideen forces that battled for control of Kabul during the civil war. We turned onto the narrow road winding up the hill itself, the palace rising in front of us and its damage becoming visible. The roof had caved in, and the walls were riddled with bullet holes, but even in its ravaged state—or perhaps because of it—the palace was astonishingly beautiful. History lined its walls like wrinkles in an old man's face, each bullet hole affirming its place in history. The palace was surrounded by barbed wire and guarded by a small group of Afghan National Army soldiers who watched us from behind their gate as we got out of the minivan. Najibullah went over to talk with them.

Najibullah walked back over to us with two of the Afghan soldiers who guarded the building. Below us, there was a field with boys playing football, their shouts rising up.

"They will allow us to set up the exhibition here," Najibullah said.

I nodded my head to each solider with my hand on my heart in gratitude. They nodded in return.

Our goal here was to discover how easily we could transport and set up the images in public, and to test the reactions of the people who watched, so that we could troubleshoot potential problems with the full exhibition. Darul Aman was a very public place, but due to its placement on the hilltop, it limited the car and foot traffic that mostly kept to the main roads wrapping the bottom of the hill. We unpacked eight of the enormous images, and soon a small crowd of men and boys had gathered, curious about what we were doing, as were the soldiers. Out of each bag, Anna and I pulled the bulky, collapsible frames. Two people were required to unfold and lock each frame into place, the cloth photographs stretching taut to reveal their images and vibrant colors. We moved them, selecting locations and experimenting with different layouts and spacing. Each image was freestanding, but if we had a windy day, we would have to get creative to keep them from blowing over due to their large sizes. The palace presented a dramatic backdrop with which to frame the images, and when I finally stepped back to take in the scene, I smiled widely. The palace, and the golden dust lit by the setting sun created a timeless backdrop to the exhibition. The project had taken four years, but now here it was, larger than life and more beautiful than I could have imagined. Afghanistan in Afghanistan.

We stood back and watched the reactions. Curious schoolboys on their bikes and men wandering past stopped and gathered around each photo. Many took photos of themselves in front of the landscape images with their phones. Photos in front of photos as though they could step into the giant landscapes through a transporter. Tony documented the process and the interactions. I was planning to create a book about the exhibition and its return to Afghanistan. We stayed for several hours, talking with the soldiers and the men who asked us questions.

As the sun set on the images in front of the palace, I took a breath. Exhilaration coursed through me. I'd pulled off our first public exhibition in Afghanistan. This was the first real taste of the ephemeral nature of street art installations—the impermanence. Over the course of this trip, we would set up these images and take them down six more times, and each time I found myself disappointed at how empty the space felt without the images at the end of each day.

The next day was the first of Eid celebrations. We left Kabul early to drive an hour and a half north into the Shomali Plain, to the village of Istalif. Istalif is a quiet place known for traditional handmade turquoise-glazed pottery. We arrived in time to unload the exhibition while the majority of the village was walking toward the small blue-and-white tiled mosque for Eid prayers. The women would mostly likely be at home preparing the Eid feast.

I looked around, working through the puzzle of the landscape to figure out how best to set up the photographs. One long dirt road led through the entire village straight to the mosque. Normally, it would be lined with market stalls, but they were closed for the holiday. We could literally line the street with the exhibition so that as everyone came out of the mosque and walked back through the village, they would pass it.

Najibullah and our minibus driver, Mohammad, helped unload the exhibition. Anna and I unzipped each bag and pulled the heavy frames out and stacked them carefully on the dirt road. There were twenty-nine photographs in total. The local police showed up in a green jeep, just as the call to prayer rang through the village. As Najibullah made introductions, they smiled at Anna and me, and shook our hands. Najibullah explained to them and the gathering crowd what we were planning. One of the policemen explained that General Salangi had called and they were planning to stay with us to make sure we were safe. They curiously watched as we began unfolding the images in the dusty street. As each one expanded on the accordion frames, the crowd closed in to look at the emerging image. We set the images up one by one against the empty market stalls. Within an hour, we'd created a walkway of photos leading to the mosque. Slowly, men filled the street as they finished praying and headed toward their homes.

The surprise on their faces was clear—smiles, curious looks, and laughter—as groups gathered around images. Anna and I walked the length of the exhibit road several times, watching villagers viewing and interacting with the art. Most amazing was watching the

young kids who stood for ten minutes or more in front of the photo
of a Kabul market street, pointing out individual people and buildings while discussing the photo with one another. Young girls in
vibrant emerald green and ruby red walked by the images, running
their fingers across them.

A young man rode his bike close to us, keeping pace and observing us, but maintaining his distance. After a couple of laps, I turned
and walked over to him. I pointed at his bike, *"Makbul ast."* It's beautiful. This was no ordinary bike. This was a bike with pinwheels,
multiple horns, and a plastic flower vase containing a single plastic
flower mounted on the handlebars. There was some sort of fur
wrapped around the front of the bike, tied with a pink satin bow.
He smiled with pride and spun the pinwheel. I laughed. He stepped
off and handed the bike to me. He spoke quietly but I heard,
"Shoma?" You?

"I can ride your bike?" I asked in English. He nodded vigorously.

"You're sure?" He nodded again. I looked at Anna. How could I
say no?

"I'm going for it."

"Hell yeah, you are." She laughed.

I accepted the bike and sat down. The seat was way too low, and
I immediately discovered the brakes were barely working, but I certainly wasn't going to complain. I rode up and down the bumpy
road, avoiding the worst of the potholes and piles of rubble, not daring to go very fast as I was unsure of my ability to stop. Laughter
erupted from the men around me, and small kids chased after me.

I rode the bedazzled bike back to the man who was now standing next to Anna. I motioned to her questioningly. "Can she ride the
bike, too?" He understood and nodded with a huge grin.

"You wanna ride?" I teased, knowing her love of bikes was nearly
equal to mine.

"Are you kidding?" She laughed. "Holy shit, yes!"

While she was riding up and down the dusty road, one of the villagers spoke to me in English in awe, "It takes a lot of intelligence to ride a bike, I've never seen a woman do it." Perhaps the most significant statement any Afghan man had made to me about women riding bikes—equating intelligence with the action of riding, as though that was the reason women didn't do it. This showed me that even though I was a foreign woman, my riding in these areas and my welcoming the curiosity and the conversations could create a small shift in the overall perception of a woman's ability and her worth.

Over the course of the next week, we set up four more public exhibitions. We set up the next day, the second day of Eid celebrations, in the inner courtyard at Kabul's historic Babur Gardens. Hundreds of families came to picnic on the grass and by the end of the day we were told by the head of the gardens that almost two thousand people had come through. The next day was the final day of Eid and the most unusual venue we had chosen—the Kabul Zoo. We competed among the bear and monkey cages for wall spaces. It made for an unusual exhibition in a space that many Afghans like to visit. The last Kabul show was at the Women's Garden, an area open only to women, where they can relax without men around. Inside, there was also a driving school, training and educational workshops, and a small market for the women. The garden felt like an oasis after the intensity of the previous three exhibitions. It was the first time we got to sit and watch and talk to one another and to the Afghan women who walked through. Normally, we were surrounded by men, having our pictures taken or simply stared at.

At the gardens, I first met Mary, a woman who'd lived in Kabul nonstop since she first moved there in the 1960s. My friend Warren, who joined us for the Darul Aman bike ride, introduced her to me because Mary had ridden her bike around Kabul nearly every day and continued to today, even now, in her eighties. She shared some amazing stories of living in Kabul during the civil war and the Taliban time. She worked for a small women's rights organization, and when the Taliban kept harassing her at the office, she stood her ground and complained to anyone who would listen. Apparently it worked because Mullah Omar himself, in Kandahar, wrote a letter and sent it to Kabul saying she was to be left alone. She ate lunch with us in the garden and shared more stories. I told her that someone should write her story, and she replied that she was attempting to but it was very difficult. I hoped she wrote it or that someone else did before her incredible stories and experiences were lost forever.

The final exhibition was the most powerful. We drove out to Panjshir to set up a small staging at the top of Massoud's hill. Panjshir had become incredibly significant to me, and I wanted to set these images up there at least once. I chose the hillside of Massoud's tomb, as it was not only the first place I'd visited four years prior with Faheem Dashty, the fearless leader of AINA Photo who'd nearly been killed alongside Massoud—and who'd introduced me to Afghan photographers for the exhibition—but also because it overlooked the entire Panjshir Valley.

The tomb was completed, and this was the first time I'd seen it without scaffolding or workers. It was quiet except for a few of Massoud's soldiers who stood guard. Najibullah explained what we were doing and asked permission to set up the photographs for a few hours. The guards tentatively agreed, and I asked Anna to help me unzip the various bags. I wanted the first image we pulled out to be the shot Tony had taken at Kabul's Olympic Stadium four years earlier, with the billboard of Massoud looking down at the runners on the track below. We found it and set it up near the edge of the hill overlooking the valley.

In the shadow of his own marble tomb, Massoud's face gazed over his valley. One of the men looked at the photo and then at me, and smiled broadly, nodding in approval. I put my hand on my heart and smiled back. He called one of the other soldiers and together they looked at the photo and then curiously at the others we were unpacking: Beth Wald's beautiful rolling green hills; her landscape of the Buddha caves from Bamiyan; Tony's photo of the burqa-covered mother and child in the Kabul street; and Paula Bronstein's vivid portrait of a young girl peering at the camera surrounded by a sea of lapis blue burqas. As we lifted each one out of its bag and unfolded the enormous frame, the image emerged, met with curiosity from the soldiers and the visitors who'd come to pay their respects to Massoud.

It was windy at the top of the hill, so I asked Anna to help me carry some of the photos over to the old Soviet tanks that rested at the side of the hill. As "frames," the tanks made for a stunning backdrop to the images, and it was a disappointment that we couldn't leave them up, since they would blow away overnight. Instead, we set up the exhibition like we did at Darul Aman, a limited staging with the soldiers in a historic place. As the light started to fade, we packed the images back up, thanked the soldiers, and headed home. We stopped briefly at a kebab house along the Panjshir River to celebrate the finale of the exhibition I'd dreamed up exactly four years prior, now come to life in the country I'd come to love.

The final show occurred the day after we flew home, at the U.S. Embassy, in conjunction with a rooftop rock concert with the Afghan metal band *District Unknown*, and the first female Afghan rap-per, Susan Firooz, to celebrate the life of Daniel Pearl. The embassy liaison had agreed to keep the exhibition for me until I returned.

In the end, my goal was to show that art had a place in conflict zones—to showcase the work of Afghan photographers and to bring the images "taken" in Afghanistan home to the Afghans. They deserve the same access to art and beauty that we all crave. Public art isn't limited to the urban cultural centers of New York or London. Shows like this one can be done safely and publicly in Afghanistan, and should. Art has the power to inspire and create a ripple of change that resonates through communities. Public art serves the purpose of bringing art out of private places and into public spaces among the people who are least likely to engage with art.

While Afghanistan is not the place that many think of for emerging artists and activist culture, few countries in the world are more ripe for an artistic scene. In the time since I started working in Afghanistan—a period of approximately six years—a space has emerged for modern and edgier artistic voices and an activist movement. Today all you have to do is look on the billboards and concrete walls around Kabul to see how contemporary art is emerging in public spaces. Banksy-inspired artists, like Kabir, have embraced graffiti art as a public statement on peace. His stencil art silhouettes feature intertwined hearts. Billboards around town were sporting a collection of street art; machine guns shooting rainbows, a tank with a rainbow of colored pencils erupting from the cannon, and another with a row of grenades interspersed with a heart. One of my favorites is a map of Afghanistan with a giant Band-Aid across it. There is space for art to emerge in Kabul, and amazing Afghan artists, musicians, poets, and photographers are using art as their voice, and as that goes more public, their voices amplify.

In Kabul, I took Anna to one of the newer coffee shops, Venue, a coffee shop turned artist refuge that was opened by my friend Humayun. Sitting in the outdoor courtyard, we were surrounded by the work of emerging graffiti artists like Shamsia and Kabir. The pulse of an artistic heartbeat was clear. Just inside the entrance was the artist statement spray painted on the steel doors. "Beware of Artists: They mix with all classes of society and are therefore the most dangerous."

We had come to meet up with my friend Warren and a few friends spearheading an incredible street art initiative, part of the visionary, yet anonymous, street artist JR's global public art project, *Inside Out*. The project was the result of JR winning the renowned TED prize as a way of illustrating the power of photography and street art to represent community and illustrate the faces that make up our global neighborhoods. The group was meeting to discuss the logistics of putting up hundreds of poster-sized, black-and-white portraits around the city. Sitting around the table in the courtyard were members of District Unknown, visiting Swiss artists Shaykla and Shervin who were spearheading the Kabul *Inside Out* project, and emerging graffiti artist, Shamsia, and her friend, another talented artist, Nabila.

To great excitement, Shaykla put two large mailing tubes on the table. Each one contained a roll of a hundred or more large poster-sized black-and-white portraits of Afghan men, women, and children. Locations were discussed for maximum impact—those that were accessible and still relatively safe for the art to be stationed at for an extended period of time. Someone had brought a sample of the glue they planned on using, and everyone agreed that a test was necessary to check how the glue would react with the ink. A space on the courtyard wall was chosen, next to a large in-progress mural by Shamsia and one of Kabir's stencil art pieces of a young boy carrying buckets of hearts. An old man in a pakol hat was chosen as the poster, and five minutes later, it was deemed a success, and plans resumed for large-scale logistics of hundreds of portraits. It was beautiful to bear witness to and exciting to envision.

Three days later, on an early morning bike ride through Kabul, I got to see the images close up on the walls of Kabul. I had made plans to ride to Darul Aman Palace with a friend of mine, Mikhail Galustov, a Georgian photographer who lives in Kabul and loves to ride. Mikhail told me about the men's national cycling team, the first I'd ever heard about them. He'd introduced me to one of the young men on the team, Ashraf Ghani, who worked as a waiter at Design Café, a few doors down from Venue. Ashraf and I spoke at length about biking, the men's team, and racing. Ashraf had asked if I wanted to ride with the team, and I enthusiastically agreed. We made plans to ride the next morning at six o'clock. I invited Mikhail to come with us. When I woke at 5:30, there was a light rain, and ten minutes later a text from Ashraf cancelling due to weather. Mikhail was already en route to meet me at our guesthouse and was more than happy to ride as the rain looked to be clearing by the time we set out a little after six. We decided to ride to Darul Aman as the roads should be quiet this early in the morning.

Tony, Anna, and Warren came along to play and take photos. They wanted to meet the men's team and watch a training ride. Warren also wanted to see the finished *Inside Out* project while the streets were quiet. When we told them that the team cancelled, they decided to come along anyway since everyone was already awake and assembled at the guesthouse. Mikhail and I took off, the roads empty but relatively dry. I was on my brand-new Alchemy 29er single-speed mountain bike, and Mikhail rode his Cannondale 29er fully geared bike looking ever the European in a fashionable sweater over a shirt and fitted khaki pants, a kaffiyeh scarf around his neck. I was in my usual layered getup: long black pants under my black halter dress, tunic, and a thin puffy jacket. I had a kaffiyeh scarf tied around my head and another around my neck. With no more than an occasional car passing, we chatted amiably as we pedaled side by side, mostly about bikes. As we rode past a mosque and a long stretch of wall, the series of portraits emerged. Tony, Anna, and Warren cheered out the bus door, taking photos and celebrating as we rode by. I laughed out loud at the absurdity of keeping a low profile biking through Kabul with a minibus of photo-taking, cheering friends.

Twenty minutes or so later we turned right onto the dirt road in front of the hill where Darul Aman Palace sat. It was probably just after seven o'clock, and traffic was getting busier. Kids were walking and biking to school. I blinked hard and realized there was a girl on a mountain bike in front of me—on a bike miles too big for her, wearing a backpack, but it was definitely a girl.

"Mikhail, did you see that?" Disbelief mingled with excitement.

He nodded. "This is a Hazara neighborhood. They are a little more progressive here. Occasionally, you see something like that."

"Holy shit! That's the first girl I've ever seen on a bike here."

His Georgian personality showed little emotion. "It is pretty cool."

"I didn't realize this area was Hazara." Hazara is an ethnic group, like the Tajik who predominate in the north and Pashtun in the south. Bamiyan province is predominantly Hazara and is one of the safest in the country and one of the most progressive in terms of sports, youth radio, tourism, and apparently their women. It was where the Taliban blew up the Buddhas. It was also where, for the past three years, a ski competition had taken place as ski tourism developed. Girls had been allowed to learn to ski, and the

Band-e Amir lakes in that area had been designated Afghanistan's first national park. Bamiyan also had a female governor, Habiba Sarobi, who had been in charge since 2005.

My mind blown, we rode down a bumpy road and toward the hill to the palace. Mikhail's chain broke, so he walked back to the minibus at the bottom of Darul Aman to see if our driver Mohammad could help. Meanwhile, a group of young boys on their way to school joined me, and together we rode laps like a biker gang. They turned out to be avid football fans.

"Who plays football?" I pointed to each in turn and asked in Dari, "*Shoma?*" You? And each replied "*Bale.*" Yes.

"Are you proud of the Afghan football team? They just played at Kabul Stadium, right?"

"Yes," one of them replied in English, "but I like AC Milan better."

"Really? What about you?" I pointed to another boy. "What team do you like?"

"I like Barcelona."

"Wow, a lot of European teams.

"What about you two?" I pointed at the two shyer boys at the back.

"Barcelona."

"Bayern Munich."

"Well, all right then." I laughed as they shouted out their favorite teams.

"Where are you from?" the leader of the gang asked.

"I'm American."

"What are you doing here?"

"I work in Kabul. I have a nonprofit."

"Do you always ride your bike in Kabul?"

"No, not always. But I wish I could. I love riding bikes. What about you? Do you like riding bikes?"

He smiled big. "Yes, I love riding bikes."

"Very cool. Follow me."

We rode up to the top of the hill where Warren was already talking to the guards. Anna and Tony were talking with Najibullah, and Mikhail soon joined us, the chain repaired. We all chatted for a while. An old man, with a long white beard and a black turban with white stripes, pushed a bike up to me and asked what was going on. I exchanged greetings with him and told him my name, then I called Najibullah over to help translate. He talked for a few minutes with the man.

"This is the gardener. He has been working here at the palace since he was a small boy."

"Seriously? Please tell him we are honored to meet him."

For twenty minutes or so we listened to stories about the palace, his childhood, the civil war, and his family. Then he asked me about my bike, and I asked about his. Bike bonding in Kabul—nothing unusual there, right? In hopes of getting us access, Warren had been buttering up the soldiers who guarded the palace and who were curious about what was going on. They were insisting we weren't allowed, mostly because it was unsafe.

"What if I ask them if they want to ride my bike?"

"Definitely." He nodded. "They'll love it."

I walked over to the barbed wire gate with my bike and offered it up with a smile. "Anyone want to ride a bike?" Two of the guards smiled and nodded. They walked out, and I tried to explain "disc brakes"—basically saying "softly softly" while pointing at the brake levers, hoping that this translated somehow. Brakes on Afghan bikes take serious grip strength to engage, and these were brand-new Avid disc brakes that barely had to be touched with one finger. Squeeze too hard, and someone would be flying over the handlebars. I didn't need an Afghan soldier face planting on my bike and getting pissed off.

With a large grin, and to the cheers of his fellow soldiers, one mounted my bike in his fatigues and plastic sandals. He pedaled in circles around the large stone courtyard in front of the palace. Everyone was cheering and laughing, and I glanced at Tony to see if he had his camera out. Of course he did, but before I could turn back, I heard a collective intake of breath and a "Oooohhhhhhhh." Shit, a crash? I swung around, and sure enough the soldier was righting himself and my bike, having squeezed the front brake too hard. He'd somehow leaped off and landed on his feet like a cat. Relief flooded me, and we all cheered again as he rode over with a sheepish grin into a crush of hugs from the other soldiers, Warren, and Tony.

He stepped off with a shy smile and walked over to me, but before he could hand the bike back, his commander, a much sterner looking man with a beard and stocky build, took it. He glanced at me mischievously and off he rode. The soldiers had a turn, and the gardener and the biker gang watched while Tony and Warren took photos. Warren was shaking his iPhone each time he took a photo, and I realized he was taking photos with the Hipstamatic app set on random. I grabbed my bike and rode some circles, and the boys followed me, a little train of bikes cruising. A few minutes later, while the gardener spoke with the guards, I asked the boys if they needed to get to school. I assumed we had delayed them en route since they were all wearing backpacks. They nodded reluctantly, and with waves to our crew and many "*khoda hafez*," they pedaled off down the other side of the hill.

Najibullah walked over. "If you want, they will let us inside the palace."

"Really? Yes, please!" I nearly hugged Najibullah with excitement, but over the past four years I'd learned how to celebrate solo so that I didn't embarrass him. Usually, I gave a little high five to whatever female was nearest and did a little jig on my own—much to the amusement of Najib. I shouted over to Warren, Mikhail, Tony, and Anna. "Guys, they are going to let us inside!"

Najibullah continued. "They said you can bring your bikes inside, too."

"Can we ride in there?" I hardly dared to believe things could get any better.

"They say yes, but to be careful. There are places that are not safe."

Without further ado, we got a personal tour of the palace. The soldiers weren't wrong. There were sections of missing floors, collapsed ceilings, and piles of rubble lined every corridor. Graffiti writing covered a lot of walls, and bullet holes were scattered throughout. We gingerly carried our bikes up the exposed, disintegrating staircases to the second and third floors, where open windows and missing walls gave stunning views in all directions across the city. Mikhail, Anna, and I took turns riding down the rubble-strewn corridors, exploring, and giggling like school children at the serendipity—the doors that open when you ride a bike.

As if the universe was conspiring to support my work and give a stamp of legitimacy to all that I'd done so far, I woke the next morning to the public announcement that I'd been chosen as one of National Geographic's Adventurers of the Year. This wasn't just because I was the first woman to mountain bike in Afghanistan and all the sorts of things that are typically labeled "adventurous," but the profile on the *National Geographic Adventure* Web site focused on the overall work I was doing in Afghanistan as an activist, with women and voice, and in particular with the *Streets of Afghanistan* exhibition. Seeing my name with the group of explorers and adventurers I admired under the umbrella of National Geographic

Adventurer of the Year strengthened my resolve to continue to explore, use my voice, and push boundaries.

Before we left Kabul, I tried one more time to ride with the men's team. Ashraf had told me to meet the team at 6:30 A.M. at a petrol station on the road to Panjshir. I pulled up with Najibullah, Anna, and Tony. Ashraf introduced the team, and we discussed the ride I would join on the highway to Bagram. They were a motley crew of riders in assorted clothing and bike gear. They reminded me of the group I used to ride with in Germany—garish cycling clothing in neon colors, a mix of tennis shoes and cycling shoes, and various styles and mismatched gear. Most of the guys were on legitimate road bikes of varying ages and materials, but they could all have done with a basic bike fit; some had their seats too low, and others were too far away from their handlebars. As we waited for two more riders to arrive, a car pulled up and a man and young woman stepped out. He saw me, looked at my bike, and started shouting at the boys. I backed up and stood with Najibullah, waiting to hear what was going on.

"This is their coach," Najibullah said quietly as he listened.

"He wasn't told about their plans for a training ride, and he is upset."

No shit, I thought. He was shouting his head off. The young woman was quietly standing beside him. She was wearing black high heels and was very put together. I noticed her angular face accentuated with strong black eyebrows and bright red lipstick. Beautiful but tough.

"Who's the young woman?"

"Let's wait and we'll talk to him."

As if on cue, the coach turned to us, got right up in my face and continued in a louder than normal voice, although he had toned down the shouting. Najibullah calmly introduced us all and explained what we were doing there. Coach shouted; Najibullah listened.

"This is Coach Seddiq. He is upset that the team is arranging a ride with a foreigner without telling him. They disrespected him by not asking his permission. The fact that you are a woman is a concern to him as he is afraid something could happen to you and it would reflect badly on the team. He was driving to Mazar to meet with some other riders when he noticed his team meeting here. That's why he pulled over."

"Coach, it is an honor to meet you. I am sorry you were not made aware that I was joining the team. I was invited by one of the riders for a fun ride since I ride and race in the States. I simply wanted to ride with them and experience what it is like for them to train in Afghanistan. I meant no disrespect to you."

Coach listened and then shook his head. "No problem, no problem," he said in English. Then he told Najibullah that I was most welcome to Afghanistan and he was at my service.

"Who is the woman?" I asked. Najibullah spoke with the coach, and the young woman looked up as the conversation turned to her. I smiled at her, and she shyly smiled back.

"The young woman is Mariam. She is assistant to the coach. She helps with the woman's team."

"Wait. What?" *Women's team?*

More talking.

"Yes, she is on the woman's team and helps the coach as his assistant. He coaches the men's and the women's national cycling team."

My mind was reeling. No one I knew had ever heard of a woman's team. No one I had talked to in Kabul besides Mikhail had even heard of the men's team.

"Can the coach tell me more about the women's team? Tell him I am a bike rider and I have been looking to find Afghan women who are allowed to ride bikes."

"The coach says that he started coaching a woman's team because his daughter wanted to ride. They have competed in Pakistan and hope to race more outside of Afghanistan. He is going to Mazar because he heard about a group of women who want to learn to ride bikes."

"Holy cow. Can you explain to him that we are leaving, but we would love to find a way to help the teams? I will be back in a few months and would like to meet with him and meet the women's team."

Najibullah translated, and the coach smiled at me and started nodding his head excitedly. His demeanor softened, and he grabbed my hand. "Thank you, thank you," he said in English. He continued to Najibullah in Dari.

"Coach says that you are most welcome to come back and ride with the women's team. It would be an honor. We can all sit down and discuss with him when you return, and you can ride with the men's and women's team. No problem." Najibullah continued to me, "Coach was just upset to be disrespected by the boys."

Ashraf was embarrassed and was hiding off to the side, his swagger long gone after having been chastised in front of us. He'd brought us there, as the de facto leader of the team, and his ego had taken a bruising.

"Coach, I look forward to meeting with you when I return and riding with the teams. I will see what I can do to help both teams, and I wish you and your team all the very best. Najibullah can stay in touch while I am back home. I will be hoping that all your riders stay safe, *inshallah*."

My mind was already thinking of the donated bikes and clothing we could rally as an initial first step.

We said our good-byes and loaded into the minibus to get some breakfast. I was bummed to miss riding with them but excited to discover women riding, in public, and doing so as part of the national cycling federation. This was huge! These women were the first Afghan women to ride bikes. I babbled nonstop all the way to breakfast, my mind still reeling with the possibilities and already plotting my return. Here were women challenging the status quo and taboos that prevented other women and girls from riding. My heart swelled with pride at what they were both accomplishing and risking. Coach Seddiq was another example of an Afghan man like Faheem Dashty, Najibullah, and the myriad of male teachers and doctors I'd encountered who were fighting for the rights of women and girls—men who realized that Afghanistan cannot truly succeed unless all of its citizens had access to the same opportunities for education, training, and sports.

I'd been gifted a book, *Wheels of Change*, by a woman who'd read about my mountain biking adventures in Afghanistan and my disappointment with the cultural barriers that prevent Afghan women from riding. The book illustrated the cultural shift when American women began riding bikes at the turn of the century. As in Afghanistan, women who rode were considered immoral and promiscuous, in part because of straddling a bike seat in public, and in part because of the individual freedom the bike allowed. The bike became more than a hobby or sport; it became a vehicle for change and an integral symbol of the women's suffrage movement. The bicycle gave women true freedom of physical mobility so that they no longer depended on male family members for transportation. It truly expanded their world. Bicycling gave a woman the freedom to go off on her own, as far as she could pedal, unaccompanied by a chaperone.

The women's rights activist Susan B. Anthony famously stated in 1896, "I think the bicycle has done more to emancipate women than anything else in the world. . . ." It gives a woman a feeling of freedom and self-reliance. The moment she takes her seat she knows she can't get into harm unless she gets off her bicycle, and away she goes, the picture of free, untrammeled womanhood."

The bike sparked a change in women's fashion as well. Riding in petticoats was cumbersome and difficult, so split skirts or pantaloons were invented, heralding a new era in women's fashion. As a woman who is happiest in a pair of jeans, I, for one, am grateful. But these changes weren't without controversy, as one famous quote I found stated, "The wearers of the bloomers are usually young women who have minds of their own and tongues that know how to talk."

It wasn't long before those independent minds and talking tongues were changing the entire idea of feminism, fashion, and sports in the United States. Although even in the United States, where we tend to view women's rights as progressive, it wasn't until 1984, the year my sister was born, that women were allowed to cycle in the Olympics. It took nearly a hundred years from the time American women started riding before it became acceptable for them to compete in the Olympics alongside their male counterparts.

Today, the bike is used as a tool for change around the world, and organizations like World Bicycle Relief and 88 Bikes use the bikes directly with girls as a vehicle to change lives. In communities throughout Africa and Southeast Asia, the bike increases the access to school for boys and girls alike by simply reducing the commute they have to make on foot. In rural Cambodia, school typically ends at the primary level for many girls simply because the nearest secondary school is too far to commute to by foot. Typically, the commute is not just long but increasingly dangerous as rape and gender violence have reached near epidemic proportions in the countryside. The vast majority of underage rape victims were assaulted while walking home from school. But with access to a bicycle, one of the key barriers to education disappears, as do the attacks against girls.

In Afghanistan, girls on bikes—despite bikes being a logical and affordable tool—are just not culturally acceptable. Time and time again, men who accept me as a foreigner riding a bike admit freely that they wouldn't allow their girls to do so. Constantly, I have questioned the men I met—Why? What if? There is a women's boxing team and women skateboarders, but what is it that makes the bike so taboo in Afghanistan? Yet these young women like Mariam were riding as part of a national cycling team, for the simple joy of learning a new sport and hobby—the same as women anywhere else. This was unimaginable ten years ago but a sign of progress in the post-Taliban era. These were the first Afghan women to pedal bicycles. Change is slow, often generational at best, and when I consider the parallels between the women riding bikes in Afghanistan and the women who started to pedal a revolution in the United States, I can't help but get excited at the spark that has begun—even if it's a slow burn.

Human Rights Watch employee Heather Barr stated in *The New York Times* that, on the morality ladder, riding bikes is just one step above the morality crimes that Afghan women are jailed for. That in itself sums up the courage and the controversy these women embody when they dare to ride. These are young revolutionaries on two wheels, even if they don't realize it. They are revolutionary simply by the very nature of the taboo they are breaking every time they pedal. Many may say, "Well, it's just a bike." But I see it's another drop in the bucket. It's one more way women are illustrating their equality and making that equality the norm, not the exception.

I sensed that my work in Afghanistan was about to ramp up rather than wind down as I'd envisioned at the beginning of the trip. If anyone embodied Strength in Numbers and the power of the bike to create change, it was these women. Was it a coincidence that I'd just decided to create Strength in Numbers as a vehicle for women to use their voice and become agents of change a few months before finding Afghan women riding, after years of riding my bike there? Or was life simply unfolding organically, revealing to me what I needed to see at its own pace?

Things unfold in a way that we often can't see until we take the time to look back at all the steps that have led up to the present, as if a road map had been laid out. I never planned to work in Afghanistan or to become an activist for women's rights. I never thought I'd be a mountain biker, much less the first woman to mountain bike in Afghanistan. But things were set in motion decades ago that led to me standing at a dusty petrol station on the outskirts of Kabul, speaking with the coach of the women's national team and plotting a two-wheeled revolution.

Twenty years ago, I lost my voice, somewhere in the dirt, behind a bush. Perhaps it simply ran out with my blood.

How was I to know it would be in Afghanistan that I found it again?

In a strange way, I have my own attacker to thank. He tried to break me, to kill my spirit and possibly my body, to leave me less than whole. He nearly succeeded. I've just started to realize how much it affected me and my relationships with the men and women in my life over the years. But when I became ready to face it and the horrors of that night, I became fearless. I realized that I wasn't scared. Of anything. Except maybe of doing nothing, of turning a blind eye to the injustices I saw in the world, of becoming apathetic and desensitized.

I took the wrong bus. That simple act created a domino effect that rippled through the rest of my life and led me to a dusty, war-torn corner of the world where women who are raped are often jailed. Where women aren't allowed to drive, or ride bikes, and in some cases are not allowed to even leave the home without their faces covered and a male escort. Where girls have acid thrown on their faces to scare them away from school. Where women set themselves on fire to escape their husbands. To a country where women's rights aren't just trampled—they're crushed into a fine dust that blows across the country.

Yet this place, whose pollution turns my nose black and fills my lungs with a cough that impedes my mountain biking each time I return home, is the place I chose to risk everything and fully commit to be an active participant in the world that surrounds me. It is the place that showed the best of humanity in the worst of circumstances. It is the place that showed me hope is always stronger than fear; that my vulnerability could be my biggest source of strength rather than my weakness; that a bicycle can be a vehicle for social justice; and that a two-wheeled revolution is possible. By doing so, Afghanistan illustrated for me the parallel situation for women in my own country, and how sparking a two-wheeled revolution in the United States was perhaps my next step and the evolution of Mountain2Mountain.

Every day has become a reminder to never forget how fortunate I am to have the freedom to ride my bike, anywhere I wish, dressed however I like—a reminder that I should never take for granted the life I have, and the opportunities that unfold. This life is a ride, and I am so very glad I'm on it, balancing on two wheels, trying not to crash, but pedaling as hard as I can, with the wind in my face, and a smile as big as the sun. As a dear friend always says, "Just ride. Just ride. Just ride."

Epilogue

A Two-Wheeled Revolution

Afghanistan 2013

The final day of filming the Afghan National Women's Cycling Team was one of the best days of my most recent trip and an unexpected culmination of my own years of biking in Afghanistan. We met up with Coach Seddiq whose white Land Cruiser held four members of the women's team, their bikes strapped to the roof. We drove outside of Kabul to start their ride. Heavily loaded, brightly painted, Pakistani trucks thundered by as the team prepared their bikes and the coach spoke with them.

After meeting the coach and some of the girls in October, I'd returned home to Breckenridge. That January, I'd lunch with two girlfriends, Anna Brones and Sarah Menzies. I told Sarah about these girls and what an amazing film their story would make. As Anna had been with me on the previous visit to Afghanistan and had met the coach and the girls, she added her thoughts. By the end of lunch, our decision was made—Sarah would join me in Afghanistan to make a film about the women who dare to ride. We'd figure out the details, but for now, we have three and a half months to do logistics and preproduction, and get funding secured.

I had set up a gear drive with local bike shops, and I reached out to my friend Claudia Lopez. A fiery Colombian photographer, she was living in Boulder and we'd met several times for coffee and chats about travel, photography, art as activism, and the power of voice through different mediums. When I explained the project and proposed that she joined as a photographer to document it, she immediately said yes.

Sarah brought on board Whitney Connor Clapper as codirector. Whitney was another Anna type—a woman who simply "gets shit done." She was affable, smart, and ready for anything. More important, as I discovered throughout our time in Afghanistan, she created a safe space for everyone to collaborate and create without ego—allowing the best of everyone to shine. With four passionate, high-energy creatives working together for the first time, our crew's synergy may not have gelled the way it did without her subtle influence and incredible tirelessness.

The crew complete, we made plans in the months leading up to the trip about logistics, filming, and the arc of the story. I worked hard to get yet another crew of first-timers up to speed on all things Afghan. I collected four hundred pounds of cycling gear and soon had a storage unit full of bikes and gear that we packed up to bring over to Kabul to distribute to the cycling federation for the men's and women's teams. Three months later, all four of us were standing on the side of the highway leading north out of Kabul, watching a train of girls on bikes pedaling away for the first time.

For the following two weeks, we filmed daily: training rides, b-roll of daily life and scenery in the city, and interviews—hours and hours of interviews. We interviewed the coach and four of the team riders, Mariam, Nazifa, Sadaf, and Farzana. We also secured an interview with a female member of Parliament and women's rights activist Fawzia Koofi, to give us her perspectives on progress for women's rights in Afghanistan, the uncertain future of these gains over the past ten years, and her thoughts on this team of women cyclists. Fawzia helped put into context the risk these girls undertake by challenging the taboo against women riding bikes. She'd been left outside in the sun to die by her family at birth when they discovered she was "just" another girl. To her family's surprise, she survived the exposure but had burns on her skin that remain today. They took her inside and raised her as part of the family. She survived the era of the Taliban regime, married a man she loved, had two daughters with him, and eventually became a member of Parliament, an author of the bestselling memoir *The Favored Daughter*, and a strong political force who seriously considered making a run for president in the 2014 elections. She freely admitted that these girls were on the front line, risking their lives to challenge the status quo, but that without women willing to take on those risks, change would never occur.

While it's hard to imagine these young women having to fight that fight, the truth is that all Afghan women have to fight that fight. Young girls my daughter's age who walk to school and risk harassment, threats, and acid attacks have to fight that fight. Women forced into arranged marriages with men forty years their senior have to fight that fight. Women who risk their lives and their honor to run for political office in order to fight for their rights and the future of their country are fighting that fight. If no one takes on the risk to make a stand, to use their voices, and to fight against the norms that oppress them, change will never occur. Change doesn't happen without risk.

Risk was a key theme we examined in the interviews with the girls and their families. They ride with their families' permission, something their coach himself insists upon. Each time we spoke with the girls, they acknowledged the risks they were exposed to, whether it be traffic or harassment. While they downplayed that it was controversial, they also admitted the frustration of the logistics of being a female cyclist. The girls couldn't meet up on their own for a group ride or even venture out by themselves. Sadaf and Farzana talked about riding with a brother or father occasionally, but the inability to train without their coach providing safe logistics was extremely limiting. The girls still tended to focus on the opportunities that cycling had provided, namely travel. Being part of the national cycling team had allowed them to acquire passports and travel outside Afghanistan for the first time. Exposed to other female cyclists at races in Pakistan and India, they were able to interact with their regional counterparts and learn from them.

One rider, Nazifa, inspired the entire crew during her interviews. Nazifa was one of the smallest riders but had exhibited some of the deepest drive and strength as a rider. She completely opened up to us and bonded particularly with Sarah. Her large smile and tinkling laughter was a constant source of joy during filming with her. She had lost her father, and so her uncle was the main source of support for the family. He'd obviously instilled a sense of national pride in her, and this came out when she spoke of her desire to represent her country in the Olympics, to "show the world that Afghanistan is not just a drug country."

These girls are the next generation, the first to have access to computers and the Internet—and therefore the first to know more broadly what is happening in the rest of the world. All that they are doing—going to university, riding bikes, racing, working outside the home, traveling outside of Afghanistan—are risks, challenges to the status quo that most Afghan women have found themselves living under for at least the past forty years. Yet each time they are asked, they willingly accept the risks, in order to gain the opportunities.

As Fawzia Koofi reiterated often in our interviews, "The time has come to stop referring to Afghan women as 'poor Afghan women.' That changes nothing. It is time to start calling them 'strong Afghan women' because that's the only way to change the perception of Afghan women, and encourage them to succeed."

So there we were, standing on the side of a highway leading out of Kabul, watching the girls get their bikes off the roof of the coach's white Land Cruiser for a training ride. We watched them pull out on the highway with apprehension. Men stared at the girls from all directions, cars honked, trucks swerved around one another in typical Afghan mayhem. The girls seemed so vulnerable on their skinny tires entering the fray. Standing on the side of the road, I felt the mayhem as dust swirled, and the wind gusts challenged the girls to hold their line. There was a sense from the crew of heavy responsibility, and we all gut-checked ourselves as they pedaled off. None of us felt good about watching them ride here. This was seriously dangerous riding, not just because they were girls doing something Afghan women didn't do, but because it was a trucking highway where driving a car was dangerous enough. The brightly painted, intricately decorated Pakistani trucks roared down the highways, creating huge gusts of dusty wind as they passed. I reminded myself that the girls weren't doing this for us; this was their training ground and they faced these risks every time they pedaled. We just needed to document and share their incredible story.

Standing on the side of an Afghan highway, I thought back to all the things that led me to this place: my rape, Larissa's rape, Devon's birth, ten years working as a sports trainer, a life lived in multiple countries, my love of mountain biking and exploration—all bricks in the foundation that brought me to Afghanistan and brought me deeper into my truest self. Working here, I began to realize that my deeper motivations could be a simple desire to believe that my own beauty could emerge through my heartbreak; that women's voices matter; and my own need to express and thus be understood through my own layers of complexity. The hope that reconciliation and forgiveness can be found within me for those who tried to break me. That if I can find forgiveness for the man that raped me and nearly killed me, I can find compassion in humanity itself.

The young women who dare to ride their bikes are pedaling a revolution. They train on some of the most dangerous highways in the world, in a country where their existence is a challenge to the status quo, breaking a major cultural taboo. Like the American women who dared to ride in the late 1800s in America, they are refusing tradition in the post-Taliban era, taking advantage of all the opportunities before them. They serve as inspiration to women around the world, and to me. My hope is that the gains made for women in the past decade aren't lost in the upcoming one as the international focus shifts, international support wanes, and the Afghans take on more control of their country. As they work to ready themselves for international competitions—with their eyes set on representing their country in a future Olympics—they are already demonstrating to the world the strength of Afghan women. They are the best possible example of the heart and soul behind Strength in Numbers—showing the world a different view of women in Afghanistan while showing Afghans the strength of women. One pedal stroke at a time.

Acknowledgments

First and foremost: Devon, you are my reason for everything. Not one day goes by that I am not grateful beyond measure that you came into my life, and I am honored to be your mom. I love you, I love you, I love you. To the moon and back a million times over.

Larissa, we grew up ten years apart, and half a world away for much of it. I am so blown away by our relationship now. Sisters, best friends, neighbors, and you're the best aunt that Devon could ask for. Thank you for believing in me and for allowing me to share the part of your story that intertwines with mine. Silver linings out of violent histories.

Christiane Leitinger, my soul sister and the woman that believed in me through the toughest of times, when everyone thought I was crazy, including myself, for continuing down this path.

Mom and Dad, thank you for believing in me and supporting the work I chose to dedicate my life to, for making me believe from a very early age that a young girl from North Dakota could do anything she wanted.

A huge thanks to Dede Cummings for coming on as my agent, pitching my book to St. Martin's Press, and firmly getting behind the project. And to my editor, Daniela Rapp, who understood what I wanted this book to be, and supported me throughout!

Jason Dilg, for challenging me to speak not once, but twice at TEDxMileHigh, which helped me to find my voice and stand up for those that don't know how to use theirs yet. For your friendship, your advice, and mind blowing brainstorming sessions! #giveashit.

Allen Lim, for reminding me that suffering is part of the journey and letting me cry on your couch when I wasn't sure I could keep doing this alone. And for believing in the power of bikes to transform the world! "Just ride, just ride, just ride."

Travis Beard, the man, the myth, the legend. Thank you for your years of friendship, advice, and inspiration. You kick serious ass and have done far more for mentoring and inspiring the next generation of artists and musicians than anyone I know. You are Afghanistan's best-kept secret and I am grateful for your sarcasm, your support, and your assistance. Rock on.

Hamid, for teaching me to ride a motorcycle, being my translator on many trips to Panjshir, and endless laughs, many of them at my expense, and the best nickname I've ever been given. CIB.

Najibullah Sedeqe, my translator and fixer extraordinaire. Thank you for the initial introduction into Afghanistan, the friendship, and the advice when I continued to encounter unknown situations. Six years we have worked together, and I hope that we have many more years working together.

Tony Di Zinno, the photo sherpa. Thank you for the photos and the support, documenting my first trip, and coming back four years later to see the *Streets* exhibition in the streets, parks, and villages of Afghanistan.

Justin Balding, for believing in my work and my story enough to introduce me to Ann Curry, an interview that unexpectedly sparked so much change, personally and professionally. Even more important, you became a dear and trusted friend and I hope I can return the favor someday.

James Edward Mills, for believing in me from the beginning, continuing to publicly share my work and my story, and for calling me Blondie, which always makes me smile.

Sarah Menzies, Whitney Connor Clapper, and Claudia Lopez, for showing me how amazing creative women can be and what a powerful force we can become when we drop our respective egos and collaborate our asses off. So proud and humbled to work with you on Afghan Cycles, and most important, honored to call you friends.

Anna Brones, you fabulous woman, you! I dub thee, the woman who "gets shit done." Thank you for joining me in Afghanistan on the promise of kebabs and pomegranate juice and not once complaining after setting up the *Streets* exhibition about a billion times.

Mark Wiggins, for years of new trails on two wheels. You are an amazing friend, and I will always love riding single-speeds with you!

This book, and many of my ongoing efforts, wouldn't be possible without the kindness and patience of Ket McSparin. Thank you for being the best landlord ever. Devon and I are grateful beyond words.

To all the Afghans who opened their homes, their lives, and shared their stories and their tea with me. It has been my greatest honor to work in and explore your country. Thank you for your friendship, your advice, and your patience.

Last but not least, Deni Béchard, for your incredible patience and help in the last-minute push with the editing while I was in Kabul. In particular, your cleanup of my wayward grammar and liberal sprinkling of random punctuation. I promise I was paying attention. Sort of.

Glossary of Dari Words and Phrases

aks. *photograph*

anor. *pomegranate*

bale. *yes*

bolone. *fried dough stuffed with potatoes*

burro. *go*

baisekel. *bicycle*

buzkashi. *traditional horse polo played with headless calf or goat*

chaikador. *watchman or gatekeeper*

chaihanna. *tea house*

chai. *tea*

chirany. *gift*

Dari. *national language of Afghanistan*

Hazara. *ethnic group of Mongol descent from central Afghanistan*

hosh mekanam. *you're welcome*

hubas. *good*

imam. *Muslim religious leader*

jihad. *holy struggle or holy war*

jirga. *council of community elders and leaders*

kharajee. *foreigner*

khoda hafez. *good-bye*

koh. *mountain*

Kuchi. *nomad*

kojaa. *where*

lotfan. *please*

madrassa. *Islamic school*

makbul. *beautiful*

mazadoras. *delicious*

muezzin. *the one who calls Muslims to prayer*

na. *no*

pakol. *flat hat worn by Afghan men*

Pashto. *second language of Afghanistan*

Pashtun. *dominant ethnic group, predominately from southern Afghanistan*

pilau. *meal of rice and meat*

Quran. *the holy book of Islam*

salaam. *hello*

shalwar kameez. *traditional male garments made up of knee-length shirt and baggy trousers*

sher chai. *milky tea*

shoma. *you*

Tajik. *second-largest ethnic group, predominantly from northern Afghanistan*

tashakur. *thank you*

tashnab. *bathroom*

toshaks. *sitting/sleeping mattress*

Uzbek. *ethnic group concentrated in northwest Afghanistan*